APPLICATIONS IN FINANCE, INVESTMENTS, AND BANKING

Advances in Computational Economics

VOLUME 9

The titles published in this series are listed at the end of this volume.

Applications in Finance, Investments, and Banking

Edited by

Diem Ho

IBM Management Technologies Consulting Group - Europe

and

Thomas Schneeweis

CISDM, School of Management,
University of Massachusetts

KLUWER ACADEMIC PUBLISHERS

BOSTON / DORDRECHT / LONDON

A C.I.P. Catalogue record for this book is available from the Library of Congress.

ISBN 978-0-7923-8294-2

Printed on acid-free paper

Table of Contents

Preface and Summary

Financial innovations have historically been driven by economic changes as well as technological progress. Today, advances in trading technology and regulatory changes, affecting banks as well as the corporate and investment community, have led to dramatic and rapid changes. Similarly, the applications of quantitative investment and computer technologies have given us a new array of tools and techniques with which to manage risk and return in asset management.

The papers contained in this volume concentrate on research and applications in three areas: mathematics and optimization in portfolio management, regulatory issues in financial product management, and investment management issues in both domestic and international markets. Each article offers a unique understanding to various issues confronting investors in the international marketplace. In "Advanced Applications in Finance: An Overview of Problems and Solution Techniques", Diem Ho offers a wide ranging survey of the state of the art in financial applications of quantitative methods. In this article, Ho gives us a sense of the range of areas which have made use of quantitative methods, as well as the power of such methods in formulating and solving problems which had been heretofore impossible to address--or otherwise addressable only by a few institutions possessing the necessary physical and human resources, such as supercomputers and specialists trained in both financial *and* quantitative problem solving. In so doing, Ho explains how changes in the nature of financial markets (globalization and deregulation) and technological advance (the widespread availability of extensive computing resources--including software as well as hardware) have combined with advances in financial theory and practice, to yield the present environment. He focuses on six specific areas: Portfolio Optimization, Asset Pricing, Risk Assessment, Securitization, Asset-Liability Management, and Data Visualization, and provides us with a discussion of both the mathematical and computing techniques that make up these application areas, as well as how those techniques have enhanced financial practice. The reader may also find the chapter as a quick refresher course in some areas of finance and mathematics. As such, it serves a useful preface to many of the other chapters contained in this book.

In their paper on asset-liability management (ALM), "Principles for the Control of Asset Liability Management Strategies in Banks and Insurance Companies," Goran Bergendahl and Jacques Janssen give us a detailed discussion of sophisticated techniques for insurance companies, banks and other financial institutions to effectively and simultaneously manage *risk* and *return,* focusing in particular on the consequences associated with interest rate risk, liquidity risk and default risk. They explain many of the short-comings of traditional approaches to ALM, which do not thoroughly address the fact that risk and returns are jointly determined, and provide a detailed framework of their own approach which directly remedies such a gap. In particular, drawing upon the mathematics of stochastic calculus, the authors give us an methodology for evaluating and selecting ALM strategies. Many explicit examples are provide to both illustrate the conceptual issues involved as well as facilitate the readers understanding of how financial institutions might actually operationalize their approach to ALM. Further, Bergendahl and Janssen do not neglect to provide us with their own specific recommendations on organizational and managerial elements that must be integrated into any firm's ALM system.

In her article, "Asset & Liability Management: Regulatory Guidelines On Interest Rate Risk Control and Their Impacts on Financial Institutions," Elisabetta Gualandri offers us a broad discussion of the many regulatory issues that confront financial institutions, paying particular attention to the problem of Interest Rate Risk (IRR). Such issues have become even more acute in recent years, with increases in volatility of interest (and exchange rates), as well as the potential for financial institution missteps afforded by an international market for derivatives comprised of OTC interest rate contracts with a notional value of 28 *trillion* dollars. Gualandri emphasizes the need for both supervisory authorities and financial institutions to confront matters of prudential regulation with an intimate and holistic conception of actual and evolving asset and liability management practices of the financial institutions themselves--a natural and essential complement to the discussion presented in the paper by Janssen and Bergendahl. Optimal enterprise strategy has and will necessarily continue to be affected by the regulations in place, both at the national, and at supranational level (e.g., as established by the G-10 central banks through the Bank for International Settlements and associated institutions), as well as those due to be implemented, such as the BIS provisions on Market Risk. Gualandri provides us with some specific ways--at practical, (i.e. operational) as well as conceptual levels--that this may be done, as well as providing us with discussion of many related concerns.

In his paper, "OTC Derivatives and the 'Competitive Payments System' Debate: The Lessons from History and Implications for a Supervisory Framework," George Martin offers us an analysis of the importance of monetary settlement institutions for understanding the evolution of financial markets and instruments, and in particular, the global market in over-the-counter derivative securities. In doing so, he offers an alternative to the monetary theorists who argue against the essential uniqueness of central bank backed and supervised fiat money as a viable medium of exchange, arguing that previous experiences in American economic history with multiple media of exchange have resulted in monetary instability. He argues that the U., S. Federal Reserve, and by extension other central banks, has evolved in function to eliminate monetary instability by promoting efficient and reliable settlement mechanisms, and has been so successful in such. Having developed a perspective on the nature of the settlements process, Martin takes the view that derivatives should be seen as an extension of the payments system, and thus, given the unique interest and responsibility of the Federal Reserve in supervising that system, that is this economic function of derivatives, rather than other characteristics (such as 'suitability' for commercial banks), which properly brings their supervision within the province of the Fed.

In this modern world of global communication and asset management, investors are also becoming increasingly sophisticated in their understanding of markets and their performance. In a "A Unified Approach to Performance Attribution", Thomas Philips describes a performance attribution methodology that can be used to analyze the performance of domestic and international equity managers and asset allocators. In addition, he describes methods to deal with cash flows in to and out of the portfolio, and to perform multiperiod attributions. These methods are general and can be applied to any additive single period performance attribution methodology. As with any analytic tool, the simple use of such an analysis can sometimes mislead. With a little care, though, it can give many insights into the nature of a manager's skills, facilitate the choice of a manager and the definition of his mandate, and help monitor the manager's performance on an ongoing basis.

Advances in investments have gone far beyond even that of traditional asset management and traditional asset products such as stocks and bonds. Against a backdrop of option pricing applications, Ronald Heynen and harry Kat give us a thorough analysis of the concept of asset volatility and its operationalization in option pricing. In such applications, it is typically the only parameter value that needs to be *estimated* in order to price options–the other values being explicitly given by the terms of the financial contract being analyzed. Conversely, if market prices of options are available, then, as Heynen and Kat show, one can infer the market's estimation of the volatility of the underlying asset. Such estimates are forward looking, and find ready application in all areas of asset pricing or management, as volatility is elemental to any notion of *risk*. Moreover, Heynen and Kat address the fact that asset return volatility is time varying, and in so doing provide a review of the GARCH (Generalized Auto-Regressive Conditional Heteroscedasticity) literature that currently occupies a central place in the modeling practice for financial time series. They also address the fact that the classical Black-Scholes (BS) model of option-pricing seems to be rejected as a model of how markets actually price options, since empirical evidence suggests that the option-implied unconditional distribution of underlying asset price dynamics requires either time-varying volatility or a departure from the assumption that the driving process behind asset prices can adequately be represented as geometric Brownian motion. The practical result--documented by Heynen and Kat--of these violations of the BS model include the fact that option prices imply a "volatility smile" (in which the implied volatility varies with the strike price of the option) or a 'term structure of volatility' (in which the expected volatility for an asset varies with the time to expiration of the option.) All told, Heynen and Kat bring us to a better understanding of the nature of asset price volatility and its impact on option pricing theory, and provide us with kind of insights that allow us to quickly put that knowledge into practice.

In investments, the foundation of equity valuation as well as investment management performance is often found in a through understanding of firms' actual and forecasted earnings. In "Diversifying Earnings Forecast Errors via Composite of Market-based, Analyst, and Time-Series Predictions", Pieter Elgers, May Lo, and Dennis Murray show that alternative earnings forecast methods may be complementary rather than competitive. In this paper, Elgers, Lo, and Murray evaluate financial analyst, market-based and time-series forecasts as potential complements in the construction of composite forecasts. Both relative prior error (RPE) and regression weighting schemes are examined, and results are provided separately for firms in different size groups. They conclude that RPE-weighted composites enable significant reductions in earnings prediction errors for all size groups. Regression-based composites fail to improve upon the prediction errors of the single-method forecasts due to pronounced temporal instability in the covariances among the forecast errors of the single-method forecasts.

One natural consequence of the increasing internationalization of securities and derivative markets is the growth in financial products designed to allow its purchaser the opportunity to take positions whose value explicitly or implicitly depends on combinations of international interest rates and exchange rates. In his paper, "The Valuation of Cross-Currency Interest-Sensitive Claims, with Application to "Diff" Swaps," Simon Babbs provides us with an analytical framework to price such assets, focusing in particular on diff swaps, instruments which allow parties to exchange cash flows based on movements in cross-currency interest rates (e.g., exchanging six-month USD Libor for 3 month DM Libor denominated in dollars). The model which Babbs develops allows for very general specification of inter-asset correlations, and through use of a one-factor (Vasicek) model of the term structure of interest rates, provides us with tractable expressions for the value of diff swaps. The essay also gives the reader substantial exposure to some very recent mathematical techniques--that are on the cusp of those used in financial theory--used in the pricing of interest and exchange rate assets and contingent claims based on those assets. In particular, it presents a sophisticated analysis of the financial questions at hand by exploiting the interrelation between the absence of arbitrage in a price system and the "risk-neutralized" martingale dynamics of prices within that system--a framework for analysis that was presaged by Black and Scholes. Readers interested in pursuing term structure modeling in this general framework should know that it has moved far from the pages of academic journals, providing, as it does, the basis for models used at most of the major investment banks and other large financial institutions.

It is hoped that the readers of this volume will better understand the basis behind the creation of new financial instruments and the role of computer technology, accounting, mathematics and optimization in practical financial applications. Special thanks are given to those individuals who gave of their time to review the various articles submitted for this publication. As in most endeavors, however, several individuals deserve special note. We especially thank George Martin at the Center for International Securities and Derivatives Markets for his efforts at transcribing what are difficult research articles and to the offices of Kluwer publication for their patience and support in publishing the authors' efforts.

Diem Ho
IBM Management Technologies Consulting Group - Europe

Thomas Schneeweis
CISDM, School of Management, University of Massachusetts

Authors Background

Simon Babbs, First National Bank of Chicago, London

Goran Bergendahl, Department of Business Administration, School of Economics and Commercial Law, University of Gothenburg, Gothenburg

Pieter Elgers, School of Management, University of Massachusetts, Amherst

Jacques Jansen, Universite Libre de Bruxelles, Ecole de Commerce SOLVAY (CADEPS) et Dept. de Mathematicques, Brussels

Elisabetta Gulandri, Department of Economics Asiendale, University of Modena

Ronald Heynen, Banque Paribas, London

Diem Ho, IBM Management Technologies Consulting Group - Europe, Paris

May Lo, Western New England College, Springfield, Massachusetts

Harry Kat, Bank of America, London

George Martin, CISDM, School of Management, University of Massachusetts

Dennis Murray, University of Colorado-Denver, Denver, Colorado

Thomas Philips, Paradigm Asset Management, New York

ADVANCED APPLICATIONS IN FINANCE: AN OVERVIEW OF PROBLEMS AND SOLUTION TECHNIQUES

Diem Ho
IBM Management Technologies Consulting Group

D. Ho and T. Schneeweis (eds.), Applications in Finance, Investments, and Banking, 1–19.

I. Introduction

In the last two decades, we have witnessed spectacular innovations in Finance. These innovations may have been rooted in the process of economic growth; from the uncertainty and volatility associated with foreign exchange rates, interest rates and other asset prices; or even from the desire to get around government-imposed regulation (Miller, 1992).

These innovations have created a dynamic market place. The deregulation and the globalization in the 80s of the financial market have generated more intense competition. The market-related information to be processed is ever increasing. With advanced technology, many techniques have been developed to take advantage of the growing availability of information. Concomitantly, business endeavors--and in particular, strategic and tactical decision-making--have become increasingly information and time-sensitive. Application of the techniques outlined below can contribute to the efficiency, profitability and competitiveness of the enterprise in the current market situation.

The primary objective of this chapter is to go over a number of applications in Finance in which information can be converted into profitable knowledge. In the next section we shall discuss the environment. We follow with section 3, where some building blocks frequently used in financial products will be described. In section 4, typical applications will be discussed. Concluding remarks will be offered in section 5.

II. Environment

Since the collapse of the Bretton Woods regime of fixed exchange rates (in 1973), we have witnessed a considerable turbulence in foreign exchange and commodity prices. There have be no shortage of other shocks since then: The OPEC-induced increases in oil prices, the U.S. Federal Reserve's efforts to control inflation through money supply targets (rather than interest rate targeting), the world-wide volatility in equity and equity-linked markets in October 1987, etc. In such a volatile environment, the business of finance must necessarily become a business of risk taking.

As such, risk must be managed. The uncertainty in financial markets has provided impetus for financial innovations and re-innovation. A number of derivative products such as forward contracts, futures contracts, options and swaps were more actively marketed, though these products may not be new. (For example, forward or future contracts have existed for centuries (see, for example, Smith et al., 1990)). The globalization and the deregulation of capital markets, on one side, can help businesses to reduce certain risk by diversification, but on the other side, generate more information and create stiff competition and a precarious environment that may have not existed previously. The response from the market is to create solutions and instruments that are more and more complex in order to satisfy sophisticated demands of customers. The existence of these instruments may serve to redistribute risks, to render the market more efficient, or just to make a fast buck from the unwary. In this environment, advanced mathematics, statistics and optimization have become crucial tools. In addition, with the information revolution in the 70s--the advent of high technologies and advanced and user-oriented software-- financial innovation has had an ideal place to breed. Before going into applications we shall discuss certain basic notions in finance so that we might lay down the framework for further discussion in this chapter, as well as later chapters in this book.

III. Basic notions

The basic concepts include two elements: the stochastic process and the contract-based payoff structures that serve as the building blocks for financial instruments and solutions.

1. Stochastic processes

Since the market is volatile, underlying asset values change with time in an uncertain--i.e. random--way. They may be thought of as following a stochastic process--which is itself a fancy way of saying nothing more than that the values of an asset may be conceptualized as a sequence of random events which occur over the course of time. These events can occur continuously or in discrete intervals of time. For example, currency trading takes place continuously, and one has a continuous record of prices. Sales of less liquid instruments, or instruments that are traded through exchanges that limit the frequency of trading (i.e. through batch auctions) maybe be thought of as occurring in discrete time.

Out of a quest for descriptive specificity as well as analytical tractability, one can use a more refined--and therefore restrictive--class of stochastic processes to describe the evolution of asset prices. In financial applications, one typically works with stochastic processes that have the so-called "markov" property--the term derives from the name of the Russian mathematician who studied the consequences of the property. This property can be intuitively described as: next period's events (i.e. the new price or value) depend only on the current period's event. That is to say, the event process has no memory. This memoryless property seems to comport with observed financial price series--there is little evidence that a previous period's return--say that which occurred 5 days ago--has any implication for that which occurs tomorrow.

One particular type of Markov process which describes asset prices is Brownian motion. The terminology comes from the name of the botanist who sought to describe the erratic movement of small particulates suspended in liquid. To make this notion more precise, we offer the following equations which are used to describe such a process mathematically. Let z be the quantity of interest (viz., an asset price), and t be the current time. Then, in the discrete time version of the Brownian motion--commonly referred to as a random walk--we can write:

$$\Delta z = \varepsilon\sqrt{\Delta t}$$

- ε is a random sample from a standard normal distribution
- mean of $\Delta z = 0$
- variance of $\Delta z = \Delta t$ and
- Δz_1 is independent of Δz_2.

This process can be generalized to incorporate a wide variety of volatilities and drifts, i.e.,

$$\Delta x = a\Delta t + b\Delta z$$

in the limit of $\Delta t \rightarrow 0$

$$dx = adt + bdz$$

where

- x is the quantity being tracked
- a is the rate of drift
- b is the per unit disturbance or variability of the path followed by x

When the drift rate and the variance rate are also functions of the underlying variable and time, we have the diffusion process:

$$dx = a(x,t)dt + b(x,t)dz$$

This is the basic motion which is assumed to explain the behavior of most financial assets in an efficient market. Geometric Brownian motion, which is generally thought of as a good model of the evolution of equity prices, is a special case of this last equation: by setting a(x,t)=ax and b(x,t)=bx, we have model which describes a quantity such that the incremental changes/returns, expressed as percentages, are normally distributed--implying that the prices themselves are *log*normally distributed.

2. Building Blocks

As mentioned above, a number of important financial product innovations have occurred in the market in the last two decades. There are four basic building blocks: forwards, futures, options and swaps.

- A *forward contract* obligates the owner to buy an asset at a pre-specified date in the future at a price set now.

- A *futures contract* is similar in structure to forward contract, except that the losses of gains are settled on a daily basis, and that the contracts are traded through an exchange.

- An *option contract* gives the owner the right (but not the obligation) to buy or to sell an asset at a specified date in the future at a pre-specified price.

- A *swap contract* is a combination of forward contracts obligating the contracting parties to exchange payments based on the relative movements of a set of underlying assets or indices, e.g. LIBOR vs. 5 yr. CMT rates.

As might be gleaned from the descriptions, the payoff profiles of forwards, futures and swaps are similar, where the payoff is the difference between the contracted price at expiration of the contract and the actual market price that prevails at that time. However, each set of contracts has different non-market risks associated with them. For example, because futures contracts are settled daily, and require the posting of margin (unlike forwards or swaps), the risk of default or non-delivery is minimized. The periodic payments contractually specified in a swap generally occur less than daily, and without the support of margin (though other credit enhancements may be employed), and thus tend to have more non-price risk than futures. Options, however, differ substantially in payoff profile from the other building blocks. Option payoffs are nonlinear, and therefore more complicated to understand. It is, however, that nonlinearity which makes them such important building blocks, since an extremely wide variety of payoff patterns can be created or hedged through the combination of options. (Futures contracts, and therefore swaps, can be built from options by combining options to sell and options to buy set at the same exercise price.)

IV. Typical Applications

There are numerous financial applications that are computationally and data intensive. We discuss six typical applications in this section:

1. Portfolio Optimization

This is a classic application, cover a whole class of asset allocation problems. In its most generic of forms, the problem is to select a portfolio of assets which yields the highest expected return for a given level of risk. (Alternately, the problem can be thought of as minimizing the level of risk for a given expected rate of return.) A key concept, effectively articulated by Markowitz (1952,1989) in solving this problem is the recognition the risk reduction that comes with effective diversification. With risk represented as the variance of expected returns, the classical portfolio optimization problem becomes a problem of optimal use of offsetting asset return covariances--a quadratic programming problem because of the quadratic nature of the variance/covariance terms. The solution to this problem has received extensive attention (e.g. Beale, 1959; Wolfe, 1959;, Dantzig, 1963; Theil and Van de Panne, 1960; Lemke, 1962; Ho, 1992a).

To be more specific, the risk associated with any security can be usefully divided into risk that affects all assets, and risk that is specific to that asset; it is the latter risk which may be diversified away.

Markowitz formulates the portfolio optimization problem as:

$\min V = X'AX$

subject to

$R = \Sigma x_i r_i$

$\Sigma x_i = 1$

$x_i \geq 0$ (i.e., no short sales)

where:

V is variance or risk

A is the variance-covariance matrix of asset returns to be optimized

$X' = (x_1, x_2 \ldots x_n)$ is the vector describing the portfolio composition

R is the rate of return on the portfolio

and r_i is the rate of return on the ith asset.

Ho (1992a) has taken advantage of the special structure of the portfolio optimization problem to propose a robust iteration procedure for the solution of this problem.

In reality, there are more constraints on the portfolio manager than what we see above in the standard model. Other typical constraints may be cash yields, asset holdings, index tracking, etc. These constraints can be easily incorporated into the problem formulation. However, if computational power is insufficient to solve the fully specified model--as was the case until recently for all but the most modest of problems--an alternate solution strategy, developed by Sharpe (1963, 1985) involves reformulating the problem as an index model, in which individual assets covariances are not specified through a full covariance matrix, but through a set of covariances with a variety of indices--thus dramatically reducing the dimensionality of the problem. These indices might include economic factors such as: a market index, like the S&P 500; an industry index; an interest rate variable; an inflation rate variable; a GDP variables; government spending; monetary variables like the money supply, etc.

In present day practice, the solution of the portfolio selection problem may involve one or more of the following mathematical techniques:

- *Linear Programming*

If the portfolio risk can be assessed simply as an asset ranking or by the linear distance from the target (minimum shortfall), the problem can be formulated as a linear programming problem. In the case of maximizing the final wealth of a multiperiod investment subjected to linear constraints of preceding periods, the problem can also be solved by linear programming (Mulvey and Valdimirou, 1992).

- *Quadratic Programming*

This technique is typically used in the case of mean-variance or multi-index solutions. It also applies when one wishes to employ a semi-variance, rather than variance constraint. The semi-variance loss function involves penalize returns below a pre-specified level, but does not offset those losses with returns greater than expected. Thus it is a more conservative criteria than covariance since it involves an unconditional minimization of downside risk (see Harlow, 1991; King and Jensen, 1992). The semi-variance method can be handled by using historical data to model the return distributions of individual assets. From these distributions, simulations of future portfolio return can be generated in order to solve the optimization problem; artificial or historical data can be used as an input into the solution process.

- *Dynamic programming*

If the problem involves more than one period, the problem is formulated as the compounded return of different periods; as such the problem is dynamic, and requires the use of dynamic programming methods. The portfolio selection problem becomes dynamic especially when transactions costs are considered, or when the manager wishes to exploit predictable variation in asset prices, such as may arise with seasonal variations or the business cycle. Another class of problems that make use of dynamic programming methods include multi-period asset-liability management. It is worth noting that problems requiring dynamic programming methods are often extremely complex, and methods employed for their solution are not always robust. Translating a dynamic programming problem in to a linear programming framework often serves to increase the stability and robustness of the solution process.

All of the solution techniques above are designed to solve problems in which the underlying, market-generated, parameters are static. Unfortunately, for the portfolio manager, parameters are time-varying. These changes must be incorporated into the optimized portfolio, but arbitrary modification of input data may undermine the optimality properties of selected portfolio (see, e.g., Black and Litterman, 1991.) Asset return changes in one group of assets may be associated with changes in the expected returns of other assets. Equilibrium models, such as the Capital Asset Pricing Model (CAPM), may be useful in the determination of just how the changes in one set of assets might be related to other assets.

In addition to the less dramatic changes in the asset universe described in the previous paragraph, portfolio managers may also be concerned with more consequential events, especially those associated with large downward market movements. Portfolio managers may wish to insure their portfolios through the purchase of put options which limit their downside risk. However, a put on their specific portfolio may not exist, be readily available, or may be "too expensive." In such a situation, the manager could choose to replicate a put option by creating a synthetic option by purchasing a basket of options that approximate the target option. This method of hedging has the advantage over "delta hedging" in that more accurately incorporates more risk parameters (see Hull, 1989). The actual composition of the basket can be found using optimization methods such as those described above.

Some other areas where optimization methods may be used include "dedication" problems in cash-flow management, strategic planning and asset-liability management.

2. Asset Pricing

The assets discussed in this section are financial products, with particular focus on derivative products such as options, futures, forwards, and swaps as well as more exotic products. Models used to price such contracts may have closed-form solutions, while most often they require numerical techniques like the numerical solution of partial differential equations or monte carlo simulations. One of the most famous, and most important, of such pricing solutions is the closed-form formula known as the Black-Scholes equation for a class of options contracts on equity assets. Under the assumption that the underlying (non-dividend paying) asset price evolves according to geometric Brownian motion, the formula gives the price of a call option, C, on that asset, S, with an exercise price X, and a time to maturity on the option of T. Additional inputs into the formula are r, the "risk-free" rate--usually the rate on government debt at the time horizon of the option-and the standard deviation, σ, of the asset price expected over the course of the contract. Additional features have been incorporated into the model, such as dividends, taxes, stochastic interest rates, etc. A good review can be found in Smithson (1991). The Black-Scholes (1973) equation, as extended by Merton (1973) and Ingersoll (1976), can be written as:

$C=ASN(d_1)-BXN(d_2)$

where

N(x) is the cumulative normal distribution function

$$d_1 = \ln(AS/BX)/(\sigma\sqrt{T}) + \sigma\sqrt{T}/2$$

$$d_2 = d_1 - \sigma\sqrt{T}$$

$$A = e^{-\delta(1-\tau)T}$$

$$B = e^{-r(1-\tau)T}$$

where δ is the dividend rate and τ is the tax rate.

The model can be extended to include a variable interest rate by substituting B(T) for e^{-rT}, where B(T) represents the price of a discount bond paying 1 unit of currency at the terminal date, T; and, substituting σ' for σ, and

$$\sigma'^2 T = \int_0^T (\sigma^2 + \sigma_B^2 - 2\rho\sigma\sigma_B)dt$$

where σ_B is the volatility of B and ρ is the correlation between the bond and the underlying asset.

Alternately, for a commodity as an underlying asset, A=1 and $S=e^{-rT}F$ where F is the futures price on the asset (see Black, 1976).

And finally, for foreign exchange, $A=\exp(-r_fT)$, $B=\exp(-r_dT)$ where *f* denotes foreign and *d* denotes the domestic riskless rate (see Garman and Kohlhagen, 1983).

While the Black-Scholes equation is useful for pricing European options, it is less helpful in pricing American options, i.e. options which may be exercised at *any time up to* the expiration date, and other, more exotic options. Other methods, mainly numeric, are necessary. These include: binomial or trinomial methods, in which the state space is discretized, and an option price is solved for using a backward recursion or more generically, a dynamic programming method (Hull and White, 1992); monte carlo or simulation methods (Boyle, 1977) wherein the expected value of the option is computed via averaging of a range of outcomes simulated in a manner consonant with the underlying model; and by finite difference or other methods used to solve associated partial differential equations numerically (see Courtadon, 1982 or Hull and White, 1990).

In asset-liability management problems, to be discussed further below, asset pricing techniques are especially important. This is true whenever the assets are directly sensitive to interest rate variation. Exactly how to model the evolution of the term structure of interest rates--the basis for actually determining the value of interest-rate contingent claims--has been the subject of much work. Some recent work includes the modeling of Ho and Lee (1986) and Black, Derman and Toy (1990). There are a number of problems that arise in deriving and using such models, including their computational complexity. One particular practical problem is the selection of inputs into the model: for example, historical data may not adequately reflect the time-varying nature of the term-structure; forward-looking inputs, like implied volatilities derived from traded option contracts, however, are not available at all horizons.

3. Segmentation and risk assessment

This is a classical application in the financial sector. From a number of quantifiable characteristics, we attempt to define as finely as possible the customer or counter-party profiles. In marketing, we can use segmentation and risk assessment methods to better target our customers and products. One such specific application is credit scoring. Another possible application might be the targeting of companies for merger or acquisition. (See Marcotorchino and Michaud, 1979,1981; and Marcotorchino, 1987 for advanced discussion of these applications.)

Such methods have been developed to handle both quantitative and qualitative data, and may be applied in financial as well as non-financial contexts. Classifications can be done automatically, with the optimal number of classes to be determined simultaneously (Messatfa, 1990, 1992). The main drawback in many of these solutions is that they are based solely on the profile characteristics of the target; environmental parameters associated with segmentation or risk analysis should be incorporated to add in a forward-looking dimension to the solution. This information, along with historical data, may help us to better model credit risk or pursue recovery should default occur.

4. Securitization

An important class of securities are so-called mortgage-backed securities (MBS); managing the risks associated with such securities requires a constellation of advanced techniques. For example, MBS securities have embedded options (associated with mortgage borrowers option to prepay a mortgage at any point in time) which complicate their valuation. They also have credit risks associated with the possibility that the borrower will default. Analysis of borrower behavior, and hence security valuation, requires a large quantity of data, as well as advanced statistical and optimization techniques.

5. Visualization

With the increasing amount of data available, methods must be developed to present such large quantities of data in a form that is both intelligible and useful to the decision maker. A global view of the financial landscape--whether it involves many assets, or several characteristics of an individual asset--may often be helpful. Graphical representations--which require substantial computing power--can be very useful in this regard.

6. Asset-Liability Management (ALM)

Perhaps the most demanding of applications is asset-liability management. The objective of ALM is to manage risks, to master growth and to meet regulatory requirements. There are three particularly important risks that affect the financial intermediary seeking effective ALM techniques: interest rate risk (the most important), credit risk and foreign exchange risk. A close fourth is liquidity risk, though it may be considered an endogenous, rather than exogenous, risk. Overall, ALM seeks not only the measurement of risks--be they associated with products, positions, or portfolios--but the development of optimization strategies necessary to meet managerial risk objectives.

Effective ALM must recognize both its strategic and tactical importance. To do so, the ALM function must be clearly defined by management, and be capable of providing management with the requisite information necessary to evaluate the effectiveness of the ALM process, and to change its objectives if either management or the environment changes. Automation is instrumental to all of this.

An ALM system must consist of at least five modules:

- *Data collector* to provide necessary data inputs.
- *Cash flow generator* to provide asset and liability variations for all financial products.
- *Analyzer* to provide all of the mathematics, statistics and simulation necessary for modeling all products and portfolios on the balance sheet.
- *Optimizer* to provide optimal hedging strategies or other management objectives.
- *Report generator* to provide all input/output reports for management (see also Dattatreya, 1991).

An ALM system should be flexible, and allow for multiple target accounts (Fabozzi and Konishi, 1991). It must be able to provide market or liquidation values to meet internal as well as external requirements. It must be able to handle embedded options (such as callability) and option-adjusted spread analysis (OAS).

In the optimization process, the financial firm should incorporate into the solution process the tax effects and regulatory constraints imposed on the firm (see for example, Gualandri, 1996; Raghavan et al. 1991, Gilligan, 1991 or Ho, 1992b). Similarly, if administrative and marketing costs can be accurately determined, they should be included as well.

We have devoted our time to these six applications because they offer six interrelated advantages, little of which could be gotten without some of the sophisticated techniques described in the text. These advantages are, respectively:

- gain from optimal selection of assets
- precise understanding of asset values
- detailed knowledge of customers and products
- efficiency and control of enterprise's balance sheet
- effective decision making in a complex informational environment
- better risk management

V. Concluding Remarks

In an increasing complex and volatile world, efficiency and profitability are all the more important. With the increase in information, we need to employ increasingly sophisticated techniques to analyze data that is growing in size and complexity in order to exploit profit opportunities. The advent of faster and cheaper computing platforms, as well as the continued enhancement of the software programs (e.g., Minkoff, 1996) that make use of such hardware, have put such techniques within the reach of a widening range of users.

References

Beale, E.M.L. (1959) "On Quadratic Programming," *Naval Res. Log. Quart.*, 6, 227-244.

Black, F. (1976) "The Pricing of Commodity Contracts," *Journal of Financial Economics*, 3, 167-179.

Black, F., E. Derman and W. Toy (1990) "A One Factor Model of Interest Rates and its Application to Treasury Bond Options," *Financial Analysis Journal*, January, 33-39.

Black, F. and R. Litterman (1991) "Global Asset Allocation With Equities, Bonds, and Currencies," *Fixed Income Research*, Goldman Sachs, October.

Black, F. and M. Scholes (1973) "The Pricing of Options and Corporate Liabilities, *Journal of Political Economy*, 81, 637-659.

Boyle, P.P. (1977) "Options: A Monte Carlo Approach," *Journal of Financial Economics*, 4, 323-338.

Courtadon, G., (1982) "A More Accurate Finite Difference Approximation for The Valuation of Options," *Journal of Financial And Quantitative Analysis*, 17, 697-703.

Dantzig, G.B., (1963) *Linear Programming and Extensions*, Princeton: Princeton University Press.

Dattatreya,R.E., (1991) "A Practical Approach To Asset/Liability Management," In *Asset/Liability Management*, Eds. F.J. Fabozzi and A. Konishi, Chicago: Probus.

Fabozzi, F.J. and A. Konishi (1991), "Introduction," In *Asset/Liability Management* Eds. F.J. Fabozzi and A. Konishi, Chicago: Probus.

Garman, M.B. and S.W. Kohlhagen (1983) "Foreign Currency Option Values, *Journal of International Money and Finance*, 2, 231-237.

Gualandri, E., (1996) "Asset Liability Management: Regulatory Guidelines on Interest Rate Risk Control and Their Impacts on Financial Institutions," *This Volume*.

Gilligan, R.L., (1991) "Using The Bank Risk Based Capital Guidelines In Strategic Planning," In *Asset/Liability Management*, Eds. F.J. Fabozzi and A. Konishi, Chicago: Probus.

Harlow, W.V., (1991) "Asset Allocation in a Downside Risk Framework," Equity Portfolio Analysis, Salomon Brothers, March.

Ho D., (1992a) "Quadratic Programming for Portfolio Optimization," *Journal Applied Stochastic Models Data Analysis*, 8, 3.

Ho D., (1992b) "A Practical Approach to Asset Liability Management," *Financial Systems Journal*, IBM-Japan, 3, 142-150.

Ho, T.S.Y. and S.B. Lee (1986), "Term Structure Movements and Pricing Interest Rate Contingent Claims," *Journal of Finance*, 41, 1011-1029.

Hu, J.C, (1987) "Derivative Mortgage Securities: An Overview," Shearson Lehman Brothers Inc., Special Report, December.

Hull, J., (1989) *Options, Futures, and Other Derivative Securities*, Englewood Cliffs, NJ: Prentice Hall.

Hull, J. and A. White (1990) "Valuing Derivative Securities Using the Explicit Finite Difference Method," *Journal of Financial and Quantitative Analysis*, 25, 87-100.

Hull, J. and A. White (1992) "A Note on the Valuation of Mortgage-Backed Securities," Recent Developments In Pricing & Hedging Options Seminar, Organized By The University of Toronto, June.

Ingersoll, J. (1976) "A Theoretical and Empirical Investigation of the Dual Purpose Funds: An Application of Contingent Claims Analysis," *Journal of Financial Economics*, 3.

King, A.J. and D.L. Jensen (1992) "Quadratic Efficient Frontiers for Portfolio Optimization," *Journal of Applied Stochastic Models and Data Analysis, 8, 3.*

Lemke, C.E. (1962) "A Method of Solution for Quadratic Programs," *Management Science*, 8, 4, 442-453.

Marcotorchino J.F. (1987) "An Unified Approach of The Block-Seriation Problems, *Journal of Applied Stochastic Models and Data Analysis*, 3, 2.

Marcotorchino J.F. and P. Michaud (1979) *Optimisation En Analyse Ordinale Des Donnees*, Paris: Masson.

Marcotorchino J.F. and P. Michaud (1981) "Agregation Des Similarites En Classification Automatique," *Revue De Statistique Appliquee*, 30, 2.

Markowitz, H.M., (1952) "Portfolio Selection," *The Journal of Finance*, 7, 1, Pp. 77-91.

Markowitz, H.M., (1989) *Mean-Variance Analysis In Portfolio Choice and Capital Markets*, Oxford: Basil Blackwell.

Merton, R.C. (1973) "Theory of Rational Option Pricing," *Bell Journal of Economics and Management Science*, 4, 141-183.

Messatfa H., (1990) "Maximal Association for The Sum of Squares of A Contingency Table," *RAIRO-Operations Research*,1,1-19.

Messatfa H. (1992) "An Algorithm To Maximize The Agreement Between Two Partitions," *Journal of Classification, 9,5-15.*

Miller, M.H., (1992) "Financial Innovation: Achievements and Prospects," *Journal of Financial Engineering*, 1,1, 1-13.

Minkoff, A.S. (1996) "A Modeling Language and Code Generator for Mathematical Programming," *This Volume*.

Mulvey, J.M. and H. Vladimirou (1992) "Stochastic Network Programming for Financial Planning Problems," *Management Science* , 38, 11, 1642-1664.

Raghavan, V., L. Miller and D.J. Askin (1991) "The New Bank Capital Guidelines and Their Implications, In *Asset-Liability Management*, Eds. F.J. Fabozzi and A. Konishi, Chicago: Probus.

Sharpe, W.F. (1963) "A Simplified Model for Portfolio Analysis," *Management Science*, 9, 2, Pp 277-293.

Sharpe, W.F., (1985) *Investments*, 3rd Ed., Engelwood Cliffs, NJ: Prentice-Hall.

Smith, Jr, C,W. Smithson and D.S. Wilford, (1990) *Managing Financial Risk*, New York:Harper & Row.

Smithson, C.W. (1991) "Wonderful Life," *Risk*, 4, 9, 37-44.

Theil. H. and C. Van De Panne (1960), "Quadratic Programming as an Extension of Classical Quadratic Maximization," *Management Science*, 7, 1, Pp 1-20.

Wolfe, P. (1959) "The Simplex Method for Quadratic Programming," *Econometrica*, 27, Pp. 382-398.

PRINCIPLES FOR THE CONTROL OF ASSET LIABILITY MANAGEMENT STRATEGIES IN BANKS AND INSURANCE COMPANIES

Goren Bergendahl
Department of Business Administration
School of Economics and Commercial Law
University of Gothenburg

Jacques Janssen
Universite Libre de Bruxelles
Ecole de Commerce SOLVAY (CADEPS) et Dpt. De Mathematique and
Vrije Universiteit Brussel Dpt van Wiskunde

D. Ho and T. Schneeweis (eds.), Applications in Finance, Investments, and Banking, 21–61.

I. Asset-Liability Management--Definitions and Overview

1.1 General Overview

Asset and Liability Management (ALM), which is sometime referred to as Balance Sheet Management (BSM), can be viewed as a process whereby a bank's total assets and liabilities are controlled and managed simultaneously, in an integrated fashion. ALM is often considered as an instrument for *medium and long term* action. In this way, it may be seen as a complement to liquidity management, which concerns the short term action. ALM combines the traditional activities of Asset Management ("asset allocation") and Liability Management ("liability choice"). Asset Management concerns many different research areas like *reserve management* and *portfolio choice* models. (Portfolio choice includes "direct control" of assets, involving the selection of short term cash management assets to long maturity equity and debentured investments, as well as matters of "indirect control", e.g. pricing of selected assets.) Liability Management includes subjects like *deposit modeling* and *capital structure*. ALM has been used mainly for the *management of risk*, but there is, as well, a growing interest among banks to use them for the *management of return* .

Consider for a moment the economic activity of banks: it is the intermediation between deposit-makers and loan takers that is a central aspect of a bank's functioning. In order to perform this process in an efficient way, a bank has to consider the existence of both the joint demand and the joint production of services, as well the generic problem of avoiding the mismatch between assets and liabilities. *Joint demand* means that a single customer demands two services at the same time, such as the deposits of funds as well as access to the payment system. *Joint production* concerns the use of personnel and computers for the simultaneous production of several services (e.g., the use of computer systems to manage both checking accounts as well as credit services). *Mismatch* exists when loans and deposits are held in different currencies and/or have different maturity structures. (The latter may suggest the use of off-balance sheet hedging instruments.)

Using our terminology, instruments under the *direct control* of a bank are: investments in physical plant, computer facilities and offices and the investment of liquidity surplus; Those available for *indirect control* are e.g. prices related to loans and deposits.

One would expect that both risk *and* return are viewed as the main objectives of ALM. However, many banks use ALM for *risk control only,* without considering if a product with a larger risk is associated with a larger return. The reason seems to be that these banks do not calculate the marginal costs and marginal expected revenues from expanding a single service. As such, these banks do not jointly manage their *risk-return transformation* and their *real resource management.*

Furthermore, several banks pursue objectives other than the *control of risk* with equal importance in their ALM strategy. Such objectives are to *match risk and return,* to *expand the balance sheet,* to *maintain the infrastructure,* to *maintain the reserve ratio* and to comply with *regulations on capital adequacy.*

To take the last of these items, for example: Capital adequacy regulation has a strong influence on the structure of ALM systems for banks, though it is also clear that such regulations bind the actions of different banks to varying degrees. In fact, there is also a concern that these regulations may increase risk instead of reducing it by inducing financial institutions to move a greater portion of their assets and liabilities "off-balance sheet" via mechanisms such as various derivative products as well as financial guarantees like letters of credit.

In summary, there is a need to effectively implement Asset-Liability Management in banks and in insurance firms. One reason is to provide control over the different risks faced by such an institution. But another and more important reason is to provide an integrated framework within which to analyze the balance sheet as a portfolio of assets and liabilities. Such a *two-sided modeling* approach has to be done frequently, at least month by month. Any change in the portfolio has to be considered in relation to the objectives of the bank or the insurance firm. Consequently, this approach will require that the decision-maker identify his or her objectives, the instruments for achieving those objectives, the associated costs, and its relation to its market environment. This is inherently a challenging task.

1.2 ALM Objectives

One of the main objectives of an ALM strategy is to match return and risks in three basic categories: interest rate risk; liquidity risk; and default risk.

The interest rate risk influences the *return* on both assets and liabilities. A "good" ALM strategy must always act on these two parts of the balance sheet when the market interest rate moves. Liquidity risk concerns the risk that a decision-making unit will not have sufficient funds available to meet commitments at any given point in time. The effect will be that the volume of assets and liabilities change without the complete control of the bank or the insurance firm -- the decision-making unit of our discussion. The default risk is also called the "risk of ruin" by actuaries; its realization implies, in principle, that the counterparty to a transaction has to stop all its activities, or at least operate under a regime governing bankruptcy or insolvency. For banks, the primary source of default risk is the loans that it has made; it may also suffer such risks from any other financial contracts, such as swaps or forwards. Insurance companies themselves face default risk in their investment portfolio, but they also face a kind of risk akin to default risk in their premium and claims process. An insurable event may not only require payout on a policy, but may as well, in the case of morbidity or catastrophe, end the stream of premiums being collected.

Banks and insurance firms must and do take all these risks in order to achieve a return. They have the advantage over their customers in that they may pool these risks. However, a perfect and complete pooling will never occur. The reason is that, given the economic function of financial institutions like banks and insurance companies, the demand for credits are essentially long-term contracts, while deposits are short-term. This is the classical way of bank management--making profits by lending long and borrowing short. An insurance firm has long term policy contracts, which means that some of its assets may be short-term and its liabilities long-term. Furthermore, assets and liabilities will rarely generate cash flows simultaneously, and more often do so sequentially. Therefore, there may often be considerable discrepancies between assets and liabilities when volumes, and timing are concerned, and risks are not readily diversifiable. Consequently, the risk exposure may be subject to substantial variations in interest rates and liquidity. Therefore, risk reduction through pooling is not a sufficient activity for risk control but has to be complemented with active hedging and pricing.

In theory, a financial institution (like a bank or an insurance firm) would also like to perfectly match its cash flows on the assets and liabilities sides. If so, there would be no exposure to interest rate risk, liquidity risks or credit risks. In practice, this is neither possible nor desirable. Both banks and insurance firms make profit by taking such risks. The management of assets and liabilities is derived from this premise. *The utmost goal with ALM is to measure how sensitive equity is to changes in interest rates, liquidity premia, or credit conditions*. As will be shown, the duration of equity is such an index of performance. This index will become a signal to the shareholders of the riskiness of that firm.

II. Basic Components for ALM Strategies

2.1 Risk Evaluation

To begin with, we must have in mind that the risk management is not possible if we cannot quantify and measure the exposure to the risks under consideration. Here, this is done with the use of concepts like duration and convexity for the interest rate risk, and with the concept of probability or ruin for the risk of default.

A readily measurable risk is human mortality risk; this is due to the existence of human mortality tables and the law of large numbers. Nevertheless, even in this case, the statistical data must be appropriately adapted to the considered population. This leads to the concept of experimental mortality tables for life insurance companies. Some risks need complete statistical study, for example for car accidents, and if possible a stochastic actuarial deduced from it. In particular, this is the case if one wants to incorporate commercial risk in an ALM model.

We must also keep in mind the fact that the risk exposure for a given set of assets and liabilities may not be static; the underlying event generating mechanism from which emerge the risks under consideration, may itself change. For example, the probability of default on a loan may be 2% per year, given the current stage of the business cycle. But this default rate may change as the business cycle itself unfolds, in a random and unpredictable manner. Our risk measurement system should actively account for both the current risk profile of assets, but also the time-varying nature of that profile.

2.2 *The Yield Curve*

The most useful information for the interest rate evaluation is the knowledge of the yield curve for the market of (essentially) risk-free securities like government bonds. Such a yield curve is a function f of t and T (t, T being positive real numbers) representing the interest rate for a maturity value T-t given at time t. So, for a fixed time t, the function of T, $f(t,T)$ gives all the values of the interest rates for any maturity T-t. Of course, these values are changing with t and in fact all the yield curves $f(t.,T)$ are random curves indexed by t. It follows that a major problem to operate ALM models is the elaboration of stochastic models for the yield curve.

2.3 *The Return on Equity*

In addition to focusing on interest rate risk, there has been recent efforts to effectively manage the value of the firm as a whole, as expressed by the value of its equity. One criterion is to maximize expected net present value of equity. Another criterion is to maximize the net present value of the return on equity *for an predetermined acceptable level on risks*. Two ways to analyze and manage the dynamics of equity risk are:[1]

a) to concentrate on the *volatility* of equity, i.e. how the value of equity will depend on variations in market rate for risk-free capital;

b) to concentrate on the *duration* of equity. This involves viewing a share in this financial institution in a manner analogous to a zero-coupon bond. The change in market rates of interest will then influence the value of equity in the same way as does a zero-coupon bond with equivalent duration.

---

[1]For a detailed analysis, see e.g. Gilbert (1988) and Bergendahl (1989).

As will be shown later on, these two approaches are equivalent.

2.4 Constraints

The main types of constraints concern:

a) *legal aspects*: this is a function of the insurance or bank's jurisdiction;

b) *liquidity*: for the banks, these explain how to satisfy deposit withdrawals on demand and for insurance companies, how to be able to pay the claim amounts;

c) *budget*: initial (and eventually) final budgets;

d) *strategy*: political choices of the company (taking into account, among other things, the problem of taxation);

e) *shareholders*: the determinations of dividends to be distributed;

(f) *asset and liability flows:* these constraints imply the modeling of the flow of deposits for banks or of the premium entrance for insurance companies as well as the modeling of the evolution of a loans for banks and of the claim amount process for insurance companies. They also concern an expansion or a contraction of the demand for savings deposits, savings, securities, fixed rate lending, etc. ...

2.5 The Decision Variables Universe

For the process of hedging and pricing and for the investments in portfolio of bond and/or other securities, the selection of decision variables must be done. They should include a range of financial products like options, futures, caps and floors, swaps.

2.6 Data Base Management for ALM Strategies

From the preceding points, it clearly appears that the practical use of an ALM strategy in real time is impossible without having a permanent data base. It must provide the decision-maker with all the information not only for solving the mathematical program but also to re-estimate the basic parameters of the model which naturally appear in the main tools described above.

III. Duration and Gap Analysis

Duration and gap analysis are the main theoretical principles utilized for ALM. Both methods, as commonly formulated, focus on interest rate risks, to the exclusion of many of the other types of risks discussed above. Duration analysis involves the calculation of the "time-weighted" maturity for each asset account and liability which gives the decision maker some sense of the sensitivity of the process of an asset to small changes in yield. These calculations are then used to estimate interest rate sensitivities for the existing values of assets or liabilities. Gap management is often performed for a single time period (usually a year), but may also be done in a multi-period framework. It involves the estimation for each time period of the difference between those assets and liabilities that are associated with fixed interest rates. There is an extensive amount of research available that concerns the use of duration and gap analysis (see e.g. Hartzog 1983, Toevs 1983, Kaufman 1984, Brewer 1985, Harrington 1987 and Wilson 1988).

To understand these two approaches, assume that :

A_i^0 = the accounting value of asset i at time t = 0

B_j^0 = the accounting value of liability j at time t = 0

Then these assets and liabilities will generate future cash flows:

$$A_i^0 : (a_i^1, a_i^2, a_i^3, \ldots, a_i^T)$$

$$B_i^0 : (b_j^1, b_j^2, b_j^3, \ldots, b_j^T)$$

each with a market value:

(1) $A_i = \Sigma_t a_i^t \; / (1 + r_i)^t$

(2) $B_j = \Sigma_t b_j^t \; / (1 + r_j)^t$

(3.1)

where r_i and r_j are market rates of interest. These rates may differ because of different credit risks. They are known at time t=0 but may change afterwards.
The future cash flows should include:

a) interest income;
b) interest expenditures;
c) non-interest income;
d) administrative outlays.

Consequently, each asset and liability is supposed to generate a *profit margin*:

$(A_i - A_i^0)$ for asset i

$(B_j^0 - B_j)$ for liability j

Example A

One bank has 100 millions in customer loans. These loans will generate an interest income of 13% per year for three years. After that the loans will be repaid to 98% (2% will become credit losses). The administrative costs are estimated to 1% per year. The loans are funded on the interbank market at a rate of 10%. That gives the following cost flows:

	interest income	_ administrative costs	+ repayment	
year 1	0.13 x 100	-0.01 x 100		= 12
year 2	0.13 x 100	-0.01 x 100		= 12
year 3	0.13 x 100	-0.01 x 100	+ 98	= 12

Then, the *market value* of these loans will be:

$$A_i = \frac{12}{1.10} + \frac{12}{1.10^2} + \frac{110}{1.10^3} = 103.5m$$

which is different from the *accounting value* that is 100 m.

The *return* on an asset or a liability will become the difference between its market value and its accounting value. The *interest rate risk* will then be the risk that the return will be reduced when the interest rate moves.

Assume in example A that the interbank rate will move from 10% to 11%. This implies that the new market value has changed by 2.5 m (from 103.5 m to 101.0 m). Consequently, the return will go down from 3.5 m to 1.0 m.

The liquidity risk will be the risk that funds will not be available when needed. Assume in example A that the average customer makes a delay of 10 days to pay interest and the final installment. Then, the decision-maker will have to use a central bank funding at say 15% to pay interest and depreciation on his own borrowing interbank. This will cause an extra cost of 5% over 10 days, which will become the liquidity risk.

Finally, the default risk will be the risk that the credit losses will increase. If they grow from 2% to 4%, then the cash flow will change to 108 m year 2 and the market value will go down form 103.5 m to 102 m.

These three risks -- of interest, of liquidity, and of default -- are the main targets for the ALM banks and in insurance firms. Out of them the interest rate risk is assumed to be the most important one in the medium term, that is over a planning period of one month to one year.

Example B

Out of the two approaches to manage interest rate risks, *gap management* presupposes that the cash flow may be calculated for each type of asset and liability. For example assume that in example A the three-year loan (at 13%) will be funded with a two-year interbank loan (at 10%). The cash flows will then become:

YEAR	1	2	3
LOAN	+12	+12	+110
FUNDING	-10	-110	
GAP	+2	-98	+110

with a substantial gap in year 2.

Gap management aims at finding, and funding, such gaps. It does *not* include any technique to choose the best funding. Consequently, as an ALM strategy, it does not guarantee any kind of efficiency.

The *duration approach* is based upon a general assumption about the duration of each asset and liability. With these assumptions, in some cases, one may estimate the interest rate risk without having to calculate cash flows. The only ingredients are the market values and the duration of each asset (A_i) and liability (B_j).

As an example, assume that an asset (A_i) had a general form of cash flow. To simplify, let us suppose that we have a constant market rate r per period. The problem at hand is: how does one measure the influence of the variation of the market rate r? By differentiation, we get:

$$dA_i = [-(1+r)^{-1} \sum_{i}^{T} \frac{a_i^t t}{(1+r)^t}]dr$$

(3.2)

$$dA_i \approx \Delta A_i = A_i(r+\Delta r) - A_i$$

(3.3)

Then the *duration* can be thought of as the time-weighted value of the cash flow in proportion to its present value:

$$D_i = \frac{\sum_{i}^{T} \frac{a_i^t t}{(1+r)^t}}{A_i} = \frac{[\text{the time weighed value of the cash flow}]}{[\text{the present value of the cash flow}]}$$

(3.4)

The larger the part of the cash flow in more distant years, the larger the duration. Then define:

p_i^t =the proportion between the present value $a_i^t/(1+r)^t$ of the cash at time t and the present value of the total cash flow, i.e.

$$p_i^t = \frac{a_i^t}{(1+r)^t} / \sum_{i}^{T} \frac{a_i^t}{(1+r)^t}$$

(3.5)

This implies that:

$$D_i = \sum_{t=1}^{T} p_i^t t$$

(3.6)

The interpretation of D_i now becomes quite transparent: it represents the average of the monetary flow: $(a_i^1, a_i^2, a_i^3, \ldots, a_i^T)$ under the probability distribution $(p_i^t, t = 1, .., T)$

Consequently, we get:

$$\Delta A_i = -(1+r)A_i D \Delta r$$

(3.7)

REMARKS:

1) $\Delta r > 0 \Rightarrow \Delta A_i < 0$

2) We can write (3.2) under another form called *Hick's formula*:

$$\frac{\Delta A_i}{A_i} = -D \frac{\Delta r}{1+r}$$

3) some authors call the number:

$$D_m = \frac{-D}{1+r} \qquad (3.9)$$

the *modified duration*; some authors call it the *sensitivity parameter* or the *volatility*. This gives a new expression for Hick's formula:

$$\frac{\Delta A_i}{A_i} = -D_{m_\Delta} r$$

(3.10)

All these formulations are, *mutatis mutandis*, similar for the liabilities B_j.

Again consider **Example B** but now as an illustration to the use of the duration approach.

Here the loan with the cash flow:

+12 +12 +110

will have a duration (D) as:

$$D = \frac{\frac{12}{1+r} + \frac{12.2}{(1+r)^2} + \frac{110.3}{(1+r)^3}}{\frac{12}{1+r} + \frac{12}{(1+r)^2} + \frac{110}{(1+r)_3}}$$

It is easy to find that D varies slightly with r as:

r	0.09	0.10	0.11	0.12
D	2.70	2.69	2.69	2.68

These measures of the duration may then be used to estimate the *volatility*, that is the change in equity when the interest rate fluctuates. In this case, the volatility (D*m*) will become:

r	0.09	0.10	0.11	0.12
D*m*	-2.48	-2.45	-2.42	-2.39

IV. *Immunization and Profitability*

Let us now consider the assets (A_i) and the liabilities (B_j). The difference: $E = \Sigma_i A_i - \Sigma_j B_j$ is, then, the market value of the equity of the bank or the insurance firm.

This implies that: $E = \Sigma_{t=1}^{T} (1+r)^{-t} (\Sigma_{i=1}^{I} a_i^t - \Sigma_{j=1}^{J} b_j^t)$

$$(4.1)$$

Certain assets $i \in \Theta$ and certain liabilities $j \in \Omega$ are interest rate sensitive.

Immunization

Immunization concerns management actions to control both a) interest rate risks and b) liquidity risks. *Interest rate risks* are the risks that the market rates for assets and liabilities will move in an unfavorable direction. (For example, consider exhibit 5, below,where market rates moved 2% upwards.) *Liquidity risks* are the risks that the funding will need to be done at higher rates and/or that the interbank exchanges will be done at lower rates than before.

There are three main classes of immunization actions available:

a) off-balance sheet (OBS) actions (futures, forwards, options, swaps, etc., ...);

b) money market (MM) actions (placements and loans interbank, placements in bonds and notes, funding by own bank certificates);

c) repricing loans and deposits.

4.1 Interest rate risk

Assume that a change in interest rates (r_j) is simultaneous for all assets (i) and liabilities (j). That is:

$$dr_i = dr_j = dr \quad \text{(all i,j)} \tag{4.2}$$

Then the *interest rate risk* may be measured as:

$$\frac{dE}{dr} = \frac{d}{dr}[\Sigma_{i\varepsilon\theta} A_i - \Sigma_{j\varepsilon\Omega} B_j] \tag{4.3}$$

Then for horizontal yield curves:

$$\frac{dE}{dr} = -[\Sigma_{i\varepsilon\theta} \frac{D(A_i)\ A_i}{(1+r_i)} - \Sigma_{j\varepsilon\Omega} \frac{D(B_j)\ B_j}{(1+r_j)}] \tag{4.4}$$

Consequently, a balance sheet will be immunized at date t=0,if

$$\frac{dE}{dr} = 0 \tag{4.5}$$

$$\Sigma_{i\varepsilon\theta} \frac{D(A_i)\ A_i}{(1+r_i)} \ / \ \Sigma_{j\varepsilon\Omega} \frac{D(B_j)B_j}{(1+r_j)} \tag{4.6}$$

Obviously, with *no risk* all interest rates are equivalent (i.e., $r=r_i=r_j$). Then

$$\Sigma_{i\varepsilon\theta} D(A_i)\ A_i \ / \ \Sigma_{j\varepsilon\Omega} D(B_j)\ B_j \tag{4.7}$$

4.2 Market rates on equity

Few financial institutions will accept the extremely stringent

$$\frac{dE}{dr} = 0 \tag{4.8}$$

as a financial requirement for the firm. The shareholders may require a higher return when the risk-free market rate moves upwards (and conversely). A relevant criterion may then be that:

$$\frac{dE}{dr} = \frac{d}{dr}[\Sigma_{i\varepsilon\theta} A_i - \Sigma_{j\varepsilon\Omega} B_j] \geq \underline{q} \tag{4.9}$$

where q is constant. In combination with such a criterion, one may assume as an objective that the duration on equity--D(E)--should be fixed to at least a certain length of time t, e.g. one year. This implies that:

$$\frac{dE}{dr_E} = -[\Sigma_{i\varepsilon\theta}\frac{D(A_i)\ A_i}{(1+r_i)} - \Sigma_{j\varepsilon\Omega}\frac{D(B_j)\ B_j}{(1+r_j)}] = \frac{D(E)\ E}{1+r_E} \geq -\frac{\tau\ E}{1+r_E} \tag{4.10}$$

Exhibit 1

Assume that the ABC-bank has the following balance sheet at time t=0:

Assets		**Liabilities**	
Bonds	100 m	Fixed Rate Deposits	100 m
Fixed Rate Loans	100 m	Floating Rate Deposits	100 m
Floating Rate Loans	100 m	Equity	100 m
Total	300 m		300 m

Furthermore assume that the bond coupon is for 12%, that the lending rate is 13% and the deposit rate 7%. Then, after one year with no rate changes, the balance sheet will take the following form (assuming a dividend of 5% and ignoring taxes):

Assets		**Liabilities**	
Bonds	100	Fixed Rate Deposits	100 m
Fixed Rate Loans	100	Floating Rate Deposits	100 m
Floating Rate Loans	100	Equity	119
Retained Interest*	19		
Total	319		319 m

*100 m.12% (bonds) + 100 m.13% (FX loan) + 100 m.13% (FL loan) - 100 m.7% (FX dep.) - 100 m.7% (FL dep.) - 5m (dividend) = 19 m

Exhibit 2

Assume again that the ABC-bank starts at time t=o with the balance sheet demonstrated in *Exhibit 1*. However, assume that the market rate will move from 12% to 13% (just after t=o). That will change the rate of floating rate loans and deposits:

Estimated cash flow for interest and dividends

Year:		t=1	T=2	t=3
Assets				
Bonds	(100 m)	+12	+12	+12
Fixed Rate Loans	(100 m)	+13	+13	+13
Floating Rate Loans	(100 m)	+14	+14	+14
Subtotal		+39	+39	+39
Liabilities				
Fixed Rate Deposits	(100 m)	-7	-7	-7
Floating Rate Deposits	(100 m)	-8	-8	-8
Equity	(100 m)	-5	-5	-5
		+19	+19	+19

The items on the balance sheet will change as follows:

Year:	t=1	t=2	t=3
Assets (m)			
Bonds (discounted to 13%)	98.3 m	99.1 m	100 m
Fixed Rate Loans	100 m	100 m	100 m
Floating Rate Loans	100 m	100 m	100 m
Interest from Interbank	19 m	40.5 m	64.8 m
Subtotal	317.3 m	339.6 m	364.8 m
Liabilities			
Fixed Rate Deposits	100 m	100 m	100 m
Floating Rate Deposits	100 m	100 m	100 m
Equity	117.3 m	139.6 m	164.8 m
	317.3 m	339.6 m	364.8 m

The loss year 1 is 1.7 m (119 - 117.3) compared to *Exhibit 1*.

Exhibit 3

Assume that the conditions for the ABC-bank are the same as in ***Exhibit 2***. However, the increase in market rates implies that the floating rate lending will go down by 10% and the floating rate deposit expand by 5%. The effect will be as follows:

Estimated cash flow:

Year:		t=1	t=2	t=3
Assets				
Interbank	(15 m)	+1.95	+1.95	+1.95
Bonds	(100 m)	+12.0	+12.0	+12.0
Fixed Rate Loans	(100 m)	+13.0	+13.0	+13.0
Floating Rate Loans	(90 m)	+12.6	+12.6	+12.6
Subtotal		+39.55	+39.55	+39.55
Liabilities				
Fixed Rate Deposits	(100 m)	-7	-7	-7
Floating Rate Deposits	(100 m)	-8.8	-8.8	-8.8
Equity	(100 m)	-5	-5	-5
		+18.75	+18.75	+18.75

The balance sheet will become as follows:

Year:		**t=1**	**t=2**	**t=3**
Assets (m)				
Interbank Market		15 m	15 m	15 m
Bonds (discounted to 13%)		98.3 m	99.1 m	100 m
Fixed Rate Loans		100 m	100 m	100 m
Floating Rate Loans		90 m	90 m	90 m
Interest from Interbank		18.75 m	39.94 m	63.88 m
Subtotal		322.05 m	344.04 m	368.88 m
Liabilities				
Fixed Rate Deposits		100 m	100 m	100 m
Floating Rate Deposits		105 m	105 m	105 m
Equity		117.05 m	139.04 m	163.88 m
		322.05 m	344.04 m	368.88 m

The loss after year 1 will be 1.95 m (119 - 117.05) compared to ***Exhibit 1***.

Exhibit 4

We develop *Exhibit 3* further by assuming that the ABC-bank would like to analyze the *interest rate risk* by the use of *duration* and *volatility*. For example, measure the duration of the bond asset at the level of 12% market rate:

$$D = \frac{\frac{12.1}{1.12} + \frac{12.2}{1.12^2} + \frac{112.3}{1.12^3}}{\frac{12}{1.12} + \frac{12}{1.12^2} + \frac{112}{1.12^3}} = \frac{269.0}{100} = 2.69$$

Then the duration on equity (the duration gap) is estimated to 2.890.

Assets		
Bonds:	100 x 2.69	=269
Fixed Rate Loans:	100 x 273/102.4	=266
Floating Rate Loans:	100.0	=0
Liabilities		
Fixed Rate Deposits:	-100x2.46	=-246
Floating Rate Deposits:	100.0	=0
Equity:	100 x 2.89	=2.89

Thus an increase of all (floating) market rates by 1% will imply a loss of 2.89/1.12 = 2.58 m, in contrast with *Exhibit 1*.

Exhibits 1-4 assumed that interest rate margins between lending and borrowing were rather large (6% in *Exhibit 2*). It was also assumed that the change in market rates were moderate (1%). If so, the interest rate margin* may be kept on a rather acceptable level (19% in *Exhibit* 1, 17% in *Exhibit* 2-3 and 16% in *Exhibit* 4).

When the margins get thinner and the markets rates move in larger steps, then the return in equity will be more critical. This will be demonstrated in **Exhibit 5**, which is identical to **Exhibit 2**, except for the assumption of lower margins and larger steps in the market rates.

---

* The interest rate margin together with the non-interest income should cover the administrative expenditures as well as the return on equity.

<u>**Exhibit 5**</u>

Assume again that the ABC-bank starts at time t=0 with the balance of **Exhibit 1**. But estimate the effect that will occur when

a) the market rate moves from 12% to 14% after the fixed-rate contracts are signed at t=0;

b) the fixed rate deposits are set to 10% and the floating rate deposits to 10% (after the change of the market rate);

c) the floating rate lending will diminish by 10% while the floating rate deposit will remain on the same level.

	year	**1**	**2**	**3**
Assets				
Interbank	(10 m)	+1.4	+1.4	+1.4
Bonds	(100 m)	+12	+12	+12
Fixed Rate Loans	(100 m)	+13	+13	+13
Floating Rate Loans	(90 m)	+13.5	+13.5	+13.5
Liabilities				
Fixed Rate Deposits	(100 m)	-10	-10	-10
Floating Rate Deposits	(100 m)	-10	-10	-10
Equity	(100 m)	-5	-5	-5
		+14.9	+14.9	+14.9

At the end of year 1, the balance sheet has changed to:

New Balance Sheet	
Assets	
Interbank	10.0 m
Bonds	95.4 m
Fixed Rate Loans	100.0 m
Floating Rate Loans	90.0 m
Interest	14.9 m
Liabilities	
Fixed Rate Deposits	100m
Floating Rate Deposits	100m
Equity	110.3m

with administrative costs at about 1.5% of total assets. This implies that equity will be reduced to: 110.3 - 0.015 x 310.4 = 105.6 m. This level will be so low that actions must be taken to *immunize* the balance sheet.

Now assume that the assets, liabilities and equity of time t=0, (A_i^0, B_j^0, E^0) will move to the levels (A_i^1, B_j^1, E^1) at time t=1. It is also assumed that the risk-free market rate (on government bonds) will move from r^0 to r^1. As the equity may be determined by the values on the assets and liabilities, we can thus write:

$$E^0(A_i^0,\ B_j^0, r^0) \Rightarrow E^t(A_i^t,\ B_j^t, r^t) \tag{4.11}$$

where A^t = (A) and B^t = (B)

Here, the *volatility* of the assets A^t and the liabilities B^t may be formulated by the assistance of (3.9) and (4.11). This means that the volatility of a set of assets and liabilities may be expressed as:

$$v'(E') = -\Sigma_i \frac{D(A_i')A_i'}{(1+r_i')} + \Sigma_j \frac{D(B_j')B_j'}{(1+r_j')}$$

However, note that this volatility measure is a measure of interest rate risk prior to the implementation of any immunization strategy.

Exhibit 6 illustrates these calculations for the case of the Deutsche Bank 1991 and 1992. If these market rates were the same for all assets and liabilities - say 12% - then this bank would have the following volatilities for a change of 1 basis point.

Deutsche Bank	*1992*	*1993*
Assets:	2.3 %	2.3 %
Liabilities:	1.2 %	1.2 %

Consequently, if these assumptions were correct, then the value of Deutsche Bank equity would substantially decrease as the market rate increases.

Given these durations, Deutsche Bank would have taken less interest and liquidity risks if the duration on equity would have been much shorter.

Exhibit 6

Deutsche Bank				
Assets				
Wholesale Placements	Sight Loans	0	18.1	15.1
	0 - 3 Mos. Loans	0.1	31.8	31.0
	3 Mos. - 4 Yr. Loans	2	48.7	41.7
	> 4 Yr. Loans	5	7.7	7.2
Fixed Assets	< 4 Yr.	2	3.9	4.1
	> 4 Yr.	5	14.6	8.4
Securities		1	7.4	8.0
Loans Retail	< 4 Yr.	2	89.9	88.0
	> 4 Yr.	5	83.6	75.6
Others		1	28.9	26.6
		--	334.0	306.6
	Subtotal: Average Duration		2.55	2.49
Liabilities				
Wholesale	Sight Deposits	0	22.6	18.5
	Time Deposits	2	87.3	77.4
Retail	Sight Deposits	0	48.5	44.7
	Time Deposits	2	91.0	86.2
	Savings Deposits	0	40.9	37.4
	Savings Securities	1	7.6	6.7
Others		1	14.5	16.2
Equity		**	21.6	18.9
		--	334.0	306.6
			21.9	21.8

** Average duration on equity (yrs); and can be estimated by (4.11)

* Artificial numbers used for illustration.

V. Simulation of Risks and Returns In a Bank

5.1. Model

We have seen that uncertainty appears for at the asset and liability flows:

(a_i^t) and (b_j^t): (i=1, ..., I; j=1, ..., J; t=1, ..., T)

and of course for the yield curve r=r(t)

The planning of future assets and liabilities is a process that includes both direct choices of investment, borrowing and lending (portfolio decisions) and indirect stimulation of deposits and credits (pricing and promotion decisions). The planning should aim at estimating expected amounts on the corresponding accounts for relevant future dates.

But the planning procedure will not only estimate assets and liabilities, it must also distribute them across maturities. Such a maturity distribution will give the decision-maker an idea of the exposure to interest rate risks.

Several banks have developed computer systems in order to measure the static exposure at a certain date and to simulate dynamic exposure across certain future dates. Certain off-balance sheet items are included like swaps, futures, forward rate agreements (FRA's), options and loan commitments.

The way to model such a complicated situation varies depending on whether the decision making unit is a bank or an insurance company.

In the case of a bank, one often uses the technique of scenario analysis, for which the bank selects one of several possibilities for the future evolution of the assets and liabilities flows and even for the yield curve. This "what if" technique is suited for finding an optimal solution -- after the choice of the decision variables related to the bank portfolio. See some recent work on stochastic non-linear programming for related theoretical results (Wets (1993)).

For insurance companies, the situation is quite different. Foremost, there exist much more long-term investments than typically are found in banking institutions. Also, we can work in the framework of risk theory with the classical assumption that the claim arrivals process is a Poisson process (or is otherwise governed by some random measure) and that we can estimate the distribution of the claim amounts. Of course, we must still adequately account for the complexities reinsurance treatises, financial revenues, dividend payments, and other features not readily representable in the classic probabilistic assumptions that are deployed in order to use such classical techniques. More recent approaches to risk theory are also available, which recast risk processes in a martingale framework, and therefore are able to exploit much recent work (in a variety of disciplines) designed to characterize and solve problems with such a structure. See, for example, Grandell (1991) for a survey on risk theory from this perspective.

Another specific constraint is, in principle, the establishment of a lower bound for the ruin probability, addressed, for example, in the classical framework through Cramer-Lundberg theory; this plays more or less the same rule as the Cooke ratio for the banks. This stochastic model further needs the introduction of a stochastic dynamic for the yield curve (see J. Janssen (1993)), which can also be used in the scenario analysis used for the banks.

The main, and perhaps perpetual, problem that remains for the analyst or manager is that no model, stochastic or otherwise, is able to correctly represent the underlying data-generating process over the course of a long time period; thus it is necessary to re-estimate periodically the basic parameters of the model and eventually to change the model if it does not seem suitable anymore. This explains that the implementation of ALM strategies needs, as we said in section 1, a "good" information system. Such a "global" model including a permanent re-estimation of basic parameters is presented in J. Janssen (1992).

With this in mind, we can represent that evolution of assets and liabilities as stochastic processes:

$$A_i^{t+1} = A_i^t(1+\beta A_i^t) + A_i^t dA_i^t dW + A_i^t \beta A_i^t dZA_i^t$$

$$B_j^{t+1} = B_{ji}^t(1+\beta B_j^t) + B_j^t dB_j^t dW + B_j^t \beta B_j^t dZB_j^t$$

where certain assets and certain liabilities are interdependent. For example, we might have dependence between:

Retail savings deposits &
Retail savings securities

Wholesale sight deposits &
Wholesale time deposits

Wholesale sight loans &
Wholesale, 0-3 months loans

Loans retail, up to 4 years &
Loans retail ,4 years and more

In order to illustrate the dynamic effects on assets and liabilities, consider the aggregated balance sheet of **Exhibit 7**. It is based upon monthly date from a savings bank. The assets are grouped into: a) claims on other financial institutions (central bank, other banks, etc...)*, b) bond, notes, and securities and c) customer loans. The liabilities are divided into d) fixed-rate deposits, e) floating-rate deposits, and f) others (including long term borrowing and equity).

---

*These assets are in fact the net amount between assets and liabilities to various financial institutions.

Exhibit 7 illustrates the planning situation for a bank, at the end of December, where the next years assets and liabilities have to be forecasted on the basis of the data from the present year.

The planning should consider the following alternatives:

a) The interest rate will remain on the same level as in the preceding year, but there will be a substantial change in the flow of funds.

b) There will be a sudden increase (decrease) in the interest rates. Such a jump will influence the rates to be received from financial institutions (mainly short-term fixed rates) and from customer loans (partly long-term fixed rates). An increase in market rates will reduce the market values of bonds and notes (and conversely).

Furthermore, increased market rates will require that the interest outlays will raise for floating-rate deposits. The overall effect will then show up on the equity side.

Exhibit 7 - Table

	Dur	Jan	Feb	Mar	Apr	May	Jun	Jul	Aug	Sep	Oct	Nov	Dec
A1	0.5	1165	1125	1035	1155	1185	1180	1210	1345	1280	1350	1390	1490
A2	1	745	795	765	765	685	710	690	700	690	700	710	700
A3	2	1680	1670	1800	1830	1790	1800	1790	1840	1850	1830	1820	1810
Sum: All Assets		3590	3590	3600	3750	3660	3690	3690	3885	3820	3880	3920	4000
B1	1	1520	1520	1500	1650	1540	1560	1510	1675	1570	1580	1570	1590
B2	0	1550	1510	1510	1470	1500	1480	1480	1490	1500	1520	1550	1580
Equity		520	560	590	630	620	650	700	720	750	780	800	830
Sum : B+Equity		3590	3590	3600	3750	3660	3690	3690	3885	3820	3880	3920	4000
Duration E		6.091346	5.674107	5.733051	5.321429	5.350806	5.138462	4.807143	4.690972	4.613333	4.429487	4.34375	4.186747

VI. ALM for a Life Insurance Firm

Universal life insurance is an activity, where the insurer signs contract with customers, collects premiums over a long time period and pays out benefits at the death of the insured. However, there are other versions of life insurance, which are combinations of universal life and pension savings. In these cases, the benefits may be paid out either at the death of the insured or over a series of years. The life insurance firm that collects premiums from its customers, will be exposed to a long term debt to them. The length of that debt is uncertain due to two reasons. First, it is uncertain when the customers will die. Secondly, some customers may terminate their contracts prematurely. The task for the life insurance firm is to place the premiums into assets that will match these long term and uncertain liabilities. Usually, such a firm will place a bulk of its funds into long term bonds. Still there is the issue about how much to place in bonds and what part to put in equity.

Exhibit 8 gives a good illustration of this planning situation. The data are taken from the French insurance firm Predica, which is a subsidiary to the Credit Agricole. Predica offers different combinations of universal life products and pensions savings. It is a company that has shown a rapid growth in terms of premium income over a period of five years.

The liability side of the balance sheet shows a complete dominance of technical provisions. When other insurance companies (mainly non-life ones) have liabilities in terms of reinsurance activities, these items are almost non-existing in the case of Predica. The customers of life insurance and savings bond are guaranteed a minimum interest rate on their premiums (4.5%). The capital will then be locked up for at least 8 years.

On the assets side, most technical reserves are placed into fixed-rate securities. The following example shows the situation in 1990 (Predica Annual Report 1990, pp 40-55):

	Expiry Date	Interest Rate	FRF bn
Government Bonds	1993 - 1999	9.45 - 11%	1.4
Long-term National Bonds	1991 - 2019	7.5 - 10%	24.5
Quoted National Bank Notes in the Public and Semi-Public Sector		7.2 - 11.5%	21.5
Bonds and Securities without voting rights		8.6 - 9.0%	1.5
Foreign Bonds		9.0 - 10.5%	0.3
Treasury Bills	1991 - 1995	8.0 - 9.0%	1.0

These data on dates of expiry will give the basis for the estimation of the *duration* of each item on the balance sheet. However, one has to have information about repricing dates of these assets in order to calculate the exact duration. The data under the heading Duration (in fact modified duration if the interest rates for asset and liabilities are different) in **Exhibit 8** are just rough estimates without knowing the exact values. They are presented in order to demonstrate the procedure to calculate the *duration on equity*.

The following assumptions are made:

a) Property and equipment are assumed to be priced in the market without any long-term price clause. Duration = 0 year.

b) Most fixed-rate securities expire in the period 1995 - 1999. Duration = 4.5 years.

c) Floating rate securities have (obviously) short duration = 0.5

d) Subsidiaries and other assets are not assumed to have any price clause. Duration = 0.

e) Premiums are assumed to be contracted for at least 8 years and with a "floor" on interest. This is approximated as a duration = 4 years.

f) Claims are assumed to be contracted for half a year in average.

g) Short-term debts is assumed to have a duration = 0.1 years.

h) No duration on generated income is taken into account.

With these assumptions, the duration on equity will become:*

1990:	9.5 years
1991:	7.0 years
1992:	4.1 years

---

*The calculation follows the same principle as demonstrated in Exhibit 4. For example, in 1990 this implies: {54.4 x 4.5 + 3.5 x 0.5 + 2.5 x 10 - 62.6 x 4 - 0.5 x 0.5 - 0.6 x 0.1} = 9.5 years. Obviously, the duration on equity is getting shorter year by year (given the assumptions made).

Exhibit 8

	1990	1991	1992	Estimated Duration
Assets (Billions of FRF)				
Property equipment	1.3	2.1	2.5	0
Technical reserves and provisions:				
• fixed rate	54.4	66.6	84.7	4.5
• floating rate	3.5	7.2	9.1	0.5
• equities	2.5	3.5	3.8	10
Loans		0.0	0.2	0
Subsidiaries, etc.	1.8	2.4	1.8	0
Others	2.8	2.4	6.3	0
Total Assets	66.3	84.2	108.4	
Liabilities (Billions of FFR)				
Technical provisions				
• Premiums	62.6	79.6	102.1	4
• Claims	0.5	0.6	0.9	0.5
Short-term debt	0.6	--	1.0	0.1
Others	--	1.2	0.1	0
Income	0.4	0.0	0.5	0
Equity (Billions of FRF)	2.2	2.8	3.6	
Total Liabilities	66.3	84.2	108.4	

VII. Concluding Remarks

The basic architecture of a DBMS for an ALM -cell in a bank or in an insurance company must have:

(i) *an internal information part*: this part must give needed information related to the daily operations of the company as well as historical information. It must also contain strategic information coming from the Board of Directors; and,

(ii) *an external information part*: this part will be focused on pertinent information used to estimate or re-estimate the basic parameters of the stochastic models used, for example, for the yield curve.

For larger companies, this is not possible without interconnections with international data servers.

Of course, this information must be filtered, identified before using it in the optimization kernel of the ALM system that will ultimately give the (constrained) optimal values of the decision variables for building the appropriate portfolio related activities of the company.

BIBLIOGRAPHY

Barge, J. (1987) "Interest Rate Exposure," in Gardener, E.P.M. (ed.), *Interest Rate Risk and Banks*, University College of North Wales, Bangor.

Bergendahl, G. (1989), "The Management of Assets and Liabilities in Banks," *Revue de la Banque*, no.6.

Brewer, E. (1985), "Bank Gap Management and the Use of Financial Futures," *Economic Perspectives*, Federal Reserve Bank of Chicago, March/April.

Gilbert, D. (1988), "The Tools of Interest Rate Risk Management," *in Managing Bank Assets and Liabilities* ,Euromoney Publ, London.

Grandell, J. (1991) *Aspects of Risk Theory* New York: Springer-Verlag.

Hartzog, J. (1983), "Asset/Liability Management: An Overview," Special Publication Series, Federal Home Loan Bank of San Francisco, November.

Harrington, R. (1987) *Asset and Liability by Banks*, OECD, Paris.

Humphrey, D.B. (1985), "Costs and Scale Economics in Bank Intermediation," in Aspinwall, R.C. & Eisenbeis, R.A. (eds.), *Handbook for Banking Strategy*, Wiley, New York.

Janssen, J. (1992), "Modeles stochastiques de gestion d'actif-passif pour les banques et les assurances," *Transactions of the 24th International Congress of Actuaries*, vol 1; pp 137-140, Montreal, ICA-CIA.

Janssen, J. (1993), "Risk Models for ALM in Banking and Insurance."

Kaufmann, G.G. (1984), "Measuring and Managing Interest Rate Risk: A Primer," *Economic Perspectives*, Federal Reserve Bank of Chicago, Jan./Febr.

Kusy, M.L. and Ziemba, W.T. (1987), "A Bank Asset and Liabilty Management Model," *JORSA*, vol. 35, 356-374.

Toevs A.L., (1983), "Gap Management: Managing Interest Rate Risk in Banks and Thrifts," *Economic Review*, Federal Reserve Bank of San Francisco, Spring.

Wets R., (1984), "Solving stochatic programs with simple recourse," *Stochastics* 10, 219-242.

Wets R., (1993), "Optimization techniques for assets/liability management," to the Sixth International Symposium on Applied Stochastic Models and Data Analysis, May.

Wilson J.S.G., Editor, (1988), Managing Bank Assets and Liabilities, *Euromoney* Publ.

ASSET & LIABILITY MANAGEMENT: REGULATORY GUIDELINES ON INTEREST RATE RISK CONTROL AND THEIR IMPACTS ON FINANCIAL INSTITUTIONS

Elisabetta Gualandri
Dipartimento di Economia Aziendale, Università di Modena

D. Ho and T. Schneeweis (eds.), Applications in Finance, Investments, and Banking, 63–91.

I. *Introduction*

The goals of this chapter are twofold: to review the regulatory authorities' approaches to the problem of measuring and monitoring of the Interest Rate Risks (IRR) faced by financial institutions; and to outline the impact of authorities' intervention on financial institutions themselves, with particular reference to the introduction and implementation of effective Asset and Liability (ALM) techniques by those institutions. To this end, I will describe the environment in which financial institutions operate, and in particular the reasons for increased attention to IRR. Afterwards, I shall focus on the policy goals pursued, steps undertaken, and policy instruments used by regulators in this matter. Thereafter, I will review the present state of the art as far as intervention by the authorities is concerned. Finally, I will draw the main distinctions and stress the common points between authorities and institutions in their efforts to manage IRR, and, in the process, outline and evaluate the impact through the optic of ALM.

II. *Asset Liability Management and Management of the Interest Rate Risk (IRR) of Financial Institutions by Regulatory Authorities*

The Eighties witnessed the transition of supervisory authorities' philosophy of intervention from structural regulation towards prudential regulation. This new regulatory framework has resulted in an increased need for the financial institutions of the industrial countries to maintain adequate capital in order to effectively and efficiently face a deregulated and global operating environment. The economic and financial environment of these last years has been characterized by more volatile interest rates, fiercer competition and narrower spreads; simultaneously, the increased integration of financial markets and the growing involvement of banks in the securities markets have implied greater opportunities and more complex degrees of risk for financial institutions.

The impact of these factors has differed across institutions depending on their countries of operation. However, it has nonetheless required the adoption of a new set of regulatory instruments by authorities, and new strategies and risk management control techniques by financial institutions themselves, in order to maintain adequate conditions of profitability, safety and soundness of financial institutions..

Deregulation and the growth in competition in the lending sector during the Eighties helped concentrate the attention of the supervisory authorities on the sufficiency of institutions' equity to cover all the risks involved in the broadening scope of activities undertaken. As a consequence, the main aim of supervisory authorities, within prudential regulation, has been the control of capital adequacy of financial institutions. The primary risk taken into account by regulatory authorities in this environment was credit risk.

Regulatory authorities in the Nineties have recast their focus in order to take IRR into account in their evaluation of the capital adequacy of supervised institutions. While this kind of risk is an aspect of normal banking operation, it has been become more important in the deregulated environment of the last decade. In many countries the changes in monetary policy management and the growing competition between institutions have significantly increased the flexibility of banks in adjusting their interest rate risk profiles, whether such entails the ability to take on or lay off chosen interest rate risks. Furthermore, this flexibility has been enhanced by the development of new financial instruments, such as swaps and other derivatives, that may be deployed for hedging purposes or in order to profit from interest rate changes. Other causes for concern about growing IRR included the growth of the securities industry and the entrance of commercial banks into this new field of activity, with its attendant high degree of market risk, are further factors stressing the problem of the interest rate risk undertaken by financial institutions. During the last few years, the importance of IRR control has been further underlined by the crises caused by this type of risk, such as the Savings and Loan Association in the US, during the Eighties. (Admittedly, in this case, however, many other factors are considered responsible for the crisis, as will be described in a later section.)

As a consequence, at the end of the Eighties, national and supranational supervisory authorities started actively dealing with the problem of monitoring the IRR undertaken by financial institutions. Very interesting contributions to the discussion of how best to do this have been produced, especially at the supranational level. First of all, the need for harmonization of the mechanisms required for the monitoring of IRR was emphasized in the preamble to the 1989 European Community (EC) Second Directive on Credit Institutions. A new Directive on the Capital Adequacy of Investment Firms and Credit Institutions, which introduces capital adequacy requirements for IRR on the trading portfolio of financial institutions, was finally approved by the Commission of the European Communities, on 15 March 1993. The Basle Committee on Banking Regulations and Supervisory Practices, Sub-Group on Interest Rate Risk, set up by the Group of Ten Countries (G-10), started working on this theme in 1988, and issued its latest proposal in April 1993. In January 1992, the Technical Committee of the International Organization of Securities Commissions (IOSCO) reached a preliminary consensus on this problem with the Basle group.

In the pages which follow, I will outline the frameworks which authorities are establishing and focus on the guidelines for supervisory intervention which they are being established. In particular, one of the first national interventions on the problem of monitoring the IRR of financial institutions, concerning the sector of the Savings and Loan Association in the US, will be analyzed in some detail.

Before dealing directly with this topic, however, it is important to stress that the financial institutions most aware of the problem have developed effective practical methods for the measurement and management of IRR. Similar, and parallel development has occurred in the related area of Asset/Liability Management. These development occurred during the last decade, well before the authorities devoted full focus to the problem of IRR.

2.1. *Approaches to the Measurement of IRR*

Before outlining the framework of supervisory intervention on the theme of IRR, it is important to focus on methods for characterizing this risk. There are two main approaches which give rise to different models,[1] defined as follows:[2]

The current earnings perspective

This approach is based on reported earnings, and identifies subcategories of income risk and investment risk.

1) *Income risk* derives from changes in the rates of accrual on assets and liabilities and off-balance sheet instruments carried on a historic cost basis. The first step is the identification of a risk related to the difference in the time scales for deciding new rates for assets and liabilities. This risk is caused by mismatching, within a period of time known as the gapping period, between accruals on assets and liabilities at variable rates of interest, but where the time for setting new rates varies. The models related to this approach are the so-called gap management models and simulation models based on gap analysis.

2) *Investment risk* relates to variations in value, caused by movements in the interest rates, in market-to-market items on the balance sheet or those assessed at the lower-of-cost-or-market-value. This risk shows up, and thus affects book earnings, whenever the accounting principles used require incorporation of the new market

---

[1]A review of the IRR measurement models is presented in R. Platt (editor) 1986.

[2]See E. Gualandri (1991,a); Comptroller of the Currency (1989); Committee on Banking Regulation and Supervisory Practices: Sub-group on Interest Rate Risk (1988).

value. It also becomes apparent in relation to items recorded on an accrual basis, whenever the institution mobilizes these investments. Implicitly, the investment risk is identified in the cost-advantages of making new investments. A typical case is when interesting opportunities are not taken up in order to avoid putting onto the books losses deriving from the sale of other assets, or for other reasons, such as the transaction costs, difficulties in absorption by the market, incorrect assessments or "sticky" decision-making processes.

The approach based on the impact of IRR on book earnings offers undoubted advantages in terms of simple calculations and direct connection with the accounting systems and information structures generally used. However, there are disadvantages related to the significance of the results obtained. Above all, the current earnings approach shows up the interest rate risk near-term, while neglecting its importance for financial periods further away in the future. This means that the risk relating to positions which are actually very vulnerable to variations in interest rates, such as portfolio equity, but which will not mature for a considerable number of years, tend to be overlooked.

Economic Perspective

This approach identifies interest rate risk as the sensitivity of an institution's portfolio equity to future movements in interest rates, by using the concept of *duration*.[3] Attention is therefore directed at the entire time range covered by the repricing of all the items present in the institution's statement of assets and liabilities.

Under the economic perspective, the measurement of IRR reaches beyond accounting conventions; in order to measure the market value of the institution's equity, all assets

---

[3]Duration is a mathematical concept designed to measure the price sensitivity of debt securities to changes in interest rates. Specifically, duration is the weighted average maturity of all payments of a security, coupons plus principal, where the weights are the discounted present values of the payments.

and liabilities in the balance sheet as well as off-balance sheet items, are calculated at their current (rather than historic) value. Interest rate movements affect the value of net equity through their impact on the current values of all the institution's rate sensitive financial instruments. It is worth noting that the economic perspective applies the *investment risk* concept to all balance sheet and off-balance sheet instruments. Therefore, the IRR calculation tends to give the same results as would be provided by the calculation of the investment risk for an institution whose instruments can all be assessed at market value.

The two approaches to IRR are quite different, but can be considered complementary: bankers and regulators should look at them both, being aware of the limits of the related models and of the difficulties in obtaining the necessary information.

2.2 *Objectives*

The essential aim of supervisors in the management of IRR is to assess the vulnerability of institutions to this kind of risk, and thus estimate their required capital adequacy in relation to the degree of risk exposure undertaken.[4] However, different sources of risk and perspectives exist for various intermediaries, such as credit institutions and investment firms.[5] As a consequence, regulatory authorities must take these various elements into account in their efforts to establish a coherent conceptual and operational framework.

The assessment of capital charges are done with the aim of inducing banks either to reduce their risk-taking, or, at least, to support their risky positions with additional capital. However, the establishment of suboptimal capital adequacy requirements may hold dangers: if they are too high, they might create an undesirable entry barrier to the sector thus limiting competition; or, if, on the contrary, they are too low with regard to the

---

[4]See EC Commission (1990); Office of Thrift Supervision (1989).

[5]For the analysis of the different sources of interest rate risk, see E. Gualandri (1991).

risks undertaken, they might be inadequate to enforce the soundness of the system. Basically, within a policy of prudential regulation, the aim of controlling IRR stands alongside the monitoring of credit risk and liquidity risk, while doing the same for institutions' profitability and soundness. As such, the collection of risk measurements can be useful as an early warning system for the prevention of potential crises.

2.3 *Steps and Instruments*

In order to achieve the targets outlined, authorities need to work through a sequence of steps and adopt the best policy instruments. First, supervisory authorities need to put forth a risk measurement method suitable for the aims of the regulatory process, which is simultaneously concrete and reliable when applied by the supervised institutions. The top priority is therefore to strike a balance between the need for strict regulation of the formulation of basic information, and the difficulty of obtaining a reliable, meaningful measurement of IRR. From the conceptual framework chosen, authorities need to determine the type of information and financial statements required. Since the reliability of results achieved is closely determined by the quality of data received, in-depth verification is needed. It is also important where possible to avoid a significant additional reporting burden, and as such both the costs and benefits of less precise measurement of IRR must be taken into account. Consideration of procedures which encourage the timely reporting of information must also be considered.

Information derived from the collection and reprocessing of data available from financial institutions must be interpreted within the conceptual framework adopted, in order to evaluate the degree of risk exposure. For this purpose, a baseline for the levels of risk considered acceptable must be defined by authorities. A further task for regulatory authorities consists of the introduction of capital adequacy requirements and checks to ensure the maintenance of adequate capital in relation to the degree of risk undertaken. Capital requirements should be linked to the type of financial activities undertaken by institutions and thus to the various aspects and degrees of IRR undertaken, in order to guarantee the same rules for different intermediaries undertaking the same activity (level the playing fields). Furthermore, different definitions of capital base are adopted for supervisory purposes, in various countries and for different types of financial institutions. These factors are clearly serious obstacles in trying to provide a definitive and unequivocal solution to the problem of IRR measurement and control at a supranational level.

As far as risk weights for the calculation of capital requirements are concerned, two different approaches have been outlined: the comprehensive approach and the building block approach.[6] The main difference is the way in which various types of risks are taken into account. Risks taken into consideration are the so-called specific risk (credit risk) and general market risk (interest rate risk).

a) In the *comprehensive approach*, both specific and general market risks are expressed in a single risk weight. Up to now this approach has been adopted by the regulatory authorities of securities firms.

b) In the *building block approach*, specific risk requirements are split out from those for general market risk. Within the trading portfolio the sum of specific risk and general market risk is defined as position risk. At present there is a general agreement to adopt this approach at an international level, as far as the trading portfolio is concerned.

One crucial point of the regulating function is verification of the adequacy of the instruments used by the individual banks for the measurement and control of interest rate

[6]See Bank of England (1992), p. 20, Basle Committee on Banking Supervision (1993), The supervisory treatment of market risk, p. 7.

risk. This means the control of the quality of risk management and the monitoring of the suitability of the information systems implemented. Clearly, this type of analysis requires direct intervention by the supervising authorities with the individual institutions in order to check their organizational structure, in order to ensure that these elements are consistent with, and efficacious of, management strategy.

The monitoring of IRR must be carried out along with the control of credit risk, liquidity risk and foreign exchange risk, and is thus a manifestation of the global ALM strategy of supervised institutions.

III. The State of the Art

At present, both national and supranational regulatory authorities are working on the problem of monitoring the IRR assumed by supervised financial institutions. In this section I will review the main interventions made by supranational authorities: the Basle Committee on Banking Regulations and Supervisory Practices, Sub-Group on Interest Rate Risk, set up by the Group of Ten Countries within the Bank for International Settlements (BIS); the International Organization of Securities Commissions IOSCO (Technical Committee); the European Communities Directive on Capital Adequacy of Investment Firms and Credit Institutions. In the very near future, EC and G-10 countries will harmonize their regulations with the provisions made by these authorities.

In the case of the US, the Federal Deposit Insurance Corporation Improvement Act of 1991 (FDICIA) required that bank regulators publish interest rate risk regulations by June 1993.[7] The objective is to introduce interest rate risk into the risk-based capital

[7]The FDICIA 1991 introduces significant changes in the US banking and financial system including: the recapitalization of the Bank Insurance Fund (BIF); the adoption of the least costly of the possible resolution methods for a failed bank or thrift; the implementation of a new risk-based assessment scheme and insurance coverage for insured banks and thrifts; the introduction of new supervisory standards. See: S. K. Huber (1992); R. Cantor and R. Johnson (1992).

framework, in order to assess the strength of the supervised institutions. Currently, regulators are working to assimilate the EC directive. However, an initial relevant regulatory intervention on this theme was made by the Office for Thrift Supervision (OTS), former Federal Home Loan Bank System, the regulatory body of the US Savings and Loan Association (see sections below).

3.1. *The Basle Committee Approach*

The Basle Committee on Banking Regulations and Supervisory Practices, Sub-Group on Interest Rate Risk (also known as the Beverly-Carosio Committee from the names of the two chairmen who have been at its head) has been working on the problem of monitoring IRR undertaken by credit institutions since 1988. The aim is to assess the possibility of calculating an IRR measurement which can be used to construct indicators, and/or to set limitations to exposure, and/or to establish capital requirements.

The problem has been tackled starting from the institution's balance sheet, and then focusing, with the 1993 document, on the trading portfolio that intersects with the provisions of the EC Directive.

As far as the impact of IRR on the whole balance sheet is concerned, the working group's first step, at the end of the Eighties, was to define the approach to be followed in measuring interest rate risk. Considering that only a small number of banks were able to supply data compatible with the economic perspective, by calculating duration of different items, the group at first decided to adopt the current earnings perspective, even if the results obtained are not always easy to interpret and are often not sufficient to establish the level of exposure of the individual institution.[8]

The second step was to develop a model for the collection and re-processing of balance sheet and off-balance sheet instruments. The reclassified scheme must be

---

[8]See Committee on Banking Regulation and Supervisor Practices: Sub-group on Interest Rate Risk (1988, 1989).

prepared for every main currency in which the bank operates, in order to assess the impact of IRR on the exposed positions in the individual currencies. The reliability and feasibility of the system proposed were checked on groups of sample banks in the individual national contexts. The system suggested involves the reclassification of the balance sheet in relation to the type of instruments and the repricing or maturity period.[9] The instruments were divided into balance sheet and off-balance sheet items. The former were then subdivided according to the accounting criterion, separating the marked-to-market items from those assessed on an accrual basis. In the first case the items subject to investment risk are emphasized, keeping the trading portfolio separate. These are in all cases instruments to which, by convention or for more convenient accounting, the bank attributes a value in line with the market quotations, or the lower-of-cost-or-market value. In both cases, the value of the instruments must be corrected as interest rates change.

The instruments generated by the institution's operations on the money and capital markets are among the items estimated on an accrual basis, since they generally require active management. These items include interbank loans, the issue of certificates of deposit, and bonds no longer included in the previous section since they are held as investments and not for trading.

The remaining instruments which generate interest are included in a section defined as customer-driven business. These are mainly retail funds which the bank is generally prepared to provide, whether they involve accepting deposits or granting loans, at an interest rate which normally varies with inter-bank rates but whose quantity behavior may be irregular.

There is then a section containing, on the one hand, those instruments on which no interest is payable, such as fixed assets, capital and reserves, deferred charges for amortization and precious metals, and on the other hand, items on which there is a

---

[9]See Committee on Banking Regulation and Supervisory Practices: Sub-group on Interest Rate Risk (1988, Annex 4; 1989).

return, but with absolutely no link to interest rate trends, such as compulsory reserves in the case of Italian banks, holdings in companies and joint ventures.

The final section contains off-balance sheet instruments, separating options from the other operations since they imply an asymmetric risk structure. Operations with symmetrical risk are recorded on the same basis as the underlying instruments. For options, the committee suggests an estimate of their risk, based on an assessment of the deltas--a measure of the sensitivity of the value of an option to changes in the spot price of the underlying asset--of the options in question. (Smaller banks are not required to calculate option deltas.)

The reference periods within which the instruments affected by interest rates are defined, and thus within which the gaps are assessed, are set according to the type of activity undertaken by financial institutions, and the targets of the supervisory authorities.

A second scheme was also developed, keeping the trading portfolio separate from other business, and also dictating that off-balance sheet instruments be divided according to the nature of business.[10] A further step was taken to strike a balance between the current earning and the economic perspectives, and the calculation of a system of risk coefficients based on duration for each time-band was envisaged.

In 1993, the Basle Committee issued a new consultative paper, with two different proposals, the first one concerning the interest rate risk of the trading portfolio of banks (market risk), and the second one the overall IRR run by banks.[11] The first proposal sets out to achieve convergence with the EC Directive on capital adequacy for investment firms, which will be described in a later section. The second proposal is a further development of the previous documents with two interesting points. The first point is the

---

[10]See Committee on Banking Regulation and Supervisory Practices: Sub-group on Interest Rate Risk (1990).

[11]See Basle Committee on Banking Supervision (1993).

intention of the Basle Committee to develop a measurement system rather than an explicit capital charge for interest rate risk affecting banks' whole financial condition. As a matter of fact, the existing capital requirements are regarded as providing adequate protection against IRR exposure in most situations. The measurement system presented is designed to identify institutions in a critical situation. The second interesting point is the new measurement system envisaged. It may be considered as a further development of the previous proposal, trying to balance the difficulties in calculating duration measurement for many institutions, and the effectiveness of duration as a measure of IRR. Various interest rate sensitive assets and liabilities and off balance sheet activities are "slotted" into the predetermined maturity bands (or "buckets") and then aggregated. Afterwards, duration-based weights are applied to the different net positions, in each band.[12] The net balance of these duration-weighted positions is the principal basis for evaluating an institution's interest rate risk, since it is an estimate of the sensitivity of the value of a bank to a specified change in interest rate. The proposals of the document are at a preliminary stage, since many problems are left open and comments were expected by the end of 1993.[13]

3.2 *International Organization of Securities Commissions IOSCO (Technical Committee)*

---

[12]The duration weights would be adjusted to reflect the relative volatility of interest rates across the term structure.

[13]The most important issues arise especially from the way in which certain items such as those at uncertain reset date and uncertain maturity are to be "slotted" into the maturity ladder; the measurement of risk for derivatives; the definition of the duration-weights and the extent to which offsetting should be permitted between long and short positions. For the last three problems, the paper refers to the proposals made for market risk measurement. In view of the similarity, they will be described in the paragraph dealing with the EC directive.

In January 1992 the Basle committee held a meeting with the Technical Committee of the International Organizations of Securities Commissions in Geneva.

The core of the problem is that minimum standards should be applied to internationally active banks *and* securities firms, with national supervisory authorities having discretion to impose higher capital requirements. The fact is that banks are becoming increasingly active in the traditional core business of securities firms. Thus market risk requirements should become an important part of capital adequacy requirements for major international banks.

The target of IOSCO and Basle Committee was to conclude a joint agreement which could establish an international standard for market risk requirements and a definition of permitted capital. On both aspects a preliminary consensus was actually achieved. Since then, work has continued with the aim of producing joint proposals.[14] Unfortunately, it was not possible to achieve a successful result because IOSCO has been unable to reach agreement within its own group. Thus IOSCO did not associate itself to the Basle 1993 proposal, for the supervisory treatment of market risk. Up to now IOSCO has adopted the comprehensive approach. In the context of convergence with the Basle Committee and the EC Proposal, the building block approach should be accepted. However, the conversion from the comprehensive approach to the building block methodology will be complex and highly expensive, from the point of view of computer systems. Therefore, IOSCO envisaged a several years transition period. Only recently (May, 1996) have IOSCO and the Basle Committee come to agree on a set of general principles on trading risk, spurred on by the collapse of Barings Bank.

3.3. *The EC Directive*

On March 15, 1993 the EC Commission approved a Directive on the Capital Adequacy of Investment Firms and Credit Institutions (93/6/EEC), as the complement to

---

[14]See Bank of England (1192: R.C. Breeden, E.G. Corrigan (1992).

the Directive on Investment Firms (93/22/EEC). Both directives were set to be implemented by the EC countries by the end of 1995.

The purpose of the directive on capital adequacy is to achieve the necessary harmonization of capital requirements for investment firms and credit institutions within the EC. The coordination of the key rules is intended to provide adequate protection for individual investors, to ensure the health of the general financial system of the integrated European Market, and to allow non-bank investment firms and credit institutions to compete on broadly equal terms.[15]

To achieve this, minimum initial capital requirements are established for investment firms which are not credit institutions, and further capital requirements are set for both investment firms and credit institutions in order to cover the market risk to which they are exposed: position risk (that is the sum of specific risk and general market risk), foreign exchange risk and risks related to unsettled transactions, arising from the danger that the counterpart will not be able to fulfill its obligations.

While the initial proposal issued in 1990 was based on the comprehensive approach, the directive has adopted the building block approach, thus keeping general market risk separate from specific risk within the broad position risk. In this context, I shall focus on the provisions made against general market risk affecting the debt instruments of the trading portfolio.

The aim of the rules outlined is to establish the amount of capital defined as adequate in relation to the degree of interest rate risk undertaken by operators for each portfolio of traded debt instruments.

The framework prescribed by the directive for calculation of general risk of debt securities and their derivatives has been drawn up with two main problems in mind: the definition of a satisfactory parameter for measurement of the risk itself and the admissibility of offsetting symmetrical positions with opposing signs (long and short).

---

[15]See EC Directive 93/22.

For convenience, the definition of capital charge can be divided into three steps, the first linked to calculation of the securities risk and the other two to offsetting.

Step 1: definition of the risk duration weights.

To solve the problem of measuring the interest rate risk affecting debt securities, the supervisory authorities are forced to make the trade-off between the need to define a conceptually acceptable measurement of the IRR identifiable within the duration, and the concrete requirements of calculating this measure in the various supervised institutions.

Faced by the problems many intermediaries still have in calculating the duration of their various securities, the directive defines "standard" risk parameters in relation to preset time-bands. Risk factors indicating the price-sensitivity to IRR of "typical" securities with maturity dates set at the midpoint of the time-bands are calculated.[16] The time-bands which identify uniform segments of the yield curve are grouped into three zones on the basis of the change in shape of the curve itself. It is therefore up to the intermediary to allocate the net positions of the individual securities within the various time bands on the basis of the expiry date; i.e., the first repricing date for variable interest securities and the expiry date for those at fixed interest. The risk component of each securities position can then be identified by weighting the positions with the respective risk coefficients already calculated. This therefore provides a measurement of the securities' price-sensitivity to variations in interest rate.

Step 2: offsetting within the bands

We are now faced with the second problem: the admissibility of offsetting a capital charge by aggregating symmetrical positions. The first offsetting operation permitted is

---

[16]The methodology followed for the determination of risk factors is presented in F. Drudi, F. Panetta (1992) and Basle Committee (1993).

carried out within the time-bands, on the positions which have already been risk-weighted. Total offsetting would overlook the fact that long and short positions are not wholly at the same point in the time-band, and their price variations in response to changes in market interest rate may therefore not be fully offsetting. For this reason, a "vertical" disallowance factor of 10% has been introduced in order to identify of the initial capital charge for the general risk.

Step 3: offsetting within and between zones

For residual positions not covered by the offsetting process described above, further offsetting is permitted between the bands inside the same zone and then between the three zones, with the introduction of disallowance factors indicating the relative capital requirements. These factors increase in proportion to the distance on the curve itself (between the zones). Any final position for which no offsetting is possible requires a capital charge of 100%. The total value of the capital charge for the general securities risk is given by the sum of the individual horizontal and vertical disallowance components.

An important issue for each bank is the determination of the contents of its trading book, because the capital charges defined in the directive apply to the current market value of items in the trading portfolio, replacing those for credit risk.[17] The credit risk capital requirements still apply in the so called investment portfolio, where securities are bought with a long term investment purpose.

Finally it is important to stress that the directive also places institutions under an obligation to introduce reliable internal risk control systems.

---

[17]The definition of trading book includes the banks' proprietary positions in financial instruments which are taken on with the intention of benefiting in the short term from actual or expected differences between their buying and selling prices or to hedge other elements of the trading book, or which are held for short term resale, or in order toe execute a trade with a customer. See EC Directive 93/22 And Basle Committee (1993).

3.4 *The OTS Approach in the US: the TB 13 Rules*

In the US, while a new regulation required by FDICIA 1991 which adds interest rate exposure to the risk based capital framework for banks and thrifts is awaited in line with the EC directive and the Basle 1993 document, it is interesting to analyze the OTS approach to this problem.

Thrift Bulletin 13 (TB13) was initially issued in 1989 by the Federal Home Loan Bank System (FHLB), which was the regulating body of the American Savings and Loan Associations, one of the sectors most seriously hit by IRR in the '80s, because of its sensitivity to variations in rates of liabilities and fixity of its income stream, generated essentially by mortgages. Actually, the deep crisis which hit the thrift institutions in the second half of the Eighties also had other causes: the deregulation of the sector which gave rise to an unwarranted expansion risk taking, the increase in credit risk due to adverse economic conditions in regions and sectors where thrifts were deeply involved (such as the oil sector in the state of Texas, and the real estate sectors of California, Texas and New England), as well as numerous cases of fraud and criminal activity.[18] The crisis led to a thorough-going sequence of reforms that took hold in 1989, which involved, amongst other things, the abolition of the FHLB itself, to be replaced by a new agency, the Office of Thrift Supervision, answerable to the Treasury.

TB 13 is intended primarily to encourage healthy institutions to use up-to-date risk analysis techniques and to adopt prudent risk tolerance levels. Secondly, it aims to ensure that marginally insolvent institutions are protected against depletion in economic value.[19] From June 1989, supervised institutions must supply the OTS with data related to maturity and repricing dates of the various items. The OTS then applies a simulation-

---

[18]On this argument, see E. Brewer III (1989) and L.J. White (1991).

[19]See Federal Home Board Loan Bank System (1989). For a comment on TB 13 Rule, see F.J. Fabozzi, A. Konishi, (1991).

type analysis of the degree of risk, both on current interest margins and on the value of equity, in eight different interest rate movement scenarios.

Institutions with assets under $500 million are allowed to rely on the OTS's exposure estimate. Bank Boards must define specific limits on the institutions' exposure to IRR. These limits are defined as the sensitivity of a depository institution's earnings and net asset value to change in interest rates. For institutions with assets exceeding 500 million dollars, or those involved in high-risk mortgage activities, the development of internal control systems was made compulsory by the end of 1989.

IV. *Supervisory Authorities and Financial Institutions: Two Perspectives on IRR*

Before analyzing the impact of IRR regulatory guidelines for financial intermediaries, it is important to define the most salient differences and commonalties between the regulators' approach to this problem and that of institutions themselves.[20]

As already mentioned, the main aim of the supervisory authorities in defining guidelines for the measurement and control of IRR is to ensure that the degree of exposure to this kind of risk is compatible with existing net worth. Thus the regulating authorities are interested in obtaining an approximate measurement of the IRR, to be used as the basis for a possible definition of maximum exposure limits. As a consequence, the problem for regulatory authorities is to define a data structure which allows them to obtain adequate parameters for an assessment of the degree of risk.

The second step for the regulatory bodies is to establish a framework for relating these measurements to capital resources, introducing, if necessary, limits to the permitted degree of risk exposure. However, different sources of IRR may be identified, in view of the different types of financial activities undertaken by the institution. Therefore the

[20]See E. Gualandri (1991). For the targets of regulatory authorities, see also, J.V. Houpt (1990).

regulatory authorities must take some account of this fact, when defining measurement techniques and setting limits.

Above all, IRR assessment should ideally form part of a wide-ranging evaluation of the quality of the institution's overall risk management and policy, in relation to capital adequacy.

On the other hand, financial institutions themselves are interested in implementing IRR measurement and control from an practical point of view, within an overall institution-wide (but institution-specific) Asset and Liability Management strategy. Therefore, they are left to develop measuring, management and monitoring techniques suitable for their own purposes. In this case, the starting point for the measurement and control of IRR is obviously financial institutions' own assessment of the importance of the problem, followed by the adoption of suitable techniques. The institutions find themselves responsible for the introduction of reliable systems for the measurement, control and management of IRR, based on solid theoretical foundations; further, the techniques adopted must also consider the specific operating conditions of the individual institution. Particularly germane is that there is no fully operationalized definition of IRR for financial institutions that is not without ambiguity and hence room for good faith interpretation: management's understanding of this risk clearly depends on the products handled and the services supplied to clients. Thus, across institutions, the definition of the optimal model may therefore vary from case to case, since operators tend to construct measuring systems as appropriate as possible to the risk elements which affect their situation most.

In spite of the differences between the two approaches outlined, there are some points in common. *De minimis,* a common data base might be defined, which might contain the information on variables in the union of interests of regulators and agents; such might at least contribute toward the minimization of the cost of information processing. As far as regulatory authorities are concerned, computer data, remotely provided, however reliable tit may prove to be, is not sufficient in all cases. Inspection in the field is necessary to allow the capacity for measuring and handling IRR in each individual bank. The management's skill in handling IRR therefore becomes one of the items to be assessed in an approach of this type.

Moreover, within the flexible approach to prudential regulation, authorities are interested in the quality of the risk management of supervised institutions, involving consideration of each situation on a case-by-case basis, while retaining a guideline measurement of IRR assessed using the methods described above starting point. Basically, the option of a flexible approach means that the authorities must go beyond merely quantifying the level of risk, and analyze the validity of the internal systems for measuring and controlling IRR applied by the management of the various banks, in relation to the level of exposure. Therefore, the quality of risk management is not only an operational target and instrument of control of IRR for the management of financial institutions, but also an important element enabling regulatory authorities to assess the ability of institutions to cope with this kind of risk.

Ultimately, then, in an ALM perspective, three variables are involved in the assessment of IRR exposure: capital adequacy, the degree of IRR, and the quality of risk management by the institution's managerial staff.

V. *ALM and IRR Control for Financial Institutions*

As explained before, the approaches for measurement and control of IRR by the regulatory authorities and financial institutions are different but closely connected, in an ALM perspective. The implementation of adequate internal IRR control strategies will be an important factor in enabling the supervisory authorities to evaluate the institution's ability, in terms of capital adequacy and operating resources and structure, to deal with this problem. As a consequence, regulatory requirements related to IRR have important implications for financial institutions, in four key areas: definition and implementation of the strategic design, construction of the coherent organizational structure, building managerial culture, and skill and creation of the suitable information system.

5.1 *The Strategic Issues*

The measurement and control of IRR is a part of the Asset and Liability Management of financial institutions. The strategic issues involved in ALM are related to global management and financial planning. In fact, ALM may be viewed as a general approach to the problem of managing financial institutions, which implies coordination of the different specific functions in order to achieve, for example, the operational targets of maximizing the interest margin and minimizing its associated risk. Within ALM, strategic targets must be defined with reference to the growth and policy of diversification of business. Moreover, ALM is concerned with definition of policy related to the exposure to interest rate risk and foreign exchange risk, and to the control of liquidity. Within specific asset management, credit risk must obviously be taken into account. A further issue of strategic importance is the assessment of capital adequacy, in relation to the businesses engaged in and the types and degrees of risks undertaken by the institution.

5.2 *The Organizational Issues*

The policy adopted with reference to measurement and control of interest rate risk relies heavily on the implementation of a suitable organizational structure.[21] In the first instance, it is necessary to define the organizational structure and to establish which individuals and committees are responsible for the key functions:

- definition of the policy to be adopted for IRR management
- identification of the method(s) to be used for IRR measurement

---

[21]On this subject, see P.L. Fabrizi (1991).

- establishment of the operating limits in terms of maximum acceptable exposure
- formulation of strategies
- implementation of strategies
- measurement and control of results

After the identification of specific committees, their functions and operating tools must be defined. Thereafter, other important aspects need to be defined, such as the links between these committees and between other committees working in the institutions, as well as the effective hierarchy between all of them. Within the organization structure a key role is played by the Asset and Liability Committee (ALCO).

5.3 *Managerial Culture and Skills*

A key point in developing an IRR measurement method and defining strategies of control is the managerial culture and the skill level of managers themselves in these matters. The precondition is the understanding, by the top management, that interest rate risk both exists and is of serious consequentiality, and that monitoring techniques must be introduced.

A second step consists of the adoption of suitable measurement systems and then the interpretation of the results achieved. Therefore, the risk managers need a good knowledge of appropriate financial tools for measuring and managing IRR.

Obviously the management must focus on the different approaches for the monitoring of the and be aware of advantages and limitations of each. Since there is no one optimal model, the choice between different models must be made on the basis of the types of financial business engaged in and therefore the most important aspects of the undertaken. Also the type of data available must be taken into account.

Finally, risk managers must establish strong links with other people involved in the capital markets, who create products and develop strategies for dealing with IRR.

5.4 *Information Systems*

Proper information systems must be implemented, in order to solve the problem of monitoring the IRR. The first step consists of testing the suitability of the existing information systems for the processing of the information required by the regulatory bodies and of the measurement methods chosen for operative purposes. Then, if necessary, the existing systems may be modified along the guidelines previously identified. A process of collection, integration and standardization of data from different areas and different information systems must follow. However, problems may arise from the different informational and accounting systems used in different functional areas.

VI. Conclusions

The supranational supervisory authorities are currently working towards the definition of common frameworks for the measurement and control of IRR. They have undoubtedly achieved good results as far as market risk is concerned. The EC Directive on Capital Adequacy of Investment Firms and Credit Institutions and the 1993 Basle document are the prime examples of such results: not only is a substantial measurement system defined, but capital requirements are also introduced. The authorities still have work ahead of them for the definition of a measurement system addressing the overall interest rate risks faced by banks. Given the complexity of the problem itself, the different approaches to the problem in the various national contexts, and the different types of credit institutions considered and accounting conventions used, the task will occupy significant amounts of resources, and, no doubt, engender continuing, and spirited, discussion and debate among all affected parties. Such discussion and debate will, naturally, on emphasize the importance that must be attached to the goal of defining a common framework for risk measurement purposes that can provide, ultimately, results which are standardized, intelligible, and maximally transparent, and therefore readily comparable. More work has to be developed in this field, in an attempt to balance the different targets and obstacles facing supervisory authorities. The work done so far, and the experience of the individual countries on the subject, provide useful bases both for the drawing up of future guidelines and for identifying the impact on the financial institutions themselves.

Postscript--1997

The Basle Committee is still working onthe problem of monitoring IRR management undertaken by banks. A supplement to the 1988 Capital Accord to cover market risks incurred by banks was published in January, 1996. The document is in line with provisions made by the EC CAD directive.

The Committee is now deepening its focus on two specific issues: the first concerns the problem of the differences in capital requirements that stem from the usage of internal (i.e. bank-determined) models and methods for assessment of capital requirements rather than a standardised (i.e. BIS-mandated) approach; the second issue relates to sound practices for IRR management, which were outlined in a January, 1997, consultative paper, entitled "Principles for the management of interest rate risk." The principles set out in that paper are conveniently categorized as concerning: 1) The role of the board and senior management of the financial institution; 2) Policies and procedures; 3) Measurement and monitoring systems; 4) Independent controls; and 5) Information for supervisory authorities.

References

AA. VV., (1991) *La gestione integrata dell'attivo e del passivo nelle aziende di credito,* a cura di P.L. Fibrizi, Giuffrè, Milano.

Bank Of England (1992) *Banking Act Report For 1991/92.*

Basle Committee On Banking Supervision (1993) *The Prudential Supervision Of Netting, Market Risk And Interest Rate Risk,* Basle.

Breeden,D. and Corrigan, E.G. (1992) *Proposed Minimum Capital Rules For Banks And Securities Firms,* Joint Statement, "World Of Banking."

Brewer, E. III (1989) "Full-Blown Crisis, Half Measure Cure," In *Economic Perspectives,* Federal Reserve Bank Of Chicago, November/December.

Cantor, R. and Johnson, R. (1992) "Bank Capital Ratios, Asset Growth, And The Stock Market," *Federal Reserve Bank Of New York Quarterly Review*, Autumn, 1992

Committee On Banking Regulation And Supervisory Practices: Sub-Group On Interest Rate Risk (1988) *Analytical Paper On Banks' Exposure To Interest Rate Risk*, Basle, 12th September.

Committee On Banking Regulation And Supervisory Practices: Sub-Group On Interest Rate Risk (1989) *Banks' Exposure To Interest Rate Risk. Practical Measurement Methods*, Basle, 22nd February, (Bs/89/3);

Committee On Banking Regulation And Supervisory Practices: Sub-Group On Interest Rate Risk (1990) *Banks' Exposure To Interest Rate Risk. Measurement Proposals*, Basle, 25th October, (Bs/90/26);

Comptroller Of The Currency (1989) *A Conceptual Overview Of Interest Rate Risk,* Occ Staff Paper, Multinational And Regional Bank Analysis Division, Washington, November.

Drudi, F. and Panetta, F. (1992) *Rischio d'interesse e coefficienti patrimoniali per gli intermediari finanziari: un'analisi dei regolamenti sim,* In Banca D'Ttalia, "Temi Di Discussione", N. 180, novembre.

EC Commission (1993) *Council Directive On Capital Adequacy Of Investment Firms And Credit Institutions,* 25 May.

Federal Home Board Loan Bank System, *Thrift Bulletin, Tb 13,* January 26, 1989; *Tb 12,* December 13, 1988.

Fabozzi, F.J and Konishi, A. (1991) *Asset And Liability Management,* Chicago: Probus Publishing.

Fabrizi, P. L. (1991) *I profili organizzativi della gestion integrat dell'attivo e del passivo nelle aziende di credito,* In P.L. Fabrizi (a cura di), *la gestione integrata dell'attivo e del passivo nelle aziende di credito,* Milano: Giuffrè.

Gardener, E. (Ed.) (1987), *Interest Rate Risk And Banks,* Institute Of European Finance Research Monographs In Banking And Finance, No. 4, Bangor: University College Of North Wales.

Gualandri, E. (1991a) "The Approaches To Interest Rate Risk Of Supervisory Authorities And Financial Institutions," *Revue De La Banque*, No.1, Janvier .

Gualandri, E. (1991b) "Aziende di credito e rischio di interesse," In P.L. Fabrizi (A Cura Di), *La gestione integrata dell'attivo e del passivo nelle aziende di credito,* Milano: Giuffrè.

Houpt, J. (1989) "A Regulatory Perspective On Interest Rate Risk: A Fed View," *Issues In Bank Regulation*, Fall.

Huber, S.K. (1992) "The Federal Deposit Insurance Corporation Improvement Act Of 1991," *The Banking Law Journal*, 1992

Office Of Thrift Supervision, (1989) *The OTS Market Value Model,* Washington, D.C.

R.P. Platt (Ed.) (1986), *Controlling Interest Rate Risk,* New York: John Wiley & Sons.

"What Every Bank Ceo Should Know About Risk," *Risk,* Vol. 2, No. 8, September 1989

S.D. Smith (1988) "Some Factors To Consider When Choosing Your Gap Exposure", *Review,* Federal Reserve Bank of Atlanta, November.

White, L.J. (1991), *The S&L Debacle: Public Policy Lessons For Bank And Thrift Regulation,* Oxford: Oxford University Press.

D0127-ts/1

[From the conclusion]
An interesting point is the introduction of different capital adequacy requirements for credit institutions in the EC. Alongside the credit risk ratio, introduced by Directive 89/647/EEC, a position risk ratio has been introduced on the trading portfolio of financial institutions by the Directive on Capital Adequacy of Investment Firms and Credit Institutions. A key point of the new capital requirements is the drawing of the in between the trading book and the banking book, in order to apply the position risk requirement to the former, and the credit risk requirement to the latter.

As far as financial institutions are concerned, it is clear that new resources, in terms of money and personnel, must be devoted in the near future to the problem of monitoring CE. The most important areas needing new resources are those of information systems and of hedging instruments. These improvements also require a well developed managerial culture and a global ALM strategy. However the pay-off from the understanding of risks and their impacts is considerable and worth more than the efforts.

A crucial point will be the implementation of systems devoted to the analysis of possible hedging strategies in order to achieve minimization of capital resource given the introduction of further costing capital requirements. In the case of EC banks, in addition to capital requirements for credit risk, the EC directive introduces a capital charge not only for position risk, but also for counterpart risk and settlement risk. Another capital charge is added for the foreign exchange risk on the whole activity.

OTC DERIVATIVES AND THE 'COMPETITIVE PAYMENTS SYSTEM' DEBATE: THE LESSONS FROM HISTORY AND IMPLICATIONS FOR A SUPERVISORY FRAMEWORK*

George A. Martin
Department of Economics
University of Massachusetts

*I am indebted to a number of individuals for conversations on the subject of this paper, though surely none of whom will agree with all of the ideas expressed herein. I must, in particular, single out my many conversations with Martin Mayer as the inspiration, from his insights as well as in our disagreements, for my deeper reflections on the subject. I owe a special debt of gratitude to Prof. Douglas Vickers for a thorough reading of an earlier version of this paper. I am also grateful to the Brookings Institution and the Center for International Security and Derivative Markets (CISDM) at the University of Massachusetts for intellectual hospitality and generous material support. E-mail: gmartin@econs.umass.edu.

D. Ho and T. Schneeweis (eds.), Applications in Finance, Investments, and Banking, 93–157.

Introduction

The numbers are staggering. According to the Bank for International Settlements (1996), the notional value of global transactions involving derivative contracts are immense: total turnover in 1995 for exchange-traded instruments amounted to 327.6 *trillion* US dollars, with a year-end amount outstanding of 9.2 *trillion* dollars; for over-the-counter (OTC) derivatives, the total notional value outstanding at the end of March, 1995 is estimated to have been 40.6 *trillion* dollars, with figures on turnover unknown.[1] With numbers so huge, one is driven to ask: what do these numbers mean? While much of the discussion of derivatives has sought to deflate the significance of these notional quantities--often for virtuous reasons--we are convinced that they do have both economic, monetary, and policy significance. This conviction arises in part from a general predisposition to take seriously the terms in which market participants frame decisions, but also from theoretical reflection on the economic nature of these contracts. It is this latter reflection which is ultimately the subject of this paper, and which guides us through the thickets, plains and grassy knolls of monetary theory.

To be more precise, in order to understand the theoretical, economic, and policy significance of these transactions we must begin by asking some deep questions about the nature of money. Especially in the present environment of such dramatic financial innovation, if we are to think with some rigor, we cannot sidestep issues of ontology and etiology. We are led, in particular, to investigate the technological and functional character of money, both as a store of value, as Keynes and many after him have rightly

---

[1]Daily turnover averages, for April 1995, for OTC forex forwards and swaps are estimated to be 670 billion dollars, according to BIS (1996), p. 6. Figures for turnover in interest rate instruments are not available. Nonetheless, if we assume that the forex averages are a lower bound, then total turnover in OTC derivatives would be greater than 250 (trading) days x.67 trillion/day = $167 trillion dollars per year.

emphasized, but more importantly for the present inquiry--though not necessarily for monetary theory as a whole--as a medium of exchange and settlement. We hope to emphasize two features of money that are underemphasized in the literature, namely: 1) money, as a transactions technology, must be jointly conceptualized with the institutions that function to process it--i.e., we cannot think about money, as a means of payment, apart from the organization of the payment system itself; and, 2) an essential characteristic of money is that it is the means through which debts are settled with the greatest certainty, and with *finality*.

And with this emphasis we will see that, in a mature economy, we must recognize that the actual clearance and settlement process for monetary transactions gives us essential insight in to the nature of money; that the clearance and settlement process gives rise to the need for a central bank to ensure not only the efficiency of the clearance and settlement process, but the finality of such transactions; and that, this, *pace* the arguments of the Free Banking school, explains why we have not seen the 'spontaneous' development and survival of other non-governmental currencies, despite the existence of sufficient technical knowledge and organizations. We apply these insights to understand the nature of the derivatives markets, and in particular, the OTC derivatives markets, and show that the markets arise as an extension of the payments system, as as a means to organize transactions in assets more efficiently and with less settlement risk, and, moreover, to allow participants to engage in transactions in otherwise non-marketable assets, such as LIBOR *rates*. As a consequence, we argue that the Federal Reserve has a supervisory interest in such (OTC or exchange-traded) contracts to the extent that they represent a growth and extension of the payments system, but that this interest in these contracts should be narrowly circumscribed to their functioning in that system. In particular, given the present financial and institutional environment, the Fed should focus on promoting institutions and practices that reinforce the finality of such transactions in a manner most consonant with economic efficiency, as well as recognizing the key role that dealer banks play in the payments process not only through the usual clearing and settlement process, but through the OTC derivatives markets.

The course of our argument will be as follows: In the next section, we offer some basic discussion of competing characterizations of money, focusing in particular on those that arise in the Austrian, Neo-Classical and Post-Keynesian literature. We then turn to the more specific concern of the significance of the interrelation of the clearance and settlement process with the understanding of money. In the fourth section, we offer a brief logico-historical account of why central banks are both necessary, and have assumed the function of both issuer of currency and organizers and overseers of the clearance, and in particular, the settlement process; we use this theoretical and empirical evidence as a basis for criticizing the Free Banking approach, which is overly optimistic about the ability of free markets to solve the problem of organizing the payment system in an environment of uncertainty. Then, as a preamble to our discussion of the particular policy questions regarding derivatives, we briefly sketch the relevant features of the U.S. payments system, and then those of the exchange-traded and OTC derivatives markets. We then explain, in particular, how these transactions function as part of the payments system, and the appropriate stance that the Federal Reserve should therefore have towards these contracts. We reflect briefly on why it is, that in a highly deregulated and dynamic financial market, the development of private currencies has not generally occurred, and why in cases where it has, it has not survived--despite the fact that OTC markets--being effectively beyond regulation by monetary authorities--in particular would seem to provide a natural environment for the development of such alternative currencies. We close with a restatement of our conclusions. Throughout the text, we do not hesitate to raise open questions which we believe are worthy of further research and analysis.

What is Money?

Updating an apocryphal story told about Baron Rothschild to the present day, we might offer it in the following rendition: In pleasant conversation about his latest investing triumphs in the currency and interest rate markets, George Soros was once asked by a young portfolio manager to explain the nature of money. Soros demurred, offering instead the statement that he knew of only two individuals who really understood the nature of money. One was a Member of the Board of Governors, the other a minor clerk ensconced deep within the Bank of Japan. "But," he paused, "they disagree."[2] Such disagreement and befuddlement afflicts the discussion of no core economic entity as severely as it does for money. While we do not expect to end such a state of affairs, we hope we can shed a little light on the subject--our perspective will be more that of the clerk, in our focus on the microeconomics of money, but we will argue that those insights are only valid with the proper macroeconomic perspective, such as that afforded to a Governor of the a central bank.

The complex of concepts that have become associated with money is enormous, and we only seek to disentangle those that are most relevant to our discussion, keeping in mind that money cannot be defined without recognizing that money is as much about what it *does* as what it *is*. In particular, we must distinguish the following characteristics associated with money:[3,4]

Money as a *store of value*. Perhaps the central focus of Post-Keynesian monetary theory

---

[2]Peter Bernstein (1968) contains an account with Rothschild as the protagonist.

[3]An alternate attempt to establish such definitions is given, for example, in Cowen and Kroszner (1994).

[4]While many other assets have some subset of these characteristics, money, as it exists today, is unique in possessing them all. But this does not preclude multiple forms of money from existing, nor the existence of 'near-monies.'

is on the ability of this thing called money to retain value over time. Of course, many assets have this characteristic. But what makes money unique in this regard is that it is the *most liquid* of assets which serves this function. Which gives us reason to analyze:

Money as a *medium of exchange*. Money is the most widely accepted vehicle for transmitting claims from one side of the market to the other. Money need not have a physical incarnation, such as in currency or 'cash', and may merely be represented as book-entries at an institution that performs monetary functions. If cash should exist, these book entries should be readily convertible at par into cash. Which raises the facet of:

Money as a *medium of account*. Money functions, as Keynes emphasized in the opening of his *Treatise on Money*, to express the *unit of account* of a given *medium of account*. Currently, the two are identical in the form of a dollar, but under convertibility the dollar was the unit of account for a given quantity of gold, the medium of account.[5]

But most importantly for the present discussion, we are interested in money as *media of settlement*. Money is, according to Keynes (1930), "namely that by delivery of which debt-contracts and price-contracts are *discharged*...."[6] As Keynes, mentions, this function of money necessarily requires the existence of the "State or Community," as enforcer of the delivery of money, and as arbiter of what will actually be delivered as

---

[5]It is also worth pointing out at this early stage that there are competing terminological traditions on this subject: traditionally the term "unit of account" has involved the conflation of what we call here, after Niehans (1978), and many more recent theorists, the medium of account and the unit of account. As Niehans (1978:118) puts it succinctly, "Money is here called the a medium and not, as customary, a unit of account because, clearly, money itself is not a unit, but the good whose unit is used as the unit of account." An alternate, synonymous term for medium of account is also *numéraire*.

[6]Italics in original.

money. But this characterization of Keynes' is incomplete. Perhaps because he was predisposed to think of "money-proper" as cash, Keynes places insufficient emphasis on the fact that money is that medium which allows for both the greatest certainty of, and especially the *finality* of, settlement.[7] It is difficult to conceive of how the bilateral transfer of bearer assets such as cash could not represent a transaction in its finality, but this clarity does not seem to extend to more complex monetary transactions, such as that which arises with the exchange of electronic funds. Moreover, when it comes to the coordination of a large number of overlapping payments, the issue of finality is far more important and significant, for in such a situation the economics blur the distinctiveness and autonomy of each transaction. In fact, we show that it is the issue of finality, as sponsored and guaranteed by a central bank or its surrogate, and not nearly so much the determination of legally-mandated medium of exchange, that explains much of the evolution of financial institutions.

How then is it that competing theoretical paradigms characterize money? Perhaps most curious is the position of money in neo-classical theory, for example, as exhibited in Patinkin's tome (1956) on the subject, or more recently, in work by new classical economists such as Lucas and Sargent, as well as *soi-disant* proponents of the New Monetary Economics, like Robert Hall and the late Fischer Black, and Eugene Fama.

In Patinkin's work, despite language to the contrary, the economy is fundamentally non-monetary, *i.e.* it is a barter economy. Hahn (1965) makes this point evident for all in that he proves that any reasonable set of assumptions (specifically, those that allow for agent heterogeneity) will result in agents in a Patinkin model

---

[7]From the quotation reprinted in Goodhart (1989), Shackle seems to have appreciated the significance of "finality" in the functions and definition of money.

having a null demand for fiat money.[8] In Lucas and Sargent models, the basic mechanism for introducing money is through a cash-in-advance constraint. Alternately, models such as Tobin's (1958) explain the holding of money as a portfolio strategy.[9]

But these inventory-theoretic analyses of which ensure the demand for money are not nearly so probing as those posed by financial economists like Black and Fama, in part because in these former models money is nothing other than a very peculiar asset inserted into an economy. Black and Fama, on the other hand, ask us to envision a world without money as we know it. Rather than struggle to determine a role for a unique asset called money, they revel in its non-uniqueness: both Black and Fama seek to show that money is not in any way 'special' except insofar as government regulation of banks makes it so, and therefore ask us to think deeply about the ways in which the functions of money as we know it might be otherwise performed. Fama, in his contribution, argues that banks are not unique in that the "monetary" functions which they perform could be performed by non-bank institutions without regard to nominal financial quantities. Specifically, he argues that currency is a *store of value* and is thus a real good. Further, the accounting function of banks, which provides a record of the

[8]Clower (1973:121) makes this critique most forcefully when he writes that: "Patinkin's conceptual universe now appears to be just a more precise and elaborate portrait of the barter world of Mill, Walras and Marshall, its only novel feature being that 'money' appears among the set of commodities bartered." Clower's (1965) solution to the non-monetary nature is to induce a household 'liquidity preference' by positing what is essential a cash-in-advance constraint. However, it is curious, as Ostroy (1974) points out, that the introduction of money should result in an economy which is strictly less efficient than a non-monetary economy. This extremely counter-intuitive result is quite simply the inevitable result of the introduction of an additional constraint, the financial constraint. As Rogers (1989:64) writes, "this is precisely what one would expect from tampering with the perfect barter world of the neo-Walrasian *tâtonnement* process where traders are provided with the real rates of exchange for all commodities."

[9]See Thompson (1993) for a contemporary version of this approach; also see Tobin's reflections in Tobin (1980).

result of exchanges that takes place, according to Fama, do not, as they are altered with trades, necessarily involve anything that is properly considered money. Moreover, banks need not hold any of the assets involved in the transaction, whether it be money (in the form of deposits) or any other intermediate good. As Hoover (1988) emphasizes, Fama's stratagem is then to argue that, as the transactions and intermediation services provided by banks (accounting, currency, if necessary, as a store of value, and portfolio services--i.e. turning deposits into loans) are each real goods, and since, by the Modigliani-Miller theorem, value is independent of the specific relative composition of financial assets that lay behind those goods, such as the financial position of the firm/bank offering those services, and, as such, relative prices may be determined as they would in a classical Walrasian economy. Thus absolute prices of goods, in terms of the unit of account, may be expressed in terms of the relative price of the medium of account (money), and that price level is independent of the composition of financial portfolios. One may therefore choose any or many numeriare as a basis for settling transactions.[10]

The implications of the Black, Fama and Hall analysis for monetary theory have been developed in particular by Greenfield and Yeager.[11] Essentially, the Greenfield and Yeager system would involve governmental designation of a unit of account based on a broad bundle of commodities (chosen to represent the real economy as a whole and, as a consequence, be less subject to fluctuation in purchasing power); mutual funds *qua* 'intermediaries' would issue claimnotes denominated in commodity bundle units

[10]It might be worth emphasizing that the 'moneylessness' of the BFH approach comes essentially from the fact that there is no *outside* money, for which inside money is exchangeable. This is also true of the Greenfield-Yeager variant of the model discussed below.

[11]Greenfield and Yeager refer to there system as the "BFH" system in honor of the contributions of Black, Fama and Hall. We refer to their extension with the acronym BFH-GY.

against investor 'deposits', and invest those deposits in financial assets. The government itself would be constitutionally prohibited from issuing its own version of money. Note issuers would be regulated by market forces--over issuance of notes would be penalized by discounting of claimnotes. Of course, if this type of arrangement sounds familiar, it is merely a gold standard generalized to a commodity bundle, a proposal that is in many ways equivalent to Irving Fisher's 'compensated dollar' plan, in which the amount of gold backing a dollar is varied by the central bank according to the price behavior of a commodity bundle with the goal of maintaining overall price stability.[12,13] The primary difference between the two approaches lies in the fact that in Fisher's plan, there is only one medium of exchange; in the Greenfield-Yeager BFH approach, there are multiple media of exchange.

An alternative analysis and policy proposal, most generally associated with White (1984; 1989), which shares some of the intellectual lineage of the BFH-GY approach,[14] derives more from the Austrian tradition, and in particular, Hayek (1978),

---

[12]Thus, an increase in the commodity bundle index will result in a revision upwards in the redemption ratio of dollars to gold, and *mutatis mutandis* for a decrease in prices.

[13]While we do not investigate it here, the issue of price level stability is a very important motivating force behind the various proposals of alternative payments systems. Cowen and Kroszner (1994) offer a sustained critique as to why many of the proposals that grow out of the BFH-GY tradition fail to achieve that end, especially in circumstance that price indices are not continuously revised. (Which, in the present day, is not a very strong a critique). More importantly, they argue that the presence of marketability premia (which is not coextensive with Keynes' notion of 'liquidity premia', but is nonetheless related) in assets (including money as the medium of exchange) will render the price level indeterminate, since there will be real balance affects associated with the mix of financial assets held. Such marketability premia are banished from the BFH-GY system by the assumption of Walrasian markets.

[14]For example, White (1989b) avers that he finds he has more in common with the BFH-GY approach than the Post-Keynesian approach, and that as a consequence, opines that Yeager (1968) is a better guide to the properties of money in a monetary economy than that offered by Keynes.

and, as so, operates with a very different sensitivity to issues of how markets actually function. In particular, the Austrian tradition recognizes that for money, in any meaningful sense, to arise in an economic environment, the economy in question must be subject to fundamental uncertainty. Agents hold and use money because it is the most efficient manner of coping with that uncertainty,[15] since all potential investment or transactional opportunities cannot be foreseen in advance. (Could the universe of opportunities be foreseen, agents would set up a web of contingent contracts which would allow for the appropriate state-dependent reallocation of resources.)

Hayek (1978) himself argues for a 'denationalization' of money, i.e. elimination of the government monopoly on money,[16] to be achieved via the competitive provision of media of exchange tied to different media and units of account, and is generally credited with resuscitating the argument for multiple means of exchange and settlement (not to mention providing a basis for Free Money that was not tied tightly to a gold standard). This prescription is, however, at odds with the BFH-GY system, since the latter would require that there be a single medium of account that is not the medium of exchange.[17] White, moreover, makes the argument that, under the efficient functioning of markets, the media of exchange will come to be associated with a particular medium of account, on the basis of costs associated with monitoring and computing accounts in

---

[15]It is worth mentioning White's (1989b:380) declaration that he views the value of money in this regard as providing "a vehicle for low-cost transacting." He continues, "It does not rest on the desire for stability" of the value of the asset, a factor which he argues is central to Keynes' conception of 'liquidity preference.' Rather, it is, for him that money is ultimate means of settlement. See below for more on this.

[16]According to many of these proposals, the primary reason for government interest in issuance of money is seigniorage rights. Hayek (1978) has a much fuller list of reasons why government control of money is driven by institutional self interest and not the public interest.

[17]Though there are variants of this proposal with regard of the convertibility of the various media of exchange into the medium of account.

different units (*vide* Menger's story of the spontaneous development of money--money in which the medium of account is 'wedded' to the medium of exchange).[18,19] But there is nothing inherent in money, as the medium of exchange, that requires the state to issue it--for private agents can readily issue there own currency, presumably in an environment with a prevailing unit of account, backed by assets (such as, say, gold) into which those notes are redeemable, and markets will 'regulate' the relative values of those currencies according to agent assessments of the potential for those claims to go unredeemed, either by insolvency or illiquidity of the issuing institution.[20] (Of course, and we defer more detailed discussion of this until later in the paper, this is the monetary regime which prevailed in the United States prior to the founding of the Federal Reserve, and specifically before the National Currency Act of 1863 and the National Banking Act of 1864.)

Money as Means of Settlement

While the identity of the specific institution issuing it is not essential to the complete nature of money, what is essential, however, is that the economy have at least one monetary medium that functions as an ultimate *means of settlement*, the transfer of which extinguishes the claim that the seller has against the purchaser. In the present environment, dollars function as means of exchange, medium of account and means of settlement; under the gold-standard, gold was that means of settlement. In a world where all money is credit (the predominate Post-Keynesian view (*e.g.* Wray (1990), Lavoie (1994))), and more precisely, the debts of *others*, the precise nature of settlement

---

[18]Niehans(1978), chapter 7, offers a neo-classical argument for why the medium of account will come to be associated with the medium of exchange.

[19]Cowen and Kroszner (1994), in their own words, "emphasize alternatives to scenarios with a unified medium of account and exchange," in a post-Mengerian (to 'coin' a phrase) account of financial evolution.

[20]Hayek (1978) does *not* argue for the ultimate convertibility of money.

comes that much more to the fore. Exchange is no longer merely about exchanging equal embodiments of 'value', but it is precisely about an implicit forward contract for a particular nominal quantity that is the means of settlement--it is not just about the transaction at hand. What proves most distressing in the BFH system is that, in essence, any good can function as a means of settlement--Greenfield and Yeager merely choose a commodity bundle for its macroeconomic properties--since there is essentially no distinction between a medium of exchange and a medium of settlement. Moreover, the effective eradication of a difference between the exchange process and the settlement process effectively excludes the inherently temporal quality of monetary exchange in a modern market economy. As a practical consequence of this elision of the media of exchange and settlement, the model effectively denies a potentially significant source of economic uncertainty in that there is no possibility in the model that an exchange will take place, but will not settle.

Hoover (1988) argues--and White (1989) seconds the belief--that an economy must have, "as a practical matter," a good or goods to which all assets are, by law, ultimately convertible, and therefore the basis for settlement. This, according to Hoover, is necessary because financial assets find their value in that they represent claims to something else other than themselves; for example, equity shares in a mutual fund may pay off dividends in shares, but ultimately those shares must be, by legal right or by established custom, exchangeable for some other useful asset. Ultimately, this chain of exchangability must end with some good.[21] But more perspicaciously, Hoover observes that, in an non-Walrasian economy, banks will need to settle accounts amongst themselves, accounts which involve claims to (a range of) assets over which they have

---

[21]See Brunner and Meltzer (1971) on the efficiency implications of the length of this transactions chain. They argue that, in an environment of uncertainty, money not only minimizes the length and costs associated with inter-asset transactions, but, it also functions to produce information about the optimal exchanges to be undertaken.

no control. Obviously, this settlement process is facilitated if there is a single medium of settlement (otherwise banks would have to keep, clear, and update multiple accounts for each customer reflecting each of the i'th good of settlement.) Together, these two argumental prongs bring Hoover(1988b:164) to conclude that "settlement services are the principal real service provided by financial assets in accounting or clearing systems [such as is the function of banks in the BFH world]. Settlement services arise from the ability of financial assets to mimic money in discharging debts that inevitably accompany exchange [in a decentralized, sequential economy]."

White, Selgin (1989) and others who have proposed the devolution of authority to issue money to private entities, however, are not so insensitive to the issue of settlement as are proponents of the BFH-GY system. Rather, it is their argument that markets themselves will ensure a settlement system that functions smoothly--with the Free Banking experience in American (1838-63) and Scottish (-1844) history being the self-chosen template against which their ideas are modeled and compared. In broadbrush the basic White-Selgin model is this: In a fractional reserve system (Hayek (1978) *does not* support fractional reserve banking), private entities will issue money, and may do so to whatever extent that they wish (i.e. there are no reserve requirements). However, the relative value of private currencies will vary according to the market's assessment that the outstanding claims on reserves will be fulfilled upon demands for settlement. The regulating force prohibiting overissuance will be a combination of market assessment of bank reserves (perhaps facilitated by other private entities, akin to credit rating industries, that may earn a return from such research, though this particular mechanism is not emphasized in the literature) as well as the desire for firms to build reputational capital (as emphasized by Klein (1974)). Issuing firms that might, for exogenous reasons, experience temporary illiquidity (as opposed to insolvency), and would thus be unable to settle transactions, would be bailed out, for a price, by other firms that recognized the temporary nature of that state. No central authority would act to stabilize or otherwise regulate the system.[22]

However, as we will argue below, the White-Selgin model is too optimistic about the ability of the market to overcome inherent tendencies toward instability. In particular, there is an inherent tendency for instability (or 'fragility') which would be difficult to remedy without the presence of a large agent capable of facilitating solutions to collective action and information problems, viz. a central bank. In particular, we will see that, as financial markets have grown, the ability of any one, competitive agent, or constellation of agents, to ensure market stability has diminished. In part, this is because no single agent or group of agents, in a decentralized financial system, has the resources necessary to insure against the possibility of a break in the settlement process, nor does it or do they have the legal means to act in proactive manner sufficient to rectify that break, once it actually occurs. This is, by no means, to suggest that decentralized agents cannot or will not individually or collective act in ways designed to mitigate the possibility and risks of such an event--in fact we will argue that they do have precisely those incentives--but that the information and collective action problem is sufficiently difficult to solve that it requires a non-market solution in the form of a central bank to guarantee (if imperfectly) the ultimate integrity of the payments system. In particular, we will see that the most important function of the central bank is to facilitate and ultimately guarantee the finality of payments and associated settlements of large value transfers--to ensure that past and present transactions will not be undone and therefore revisited in the future. While the future may be unknowable, there is

[22]It is on this point, in particular, that Free Bankers are critical of other advocates of minimizing the role of central banks in monetary management. In particular, many a Free Banker has criticized the unwillingness of monetarists to jettison their reliance on central banks conduct (albeit minimal) monetary and supervisory activities. See for example, White (1989:48 et seq.), who takes aim at Friedman's proposals set out in his *Program for Monetary Stability*, arguing that monetarism is incompatible with free banking, and that Friedman's concerns about the incentives of Free Banks to overissue notes are not justified by the historical record.

nothing more pernicious to orderly functioning of a market to have the foundation that is past action undone. This is especially true in when those actions are comprised of large value transfers.

Clearing and Settlement of Monetary Transactions: A Brief Logico-Historical Account

In the previous sections, we have presented some of the competing views on the nature of money, and how the corresponding organizational forms of the payments system should be organized.[23] It is worth, however, looking historically at the experience of particular organizational structures that have developed[24] in the provision of payments

---

[23]While many of the analyses reviewed above may themselves be cast in terms of analysis of what money is and how money does function in an economy, it does not seem too unreasonable to impute to the authors in question a sensitivity to the fact that their models represent extreme (mathematical or verbal) abstractions from the real operations of monetary systems, and that therefore, their models represent as much declarations about how such systems *should* function, in both the normative and prognostic senses of the term.

[24]Much of the literature is fond of using the term 'evolved' or other such terms that connote the evolutionary process; we prefer the more neutral term 'developed' or its variants. However, we think that, in historical explanation, such terminology ultimately performs a disservice to the analytical process, first and foremost because it effectively suppresses the idea that institutions are built, and economic processes conducted by, agents with knowledge and, most importantly, intentions. While it is of course true that human knowledge is limited, and, to paraphrase one classical political economist of some renown, that men make there own history, but not exactly as they intend, it is nonetheless essential to economic processes that agents involved are intentional actors, and that there is a link, however attenuated and constrained, between human desire, human intention, human endeavor and human history. Evolutionary explanations, as deployed by economists, all too often amount to functionalist and teleological tales, often amounting to thinly veiled vindications of the market process, rather than proper explanation. It is beyond the scope of this paper to go much further in a critique of the use of the evolutionary mode of explanation, other than to say that such an endeavor would make use of the many insights on evolutionary theorizing and its applications to social process provided, for example, by Lloyd (1986), Rosenberg (1985,1992) and Sober (1988). A particularly nuanced approach evolutionary explanations of history is given

services. We hope, in particular, to persuade the reader that an important function of the clearinghouse system was to minimize settlement risk amongst members, and effect *finality of settlement*, and not merely to economize on the transactions costs associated with clearing claims and effecting the consequent payments. In particular, during the pre-National Banking Era, clearinghouses functioned to reduce the costs associated with discounts on heterogenous bank notes by accommodating the growth in non-discounted (and stable) claims on demand deposits that arose from settlement uncertainty in currency. After such note discounts were effectively outlawed by the National Banking Act, and transactors were deprived of the ability to price settlement risk, clearinghouses took on greater significance in that they functioned to ensure par settlement through non-price and price means via the monitoring of clearinghouse members and an increasing readiness to issue credit to illiquid members in times of crisis. We will see, however, that these actions by private clearinghouses were insufficient in that private interbank discipline was neither rigorous enough to prevent banks from engaging in imprudent lending arrangements that ultimately jeopardized their ability to function as a proper node in the payments system, nor was such discipline free from conflict of interest. It was only with the establishment of the Federal Reserve, in which the Federal Reserve System interposed itself into the interbank settlement process, as the transfer agent and provider of payments finality through the irrevocable exchange of deposited reserves, and the non-competitive lender of last resort, that settlement risk within and without of the clearing house could be minimized.

A. The Free Banking Period

After the demise of the Second Bank of the United States in 1836 and prior to the National Currency Act of 1863--immediately rewritten as the National Bank Act of

---

by Teggart (1977), a joint publication of works published originally in 1918 and 1925.

1864-federal authorities effectively withdrew from the regulation of US banks--banking regulation was conducted on the state level. While state initiatives varied considerably--California banned banks in 1849, and others retained a charter system--many states on the East Coast, including New York, which regulated the bulk of the nation's financial institutions, adopted "Free Banking."[25] Key features of Free Banking regimes are distilled by Dowd (1993:184):

> 1. Anyone could set up a 'free bank' who could raise the capital to do so, provided a minimum capital requirement was met.
> 2. 'Free bank' note issues were to be secured with holdings of specified bonds which were to be deposited with the state authorities. The usual bonds specified were state (and sometimes federal) ones.
> 3. The notes of 'free banks' were to be redeemable on demand, on penalty of liquidation, and note holders had first claim on the assets of a failed bank.
> 4. The shareholders were normally allowed some form of limited liability, usually fixed at twice of the value of capital subscribed.

It is also worth noting that 'free banking' *did not* relax restrictions on bank branching.

For our purposes, we are most interested in the practical consequences of this regulatory framework, namely the proliferation of bank notes and the variety of claims on demand deposits, and the difficulties that such created for the banking system and for economic agents engaged in monetary transactions.

Perhaps no case illustrates the difficulties posed by non-par exchange of notes than that of the Boston area in the antebellum period. At that time, the bulk of notes circulating in the New England region were issued by "country banks". This included the Boston area since the balance of payments was such that there was a net inflow of country currency. While area residents could make payments through checks written

[25]There are many accounts of free banking in the US--see for example Dowd (1993) or Sechrest (1993) for general overviews. Of course, there was also a long period of free banking in Scotland, which essentially ended in 1844 with the passage of the Bank Charter Act. See for example White (1984b), as well as the previous references.

on local demand deposits, cash transactions were hampered by the difficulty in ascertaining the fair value (or authenticity) of country notes which carried discounts to reflect both the transactions costs associated with redemption and the possibility that a bank would fail to redeem.[26] Notebrokers arose to take advantage of the economies of scale available in the collection of information about country banks as well as in the wholesale redemption at par of notes accumulated at a discount. The economies of scale were such that notebrokers had the incentive to accumulate large holdings of notes before presenting them for redemption--forcing the redeeming institution to either maintain large specie reserves or otherwise call loans in order to meet the demand.

The notebroking process was centralized with the establishment of the Boston-area Suffolk Bank System, which allowed country banks to place on deposit specie to cover redemptions. While it made redemptions that much easier for note holders, it nonetheless was advantageous to the country banks since it smoothed redemptions, and it allowed for the collection of notes below par, and thus reducing their ultimate liability. Eventually, multilateral settlement between participating members of the system was introduced as a further effort to enhance the settlement process. With the complexity of such transactions, the bank system itself took responsibility for ensuring that system members were in good standing before allowing them to participate in the settlement process, and by providing overdraft facilities to clearing members.[27]

---

[26]Checks on demand deposits were cleared on a non-par basis, but the discount reflected a fixed assessment of the cost of collecting on the checks, such as those that arose from geography, and not some assessment of the likelihood of collecting on particular demand deposits at a particular institution. Demanding institutions would merely wait for a check to clear before releasing funds to the bearer of the check. Of course, with currency, imposing this cycle would drastically reduce the transactions velocity of money and the consequent supply and demand elasticity.

[27]Goodfriend (1991:13), in his discussion of the Suffolk experience, offers the valuable comment that development of the System represented an example of the natural tendency that market economies have to substitute credit money for commodity money.

Nonetheless the Suffolk System met its demise when a competing institution was organized in 1858. That institution, known as the Bank for Mutual Redemption, offered far less invasive monitoring of members, but fewer facilities. After a short battle, the Suffolk Bank yielded to the Bank for Mutual Redemption, having given up its notebroking.[28]

While *antebellum* institutional arrangements such as the Suffolk system, and notebroking in general, helped mitigate discounts associated with competing bank notes, uncertainty about the value of such notes caused disruption in the course of economic exchange, as agents either needed to assess the appropriate discount to apply to a wide variety of bearer notes, or restrict themselves to transactions in selected notes. Transactors also incurred capital risks in that the value of notes could fluctuate over time.[29,30] However, at that time, checks drawn on demand deposits were not subject to

---

[28]The BMR was short-lived, as the National Banking Act effectively abolished the notes of state chartered institutions with a peremptory 10% tax on all such issuances.

[29]Proponents of Free Banking argue that this is not a difficulty. In fact, Selchrist, among others argue that bank notes under free banking should be conceptualized as shares in a mutual fund, with reserves as assets. But this is a very peculiar notion of a mutual fund! Firstly, note holders are limited in their upside potential by the par value of notes, while not insured against downside risk. Secondly, existing noteholders do not gain *pari passu* from either the reduction of reserves (sale of assets) or the issuance of new notes--the benefits of which accrue primarily to the shareholders of the institution. In any case the free fluctuation in the internote exchange rate mitigates the "store of value" function of money that some many working in the tradition of Keynes have rightly emphasized.

[30]It is worth noting that the reserves mandated by most Free Banking statutes required that the currency-issuing bank hold bonds of the state in which the bank was located, or sometimes in-state mortgages. Dowd (1993) argues that the reason that free banks experienced as much difficulty as they did was in part due to this very restriction on eligible reserves that certainly limited the ability of banks to diversify away risk. (Amalgamation/branching restrictions also had similar consequences.) The typical example put forward to illustrate the defects of such eligibility restrictions is the case of Minnesota, in which more than 70% of free banks failed due to the failure of state bonds

such fluctuations. It is not that the checks were without risk, though--not only did the payee have to assess the credit worthiness of the individual, but also of the paying bank--but that is was effectively *impossible* to assess and price that risk. Pricing that risk would require that one or many institutions effectively assess the credit risk of all owners of demand deposits as well as the institutions at which the deposits were held.

Of course, agents may circulate endorsed checks, but the information problem increases with the remove that one has from the original issuer of the check--at least the original payee has the possibility of applying 'non-market' criteria such as those associated with reputation or repeat transactions in evaluating the credit risk of the individual. Certainly this does not mean that a market in endorsed checks could not have arisen, but does suggest that such was neither in the interest of the check writer nor its payor. The latter wished to minimize the discount or probability of refusal of her checks; the former wished to minimize the possibility that individual holders of deposits overissue checks based on their deposits. Banks themselves encouraged the clearance of checks on a transaction-by-transaction basis by offering par settlement, thus discouraging the development of any discounts.[31]

Given both the risks associated with exchange based on bank notes, and the *impossibility* of developing a secondary market in claims on checkable deposits--i.e. market incompleteness--transactions increasingly occurred via check and *not* by bank note. According to data reported by Gorton and Mullineaux (1987:460), the notes to

---

secured by the returns of private railway assets. See Dowd (1993:157-9) for more details.

[31]In the absence of complete information, an agent wishing to accept an endorsed check must assign some positive probability that the payee will default and discount the check accordingly. In the absence of an ability to credibly communicate her own information about the creditworthiness of the original writer of the check, the agent wishing to pass that check would obviously prefer to extinguish that credit risk rather than have it priced directly into her transaction.

deposit ratio fell dramatically in New York State (which saw a free banking statute passed in 1838) and in the Nation as whole (which saw only a progressive and uneven move towards free banking):

New York Banks		**National Banks**	
Year	**Notes/Deposit**	**Year**	**Notes/Deposit**
1837	1.2	1835	0.85
1847	0.74	1845	0.79
1857	0.31	1860	0.67

We complement this with data provided by Meyers (1931:89) on the breakout of note/deposit ratios for NY City vs. Country banks:

NY City Banks		**NY Country Banks**	
Year	**Notes/Deposit**	**Year**	**Notes/Deposit**
1839	.417	1839	3.19
1849	.271	1849	2.23
1859	.093	1859	.783

Further, Gorton (1996:364) reports that discounts on country bank notes were generally declining during this period, and with fewer banks having notes trading at excess discounts. As the figure entitled "NY Bank Note Discounts" indicates, discounts indicated by a Philadelphia-based note reporter show, in particular, that the number of banks, either in the city or broader state, with "nonmodal discounts" (i.e. discounts that do not reflect common factors like distance) declines substantially with time, suggesting again that banks were quite reluctant to allow their notes to trade at a discount.[32] While it is difficult to persuasively argue from a few data points the reason for this transformation--the move towards check money and away from discounted notes--it does call into question the basic Free Banking argument that competing currencies represent a stable monetary arrangement (in the sense that the basic characteristics will persist through time).[33] It is as much an open question as to whether charted banks, which had access to state Safety Funds (deposit insurance) carried lesser discounts on their notes than free banks,[34] and whether those banks exhibited less dramatic declines

---

[32]The reason that some discounts shown in the figure assume negative values is that the reporter gives prices for Philadelphia banknotes during suspension of convertibility in specie, and therefore reflect the premium attached to holding those New York notes over Philadelphia banknotes.

[33]The data do, however, suggest that overissuance of notes was not an *increasing* problem.

[34]Gorton (1996:363) suggest that all notes of both free and charted NY banks, if solvent, trade at the same discount, with only "insolvent" institutions trading at a nonmodal discount. (It is also worth noting that the correlation coefficient for the number of banks trading at the nonmodal rate and the average nonmodal discount is not particularly strong at .49 for country ("state") banks, but much stronger for city banks at .72; presumably this reflects in part the fact that the distributions of city bank discounts are likely to be less skewed because of the smaller number of banks in the sample average, but it also raises some question about the small sample inference that only those country banks that were insolvent carried non-modal discounts.) In a period with large numbers of "insolvencies" (as indicated by the "nonmodal percentages" given in the figure), the effects of such risks however are still substantial and provide the same incentives to substitute from notes towards checks--data gleaned from King (1983) suggests that at one point (1841) a conservatively estimated minimum of 17 percent of the total notes in circulation were issued by failed banks. Further, it was often the case (Meyer 1931) that country bank notes represented a disproportionate share of notes held in New York City, and thus could not be ignored by larger and more established institutions. Other assorted evidence also suggests that discounts on NY banks do not

in their note/deposit ratios; the evidence, of course, does suggest that the typical note/deposit ratio for a country bank is higher than that of a city bank, though that is almost surely due to the slower transaction velocity of country bank notes.

We can tentatively conclude, however, that there was substantial settlement risk engendered by the usage of a largely heterogenous currency supply, either because of the possibility that banks would not honor the claim against specie; or that the discounted value of the notes would fluctuate between the time they were acquired and the time that the possessor of the notes wished to use them; or that such notes might be refused altogether. With the attendant, and likely consequent, growth in issuance of checks, banks faced a new settlement problem: how to process large numbers of often offsetting claims on a wide variety of institutions in an efficient and timely fashion. We can and will see that the establishment of clearing houses (such as the New York Clearing House in 1853) was not only an effort to economize on the transactions costs associated with processing such claims, but to minimize the settlement risk associated with such transactions. It is no accident that the clearinghouse system developed in an environment when transactions based in currency were fraught with difficulty and uncertainty, and represented a non-market (or 'hierarchical') solution to a problem created by incomplete market and informational processes.

B. The National Banking Period and Growth of Clearinghouses

The National Banking Act, which established the existence of a national currency, backed by US government bonds held on reserve,[35] among other things, effectively eliminated private issuance of currency by state banks, thus eliminating one form of

---

differ substantially across charter status, despite the fact that, as King (1983) reports, loss rates on chartered institutions were far less than in free banks.

[35]The purchase of which 'conveniently' provided a major source of finance for the Union during the Civil War.

settlement risk (associated with the heterogeneity of currency) but depriving market of the ability to monitor the financial well being of banks through the prevailing discounts on its bank notes.[36] Unable to price the remaining settlement risk, banks sought a non-market mechanism that was a ready extension of the clearinghouses that sprung up in the years before the Civil War. We use the history of the New York Clearing House as a proxy for development of the clearinghouse in general, because it has been the most important clearinghouse, it has the most extensive historical record, and forms the central focus for the theoretical discussions of clearinghouses.

With the growing *antebellum* need to clear checks and other claims on a more timely and less disruptive basis,[37] banks found that it was far more efficient for their representatives to meet in a central location to exchange specie against net positions than to settle all positions bilaterally. Netting from the previous days checks was typically computed on the morning after the checks were presented; settlement in specie was typically effected at the end of those days from reserves that were often held in the clearinghouse vaults.

Essentially unrecognized at the time of its formation, perhaps the most important feature of the clearinghouse was its membership basis, and in particular the prerogative to exclude banks judged to be unable to settle balances, or to organize alternative settlement amongst its members for a member or members that might find itself financially "embarrassed." Several ways of doing this were ultimately, and hap-

[36]The act explictly required that the bank notes of National Banks be exchanged at par.

[37]See the figure entitled "New York Clearing House Clearings (1854-1899)" for evidence derived from Cannon (1900). One also notes that prior to the establishment of the NYCH, settlement was done on a weekly basis, and the comparatively large volumes that were settled often resulted in extreme turbulence in the New York money markets.

hazardly developed, usually in the face of crisis: 1) the issuance of credit by the clearinghouse to the embarrassed member(s), 2) the suspension of species payments to non-member institutions, including corresponding banks, 3) the suspension of species payments to customers of member banks, and 4) the suspension of the provision of credit information about all individual member institutions in order to prevent runs on embarrassed institutions.

To understand the dynamics of clearinghouses at their instantiation[38] it is instructive to recall the actions of the NYCH during the first major panic, in 1857. As Meyer (1931) recounts it, August saw the failure of the Ohio Life and Trust Company, which drove up rates on commercial paper and call loans. The beginning of September saw the suspension of the Mechanic's Bank--which had originally been the issuer of settlement certificates for the clearinghouse, though it was replaced in that role by the Bank of America prior to the crisis. In response to the suspension, three weeks later, the clearing banks agreed to provide additional credit to the NYCH in order to reduce the need for the use of specie in settlement; this was repeated again a month later. Concomitantly, clearinghouse members ceased to honor correspondent relations with non-clearing (country) banks by refusing to redeem notes of country banks that had themselves previously reduced their balances held at those institutions for just that purpose. The crisis, however, was unabated. Given the scarcity of specie the usual NYCH practice of issuing certificates against specie could not directly form the basis of loans to troubled institutions; instead the clearinghouse borrowed money from state banks in the form of interest bearing notes (6% p.a.) and included them as specie in the settlement process. City banks were willing to hold these interest bearing notes, and began to resume lending. In November, redemption of country bank notes, on a staggered basis, was resumed. And in mid-December convertibility of deposits was

[38]Rather than to take their development as a step towards a subsequently realized *telos*.

resumed, after having been suspended in mid October, after having dropped a precipitous 30% since the beginning of September. In the end, during the crisis, seven free banks and three chartered banks failed.

What is instructive about the experience is, of course, that neither the suspension of illiquid members, nor the voluntary extensions of credit by member banks to the clearing house itself to minimize the need for species in settlement, were ultimately sufficient to stave off the crisis--it was the incorporation of external credit backed, in part by the state of New York in the form of Safety Fund guarentees on chartered institutions, as well as the suspension of settlement for non-member banks that ultimately led to the abatement of the crisis. As we will see, throughout the national banking period, private bank clearing arrangements by themselves proved insufficient to stem crises, in part because they we unable to provide sufficient incentives for member banks to maintain strong enough balance sheets to continue to settle transactions;[39] nor were they always able to generate sufficient internal funds to overcome bank illiquidity, and often resorted to suspension of payments and conversion of deposits with obvious deleterious effects on non-member institutions.

Roberds (1995) offers a convenient summary of many of the National Banking Era Crises, which is summarized in a table of the same name. Of most interest to us are the crises of 1873 and 1907 since the former was the first to indicate the possibility that great challenges to payments system might arise out of events in securities markets; the latter offers testimony to the idea clearinghouse activity could, in the process of seeking

---

[39]It is worth noting that New York City banks seemed to guard their reserves with remarkable zeal, suspending payments rather than drop below required 25% reserves. This was especially true when the drop in reserve would have resulted in specie flow to banks outside of the clearinghouse. (Banks were prohibited from making new loans or issuing new notes when in violation of reserve requirements; however, they were not prohibited from using reserves to make payments in specie.)

to exclude institutions from the benefits of clearing, trigger crises--crises on the magnitude that they required external intervention.

The crisis of 1873 arose out of the failures due to the default of western railroads. Those failures were the catalyst for a decline in the stock market, which put increasing pressure on banks that had been financing the clearance of stock transactions, to the point that they withdrew from such financing. Roberds (1995:18) summarizes the precise problem:

> The key factor behind the closing of the New York Stock Exchange was the primitive nature of contemporary systems for clearing and settling stock trades. At the time literally every stock trade had to be offset by transfer of bank funds via certified check, a practice that resulted in liquidity demands far in excess of the funds that most trading firms had on deposit. The difference between the liquidity needs of brokers and the funds they had on deposit was financed directly by the banks. Consequently, it was not unusual for banks to extend uncollateralized daylight credit to brokers in excess of ten times what they might have on deposit. The demand for such 'clearance' funds only grew with the onset of panic, just as the banks became most reluctant to expose themselves to the risks associated with fluctuations in stock prices.

Clearinghouse certificates were issued to member banks but these proved insufficient; payments were suspended for a month, wreaking havoc with other institutions across the nation (and introducing a currency premium of approximately 5% on currency vs. checkable deposits); and the stock market remained closed for two weeks. Deep recession followed.

The crisis of 1907 exposed some of the potentially destabilizing aspects of the members-only nature of the NYCH, and in particular the possibility that clearinghouse membership could be a source of 'conflict of interest' in that members could use their membership *against* non-members.[40] Around the turn of the century, growth in a form

[40]Goodhart (1988:39-43) contains a discussion of five examples of such conflicts of interest, including the crisis discussed here.

of bank known as a Trust--which were not required to maintain reserves in liquid and low-yielding assets--led to an intense competition with National banks for deposits. Trusts were not allowed membership in the NYCH, and as a consequence cleared through correspondent banks. The exact cause of the difficulty is unclear, but evidence presented by Grant (1992:115) suggests that the problem was some time in the making, with NYCH banks threatening as early as 1903 to withdraw correspondent clearing privileges from Trusts if they did not boost their reserves. State legislation in 1906 codified this request. But in 1907, losses in the stock market by the NYCH member, the Mercantile National Bank, caused it to ask for a clearinghouse loan, and cast doubts on an associated institution, the Knickerbocker Trust Co. Knickerbocker sought a loan from its clearing agent, the National Bank of Commerce, but was declined. Despite efforts to secure a loan from J.P. Morgan, the resulting run on the bank caused its failure and that of other Trust companies. Out of town banks began to draw down deposits on New York banks in anticipation of demands for specie. In response, clearinghouse certificates were issued, and the U.S. Treasury deposited $25 million with New York City banks. Such efforts were insufficient, and payments were suspended.[41]

Over the next few months clearinghouse certificates were again issued, and

---

[41]Widespread public opinion at the time held J.P. Morgan and other city bankers responsible for the panic; the historical record appears to be somewhat more ambiguous, however. Goodhart (1969:118-119) puts it this way:

> As far as can be ascertained, the knickerbocker had neither asked for help nor really needed it, although it had suffered a succession of unfavorable clearing balances. Indeed, the Knickerbocker later easily (1) paid all of its debts in advance of the time set, (2) managed to have a large surplus left over, and (3) reorganized and began business again. One suggestion is that this move was a part of the internecine fight then being waged in New York between the national banks and the trust companies. It is possible that the National Bank of Commerce may have merely seized a convenient pretext to eliminate a rival, or rather a set of rivals; for the run on the Knickerbocker immediately turned into a stampede of depositors onto all of the trust companies and eventually back onto the national banks themselves.

The criticisms extend to the behaviour of city banks to non-city banks, as well. For example, Sprague (1910) suggests that New York banks cut off credit to their non-city correspondents; White (1983:87) suggests the opposite.

functioned as *de facto* currency in that they circulated far beyond the membership NYCH despite the patent illegality of such issuances. In fact, the certificates were considered such an integral part of efforts to contain financial crises that thier function as currency was codified in the Aldritch-Vreeland Act of 1908. It also set forth relatively lax standards on the assets required to bank such currency--not just government bonds or other such assets. It was recognized at the time that the Act was merely prelude to the more profound financial reform to be investigated by the National Monetary Commission ultimately formed in 1910. That Commission, and its Congressional executors rightly found that the existing banking regime could not be stabilized merely through the legalization of clearinghouse certificates.

C. The Formation of the Federal Reserve System (FRS)

The FRS was an effort to stanch the recurring financial crises that traumatized the nation. Rather than draw upon the central banking model that predominated in Europe, in which the central bank was controlled by the government (as has been, and still is to some extent, the case with the Bank of England) or the largest banks, the FRS was modeled after the clearing house systems that developed across the nation.[42] In particular, as White (1983:64) notes, one of the main purposes of the FRS was to reduce the reliance on correspondent banking for the clearing and settlement of transactions which had the unfortunate consequences of dispersing reserves throughout the system and allowing larger, clearing banks to hold smaller non-clearing banks hostage during times of crisis. It is worth noting that there was little contemporary discussion of any role that the FRS might play in discretionary monetary policy as we know it except insofar as to organize itself in a manner to maintain an "elastic supply of currency."

---

[42]See Timberlake (1978) for an account of the clearinghouse origins of the Federal Reserve, and a deploration of the ultimate departures of the system from the clearinghouse model.

The foundation of the Fed allowed for number of new elements that enhanced the certainty and finality of settlement. First and foremost, the FRS, with its various reserve city banks, served to reduce the importance of correspondent banking in the clearance and settlement of national transactions; all System members could clear out-of-state claims through the System without having to maintain interbank deposits under the control of other private institutions.[43] This functioned to prevent the instabilities associated with settlement crises that recurred in many if the panics described above. Secondly, all settlements were accomplished through the exchange of reserves held the Fed, which allowed the Fed to interpose itself directly into the settlement process in order to guarantee a settlement and its irrevocability with intraday or overnight discount window borrowings, if necessary. Thirdly, the Federal Reserve itself, as constituted, now had no immediate interest in seeing the failure of solvent but illiquid institutions, as might competing banks in a clearinghouse or correspondent relationship. Fourthly, the Federal Reserve had the statutory authority to inspect the books of System members not only within a given city or clearing circle, but across the nation, and take directed actions against banks which did not live up to more encompassing prudential requirements set by the Federal Reserve; moreover, the Federal Reserve no longer had the incentive to force the costs of specie imbalance from one bank unto others since it bore ultimatel responsibility for the well-being of all System banks. Fifthly, the Federal Reserve had far less incentive to pursue the suspension of payments and conversions for troubled institutions since it could more effectively monitor troubled institutions and direct credit towards that institution via the discount window. And finally, the Federal Reserve forced all members to clear checks at par (*i.e.* with zero collection fees) in order to encourage the usage of checks, an minimize the need for the Fed to manage those collection fees.

---

[43]The difficulties associated with correspondent banking could also have been ameliorated by the relation of restrictions on branch banking.

The history of U.S. banking, from the Free Banking Period to the establishment of the Federal Reserve in the early 20th century has thus been characterized by the development of various institutional and regulatory changes that have functioned to reduce the difficulties associated with various arrangements for the clearance and settlement of money.[44] The necessity for this has not so much been driven by transactions costs associated with various clearing and settlement mechanisms, but by the uncertainty engendered in and by the market process. In particular, the period represents a dramatic case for the important complementarities that exist between market and *non-market* processes in establishing the orderly conduct of monetary exchange. While these non-market processes need not be by definition administered by public authorities--in fact they are almost always organized within and through the contractual nexus of the private sector--we did see that organization of the clearance and settlement process did not succeed without the presence of a large, non-competitive entity to oversee the non-market process.

The US Payments System and the Derivatives Markets

Perhaps two of the greatest concerns to central bankers these days have been the strain placed on the payment system by the increasing volume of transactions in financial assets and the growth of derivative markets, in particular, over-the-counter derivative markets.[45,46] Both represent *perceived* threats to the payments system, in that the

---

[44]We have only discussed in passing the characteristics and difficulties of securities settlement. Moser (1994) offers a very interesting account of the history of the Chicago futures clearinghousewhich was formed at the turn of the century.

[45]A derivative contract is a financial contract with terms such that the actual cash flows (and hence its value) are explicitly and directly linked to the fluctuation in value of another asset or set of assets. Typically, but not always, the contract will *not* involve either the purchase, sale or transfer, of the underlying asset/s from which the contract derives its value. We emphasize this latter point because one of the keys to understanding derivative contracts is that they may have a dynamic that that is only loosely hinged to that of the underlying asset—e.g. it is quite possible to have an open

interest in derivative contracts that exceeds the total supply of the underlying asset. Moreover, the underlying 'asset' may not be a salable asset. For example, one of the most common 'assets' underlying derivative contracts is LIBOR, which is merely an interest rate—not a salable asset.

Thus, for example, by this definition, collateralized mortgage obligations, which represent claims against particular future cash flows associated with securitized pool of loans, are not properly derivative securities. We prefer to term them 'structured products,' instead. It might then seem odd that 'futures' contracts are considered to be derivatives securities, since they specify the forward delivery of an asset in an *unstructured* manner. Our reason for including them in the category of derivatives is that they are rarely settled through delivery of the underlying asset, whereas CMO's are—in this case by a specific pro rata share of cash thrown off by the loans covered in the pool. By this same reasoning, we would also resist describing as derivatives repo transactions, which involve an agreement by counterparties to exchange cash for collateral (usually government securities) at the present with the agreement that at a latter date the cash-receiving party will repurchase the securities (or similar subsititutes offered by the cash-provider) for a pre-agreed price. The structure of this contract is akin to a futures/forward contract (the difference between the two is primarily that the former is a contract that is traded through an exchange, the latter is purely bilateral), but their is almost always delivery of an asset at the end of the transaction. The economic function of a repo is, therefore, much close to that of a secured loan, than a futures/forward contract.

Over-the-counter derivative contracts are distinguished from *exchange-traded* contracts in a number of regards. The latter, most crucially, involve a clearinghouse, whereas the former are almost exclusively bilateral. A clearinghouse arrangement almost always involves the clearinghouse as the intermediating legal counterparty to trades that involve contracts that are standardized in form and obligation, so that any failures between 'buyer' and 'seller' of a derivative contract become the responsibility of clearinghouse. To dispatch such responsibilities, the clearinghouse collects 'margin' payments from traders for the duration of the trades in accordance with the capital exposure of trades, from which an insurance pool is created. In addition, the centralization of clearing provides the clearinghouse and hence supervisory authorities if necessary, with current information about the risk exposure of particular institutions to particular contracts. OTC contracts typcially involve large commercial banks as broker-dealers, and may be customized, and thus non-standard, but often are not. OTC derivatives normally involve the broker-dealer as counterparty, and thus, in some way, the broker-dealer functions as would a clearinghouse. Margin is rarely collected, though there has been an increasing trend towards collateralization. The secondary market in OTC contracts is typically limited, with contracts usually being extinguished through unwinding, or the assumption of directly countervailing posititions, rather than trading.

notional quantities involved are so large that an otherwise isolated or isolatable disruption in either securities or derivatives markets (either through bankruptcy, illiquidity, technological failure or malfeasance) threatens to cascade rapidly and uncontrollably through the entire financial system. It is our contention, however, that the derivatives markets, and OTC derivatives markets in particular, *instead represent an extension of the payments system*, not only to cover trade in otherwise tradeable assets, but also to allow trade in otherwise non-tradeable assets or risks. However, they do not represent, nor suggest a move, towards an *alternative* monetary regime in which alternative media of account or settlement truly compete with Federal Reserve Notes or their electronic instantiation (or their foreign counterparts) since institutional and market efforts to manage the inherent uncertainties associated with the settlement process of any alternative monetary transaction still confer substantial advantage to usage of those dollars. And finally, as such, because OTC derivatives represent an important element of the payment system, particularly with the United States and the provence of the Federal Reserve, they properly deserve to be subject to the supervisory authority of the Fed, but only insofar as they represent elements of the system, and not, for example, because they themselves represent transactions which may be "unsuitable" for supervised institutions.

The course of our reasoning about derivatives and the payments system requires that we take a moment to set out some of the lineaments of large-value transfer systems and the settlement process in the United States and abroad. One should begin by noting that most interbank settlements in the United States are ultimately cleared through

---

[46]One only need review the activity of study groups of the Bank for International Settlements, or the recurring content of speeches and testimony of officials of the Federeal Reserve, to get a strong sense of this.

Fedwire, a funds transfer system[47] that debits or credits a settling party via its reserves held on account with the Fed.[48] Transfers are done on a gross settlement basis, that is, sequentially, transaction by transaction, throughtout the course of the business day, rather than in terms of end-of-the-day net obligations between counterparties. Thus, in the case of, say, broker-dealers in government securities, which over the course of the day might buy large quantities of short term securities from another dealer and then later sell large amounts of long term securities to that bank to finance the purchase, the settling amounts would reflect a substantial debit to the reserves of the purchaser of the short term securities until the buyer of long term securities wired payment.

The other large value transfer system (LVTS) is the Clearing House Interbank Payments System (CHIPS), founded in 1970, and run by the NYCH. Clearing is done on a continuous basis, but net balances are formally settled over Fedwire on an end-of-day basis;[49] the preponderance (80%) of the daily volume (averaging about over a trillion dollars a day) cleared is comprised of spot forex transactions.[50] Small value funds

---

[47]Fedwire also settles transactions in (dematerialized) government securities.

[48]Fedwire was created with the establishment of the Fed in 1913.

[49]As Perold (1995) describes it, the actual clearing and settlement process on CHIPS is somewhat more complicated. While end-of-day net settlement is conducted through irrevocable exchange of reserves via Fedwire, interbank payments are actually settled on a continuous basis, but those settlements are provisional, though after the passage of the Federal Deposit Insurance Corporation Improvement Act of 1991, uncontestable. (FDICIA addressed and clarified the legal foundations of netting arrangements among deposit taking institutions.) The provisionality arises from the fact that failed transactions are unwound if insufficient collateral is available to CHIPS to settle the transaction. Such collateral is posted by members in the amount of 5% of the maximum net settlement the posting institution is permitted to receive ("Sender Net Debit Cap") from a CHIPS counterparty, and ranges up to $300 million dollars for individual institutions; the collateral/cap ratio is scheduled to be lowered to 3% by the end of 1996.

[50]See the Table entitled "G-10 Payment Systems" for more statistical information on the LVTS's of both US and other members of the G-10.

transfer is also handled electronically by the Fed via the ACH system on a gross settlement basis; such transfers represent the bulk of all transactions, but a minimal proportion (15%) of the total value transferred. Other major clearance and settlement institutions included the fifteen or so securities clearing houses and depositories that cover exchange traded derivatives as well as municipal and mortgage-backed securities.[51]

The alternative models of settlement embodied by CHIPS[52] and Fedwire illustrate some of the difficulties in designing an efficient and safe LVTS.[53] The basic tension is this: the less frequent, the greater the number of clearing members, and the broader the netting, the more efficient will be the settling process—but, correspondingly, the greater then the likelihood that a clearing member will fail during the batching period, and the greater the outstanding items resulting from that failure. Real Time Gross Settlement (RTGS), on the other hand, eliminates the existence of batching risk, but impose substantial liquidity demands on clearing banks since non-synchronicities in settlement (which generally occur) require that intraday debtors cover their positions out of either own funds or funds raised from elsewhere (most usually the central bank overdraft facility--viz., the discount window in the case of the U.S., or in the case of systems like that of Japan and Switizerland, through an intraday money market). RTGS however does have the virtue that settlement failures can be addressed on a bilateral rather than a mulitlateral basis, thus reducing the risks

[51]See Parkinson et al. (1992) for a thorough exposition of the various clearing and settlement procedures for US securities. It is worth noting that Gov't issued Mortgage-backed securities (issued by agents such as FNMA) settle only on an *end of month* basis.

[52]UK settlement networks like CHAPS are truer representatives of net settlement systems than CHIPS, but their consideration in any more detail than that presented in the attached tables is beyond the scope of the present paper.

[53]See, for example, Furfine and Stehm (1996), Humphry (1984) and/or Angelini et al. (1994) for further discussion of the economics of payment system design.

associated with having to unwind multilateral transactions, and, hence ensuring payments finality. Both these overdrafts and the intraday credit implicitly extended by CHIPS members has increased dramatically, and clearly raise the possibility of severe payments system gridlock should institutions fail (to settle) during the day.[54]

The sustainability of such overdrafts rest very much on the role of the central bank as settling agent, as well as participant and/or supervisor in the clearing process. As the table entitled "Role of the Central Bank in Payments System" indicates, all banks in the G-10 settle interbank payments on the books of the central bank, and most settle payments arising from securities transactions there as well, with RTGS being the preferred method of settlement.[55] RTGS systems also allow for their own set risk management facilities, as reported in the table "Risk Management in RTGS."[56]

In order to adequately account for the risks associated with clearance and settlement through either CHIPS or Fedwire, participating agents must either post collateral to the loss sharing pool (as in NYCH CHIPS) or pay overdraft fees.[57] However, the available evidence (reported by Furfine and Stehm (1996)) does not

---

[54] *The Economist*, April 27, 1996.

[55]This represents an ironic reversal from the historic tendency to make increasing use of the economies associated with batch processing of orders.

[56]A table of information of risk management for net settlement systems is also included thereafter.

[57]Intraday overdraft credits on Fedwire were not priced until 1994. Overdrafts are currently priced at 15 basis points per annum of the minute by minute negative balance over a bank-capital adjusted minimum (so as not to penalize routine settlement). BOJ-NET, the Bank of Japan's settlement facility, does not provide overdrafts, but an active secondary market in intraday overdraft money does exist. The Swiss system provides neither overdrafts nor is there a secondary market directly in such funds.

suggest that such pricing or collateralization has had much affect on banking practice.[58] We nonetheless surmise that the issuance of OTC derivatives, as off-balance sheet items and financial contracts that minimize clearing and settlement via CHIPS or Fedwire, have been partly spured by the desire of banks not to incure costs associated with overdrafts or settlement balances.

As mentioned above, derivatives come in two basic types, depending precisely on how payments arise from the contract are cleared and settled. *Exchange-traded* instruments clear through the multilateral netting procedure of most options or futures clearinghouses, and settle on through Fedwire. The counterparty to all such transactions is the clearinghouse, which requires that traders on the exchange post margin in proportion to the riskiness of the positions that they assume (and not necessarily the credit worthiness of the institution itself.) *Over-the-counter* instruments are bilateral contracts, which settle bilaterally unless specific multilateral netting arranges are made between private institutions, and typically require no collateralization.[59] Netting ("by novation" or through "Master Agreements") is often done across contracts between the same counterparties by amending the contracts to aggregate all existing contracts. Typically at least one counterparty to an OTC contract

---

[58]In fact, it seems that pricing or collateral requirements do little, in the end to control risks associated with a settling bank that is in severe trouble. Such a bank would likely be rationed from private sources of liquidity if it sought it directly in the form of loans (and hence lender scrutiny), but could readily accumulate a substantial overdraft (perhaps to see itself through a liquidity crisis) without that overdraft being priced to reflect risk. Currently such risk is only 'priced' in the form of frown costs, or in the case of chronic overdrafters, requirements on preposting of collateral. It is worth noting that Wilcox and Hancock (1996) find that securities-related overdrafts *were* reduced by the introduction of a 10bps fee (in 1994, later moved to the current 15bps in 1995), but that funds related overdrafts have been less responsive.

[59]Though efforts to establish centralized collateral management for OTC contracts by the Chicago Board of Trade have been moving ahead. Private parties sometimes demand collateral in such contracts.

will be a commercial bank.

Settlement of derivative contracts may take place either in the physical asset covered by the contract or via cash. The vast majority of all settlements for exchange traded contracts, including claims on "real" commodities like agricultural or energy goods, is done on a cash rather than delivery basis.[60] This is particularly true of some of the most popular exchange traded instruments because the asset is not amenable to delivery (such as in the case of derivatives on the S&P 500 index) or impossible to deliver, as in the case of futures on elapsed Eurodollar rates or other derivatives linked to Libor, wherein the contract is on a *rate* rather than an asset proper. In this way derivatives represent an extension of the payments system to otherwise non-tradable assets. OTC contracts are even less likely to settle on a non-cash basis--in part because the bulk of interest rate contracts are linked to Libor or another interest rate index, and because counterparties wish to minimize the possibility of a failure to settle in the contracted items which rises with the 'lumpiness' of such transactions (since it requires that the delivering party finance the acquisition of the assets to be delivered). Cash

---

[60]Cowen and Kroszner (1994) argue that futures contracts that settle in deliverables represent an extension of the payments system to new media of settlement. We find this interperetation hard to maintain in that the settlement ratio is so skewed in favor of cash, even when the deliverables are near monies like financial assets. It is also worth noting that efforts to create settlement mechanisms that are denominated in non-dollar assets have failed. A particular example: in 1992, Bankers Trust set up an automated clearing system, Globeset, in the form of shares on interest bearing assets of different currencies. Users could settle transactions directly through the system at no cost, or use the shares as margin for trades on the CME. However the settlement system was suspended in 1994 for lack of use. It suggests that there is still substantial value in settling transactions in nominally fixed terms in and with the prevailing media of settlement. Further, it is worth noting that the persistance of cash settlement, despite the widespread availability of indexed assets, calls into question the 'market's desire' to pursue monetary arrangements in the BFH-GY tradition. Perhaps one reason for this is that the Federal Reserve, as guarentor of the settlement finality, still accepts only dollars for the reserves used as the media of settlement.

settlement of derivative contracts effectively requires less exchange of money than would be required if one were to replicate the transaction through spot market transactions.[61]

The importance of this last point for the present paper cannot be underestimated. Derivatives exist primarily to economize on transactions that could otherwise be obtained through spot market transactions, and as such contribute, in general, to the efficiency of the payments system.[62] Futures positions could be assumed merely by following the hedge ratios associated with that contract; options can be replicated via dynamic replication strategies involving the underlying and a riskless bond; interest rate swaps could be replicated by the issuance of notes and appropriate borrowings. While none of these replications could of course been done perfectly since one must incur greater transactions costs to pursue such strategies, the actual magnitude of these transactions costs may be relatively small when one is attempting to replicate *portfolios* of derivatives (since the cost of hedging a portfolio of derivatives with transactions costs on the underlying assets is necessarily subadditive in the number of derivatives being hedged).

OTC contracts, in particular, allow for the most efficient reduction in the use of the payments system for several reasons. 1) They do not require transactions in securities which typically have longer settlement times than the settlements based on marked positions; 2) They do not require the daily payments associated with the mark-to-market requirements associated with exchanges; 3) They allow a determination of the

---

[61]This is not precisely true, since it is possible that the value of the option on a *non-traded* asset be greater than the value of the asset, as for example the case of options on yields on bonds in perverse interest rate environments.

[62]Perold (1995) is the only other writer known to this author who shares this perspective.

collateral/margin to be posted to be based on the entire credit standing of the counterparty, rather than the riskiness of the particular position;[63] 4) They allow for contracts that meet the specific needs of the counterparties; and, 5) They allow for bilateral netting arrangements across heterogenous contracts (one can not offset transactions, say, between unaffiliated clearing houses). It is worth noting the value of these advantages through observing that the vast majority of swaps are plain vanilla fixed vs. floating[64] that could easily be replicated through a series ('strip') of eurodollar futures contracts, but nonetheless the payment regime associated with an OTC contract is less onerous, encouraging substitution towards such contracts.

However, OTC contracts have one notable disadvantage: there is no intermediary, such as the Fed, to guarantee settlement of claims arising from such contracts. This uncertainty is only magnified by the uncertainty surrounding the legal status of such contracts. Many "unsophisticated" counterparties on the loosing side have managed to have the contracts unwound (e.g. The State of West Virginia, Hammersmith and Fulham, and perhaps Orange County, to name a few) on the grounds that the agents of those counterparties acted without the appropriate authority (*ultra vires*) required to legally enter into such contracts. Even more complicated issues arise in the context of cross-border contracts: not only does one have the legal uncertainties of each of the respective dominions of the contracting institutions, one has the compounded uncertainty associated with attempting to make the two or more legal

---

[63]One would expect that the costs of collateral, etc. for a highly rated counterparty would be less in a bilateral market than when dealing with the exchange, since the exchange clearing house must cover counterparties of lesser credit risk. Bhasin (1995) provides evidence that actual credit quality of participants in the OTC markets has declined through time which may indicate that the savings in collateral are substantial in the OTC market. It is also worth noting that the credit risk of typical interest rate swaps is usually minimal and relatively unpriced across counterparties of a wide range of credit ratings. See Grinblatt (1994).

[64]O'Brien (1994).

systems mesh. One also has the difficulty associated with international time differentials in the settlement process that are particularly accute in the forex markets (see BIS (1996b)); these differentials can be substantial, an quite consequential, as the failure of Herrstat Bank all too poignantly illustrated in 1974.[65] Federal Reserve, and G-10 banks more generally, should and have made great strides towards the reduction of such risks through the harmonization of settlement provision and the diminution in asynchronous settlements both within and across national boundaries.[66]

---

[65]BIS (1990:28) provides an example of the credit risk at settlement that arises from time differentials between hours of operation of counterparties:

> For example, given the time differences between the Tokyo and New York business days, a party that sells Japanese Yen in exchange for US dollars must irreocably pay out the Yen approximately eight hours before it receives payment in US dollars. (However, this gaps can be as long as 18 hours.) During this period between payment of Yen and receipt of US dollars, the party that has paid yen is exposed to the loss of the full principal value of the US dollar payment.

But, as the docuement continues, the implied credit risk does not merely affect the initial payer, since settlements via correspondent accounts may not be updated on an intraday basis, and thus may result in, in the present example, the irrevocable payment of dollars without receipt of yen. The total risk affecting the initial payer are typically greater than the second payer, since much larger sums may be involved in possible failures of the first kind than would in the second case, since it is typically the case that correspondent relations would only involve smaller transactions. Intraday information in both types of risk would serve to mitigate this risk. Some banks have imprudently dismissed Herrstat type risk by assuming that all bank closures will occur overnight in the time zone of the failing institution, but this assumption is neither sustainable in its own right, nor does it eliminate possible settlement risk.

[66]In fact, as mentioned, G-10 Central Banks have demonstrated a deep preference for RTGS settlement, and have moved all central bank-owned payment systems towards that goal. (BIS (1997)). As part of this strategy, the Fed has moved to make Fedwire available 18 hours a day (beginning at 12:30am) so as to minimize the time periods in which foreign markets are open and US markets are closed. What is interesting is that private sector settlement systems, especially in the FX market, (like CHIPS, but most notably Multinet) have staunchly defended delayed net settlement procedures. We only note that such systems are far more similar in structure contractually to OTC derivatives and the multi-contract netting arrangements that have arisen to handle them than they are to the continuous gross settlement of RTGS. See, for example, Board of Governors (1994) for private sector views in this direction.

OTC derivatives are also characterized by substantial market concentrations, with commercial banks playing an extremely important role in the markets.[67] The GAO reports that the top six dealers (ranked by notional amount outstanding in 1992) in OTC derivatives were commercial banks. Similar evidence of concentration amongst commercial banks is also presented in the figure "Nine Banks with Most Derivatives." While the bilateral net effect of OTC contracts is rarely large, these contracts are thus linked though a small number of very active banks in the market. Thus the failure of one of these institutions would not only jeopardize payments to and from typical customers of the bank, it could also wreak havoc in the payments system more generally though disruption of the OTC derivatives markets. The Federal Reserve thus should have deep interest in the derivatives held on the books of such dealer banks, not so much because they represent a credit risk to the bank itself,[68] but because of the integral role that the derivatives held by the bank are playing in the promotion of efficient and reliable payment services.[69]

Thus we have seen that with OTC derivatives, and too a lesser extent, exchange traded derivatives, we have substantial economizing in the demands that securities settlement would otherwise pose to the system. But they nonetheless do not escape the vulnerabilities associated with failure of large financial institutions. Without the Federal Reserve to stand ready to assist such large and central institutions, and ensure that such

---

[67]See the figure entitled "Notional Derivatives..." for a time series of commercial bank activity in the market.

[68]Net positions are not generally very large, according to Gorton and Rosen (1995). However, these positions are typically substantially less than a the credit exposure to traditional bank products, such as commerical loans.

[69]We do not discuss here, but merely note, that the substantial reduction in required reserves across G-10 countries (see Borio (1997)) has substantial consequences for settlement procedures, viz. the greater likelihood and magnitude of overdrafts.

banks and their derivatives contracts continue to function, the possibility of catastrophic financial crisis looms unnecessarily large.

Conclusions

In the previous pages we have seen that a crucial feature explaining the evolution of financial institutions and financial contracts has been the uncertainty surrounding the settlement function of money. We saw that competitive payments systems, under free banking were ultimately unstable becaue of uncertainty surrounding the settlement value of transactions. Efforts to curtail settlement uncertainty or failures that arose through the development and elaboration of clearinghouse arrangements were, as well, insufficient, since private interbank discipline was not sufficient to prevent such difficulties; nor was it generally strong enough to remedy them quickly without the suspension of payments to non-clearing banks. We argued that the formation of the Federal Reserve represented the first real chance the US financial system had to stave off settlement failures, and the Fed did this through the extension of various guarantees and otherwise interposing itself in the market process. With our sensitivities raised to issues of settlement, we saw in the final portion of this paper that derivatives, and OTC derivatives in particular, functioned as important extensions to the payments system, a rightful provinence of the Federal Reserve. In the course of so doing suggested that while the technical means exist for the proliferation of new media of settlement, the fact that the Federal Reserve still settles transactions in dollars held on reserve represented one of many reasons that alternative media of settlement have not arisen. We concluded by arguing that the Fed has a supervisory interest in derivatives held by dealer banks not so much because they represent a substantial credit risk to the banks, but because the banks function as a central nexus for the payments system that has developed through OTC derivatives.

Many issues stand unaddressed by this paper, and should be the object of further research. In particular, we have yet to develop the appropriate monetary framework that truly captures the economics of mutlilateral monetary transactions. Nor have we devoted much attention to the very important issues that arise out the 1.6 trillion dollar per day market in securities repurchase agreements ("repos") that have become the lifeblood of non-deposit taking banks and the lubricant of securities transactions and settlements. While private third-party custodians and administrators (usually securities depositories (e.g. DTC, CEDEL or Euroclear) or banks with large base of custodial activity, like State Street Bank) have recently begun to take a more active role, there are still plenty of unresolved questions about the ontology and economics of the repo market that complicate the settlement process--for example the conflicting international case law on the status of the obligations of bankrupt repo participants. These, and related issues, await further consideration.

Bibliography*

Aglietta, M., (1994): "Les Systemes de Paiements dans l'integration europeene," Working Paper.

Allen, F., and Gale, D. (1994): *Financial Innovation and Risk Sharing*, Cambridge: MIT Press.

Angelini, P. and C. Giannini, (1994): "On the Economics of Interbank Payment Systems," *Economic Notes by Monte dei Paschi di Siena*, 23, 194-215.

Baer, H.L., V.G. France, and J.T. Moser, (1994): "Opportunity Cost and Prudentiality - An Analysis of Futures Clearinghouse Behavior," Working Paper.

Bhasin, V. (1995): "On the Credit Risk of OTC Derivative Users," Working Paper.

BIS (1990): "Report of the Committee on Interbank Netting Schemes of the Central Banks of the Group of Ten Countries," Basle, Bank for International Settlements.

BIS (1994a): "Macroeconomic and Monetary Policy Issues Raised by the Growth of Derivatives Markets," Basle: Bank for International Settlements.

BIS (1994b): "Compendium of Annexes to the Report on Macroeconomic and Monetary Policy Issues Raised by the Growth of Derivatives Markets," Basle: Bank for International Settlements.

BIS (1995): "Cross-Border Securities Settlements," Basle: Bank for International Settlements.

BIS (1996): "Central Bank Survey of Foreign Exchange and Derivatives Market Activity," Basle: Bank for International Settlements.

BIS (1996b): "Settlement Risk in Foreign Exchange Transactions," Basle: Bank for International Settlements.

BIS (1997) "Real-Time Gross Settlement Systems," Basle: Bank for International Settlements.

Board of Governors of the Federal Reserve System (1994) *Symposium Proceedings:*

---

*Not all items are referenced in the text.

International Symposium on banking and Payment Services. Washington, DC: Board of Governors of the Federal Reserve System.

Borio, C.E.V. and P. Van den Bergh, (1993): "The Nature and Management of Payment System Risks: An International Perspective," Working Paper.

Borio, C.E.V. (1997) "Monetary Policy Operating Procedures in Industrial Countries," Working Paper.

Brunner, K. and Meltzer, A. (1971): "The Uses of Money: Money in a Theory of an Exchange Economy," *American Economic Review*, 67.

Cannon, J.G., (1900): *Clearing-Houses: Their History, Methods, and Administration*, New York: D. Appleton and Company.

Cesarano, F., (1994): "The New Monetary Economics and Keynes' Theory of Money," *Journal of Economic Studies*, 21, 39-53.

Clower, R.W.,ed.,(1973): *Monetary Theory*, Baltimore: Penguin Books.

Commodity Futures Trading Commision (1993): *OTC Derivative Markets and their Regulation: Working Papers*, Washington, DC: CFTC.

Commodity Futures Trading Commision (1993): *OTC Derivative Markets and their Regulation*, Washington, DC: CFTC.

Cowen, T. and R. Kroszner, (1994): *Explorations in the New Monetary Economics*, Cambridge, MA: Blackwell.

Davidson, P. (1978): *Money and the Real World*, 2nd ed. New York: MacMillan Press.

Dorn, J.A. and A.J. Schwartz, eds., (1987): *The Search for Stable Money - Essays on Monetary Reform*, Chicago: University of Chicago Press.

Dotsey, M. and P. Ireland, (1995): "Liquidity Effects and Transactions Technologies," Journal of Money, Credit, and Banking, 27, 1441-1471.

Dowd, K., (1993): *Laissez-faire Banking*, New York: Routledge.

Downes, P. and R. Vaez-Zadeh, eds., (1991): *The Evolving Role of Central Banks*, Washington, DC: International Monetary Fund.

Duca, J.V., and W.C. Whitesell, (1995): "Credit Cards and Money Demand: A Cross-sectional Study," *Journal of Money, Credit, and Banking*, 27, 604-623.

Duffee, G.R., (1994): "Idiosyncratic Variation of Treasury Bill Yields," Working Paper.

Dymski, G.A., (1992): "A 'New View' of the Role of Banking Firms in Keynesian Monetary Theory," *Journal of Post Keynesian Economics*, 14, 311-320.

Eatwell,J., M. Milgate, and P. Newman, eds., (1989): *The New Palgrave - Money*, New York: W. W. Norton.

Edwards, F.R. and F.S. Mishkin, (1995): "The Decline of Traditional Banking: Implications for Financial Stability and Regulatory Policy," *Federal Reserve Bank of New York Economic Policy Review*, 1, 27-45.

Eisenbeis, R.A., (1995): "Private Sector Solutions to Payments System Fragility," *Journal of Financial Services Research*, 9, 327-349.

Fanno, M., (1995): *The Money Market*, New York: St. Martin's Press.

Feldstein, M., ed., (1991): *The Risk of Economic Crisis*, Chicago: University of Chicago Press.

Feldstein, M. and J.H. Stock, (1993): "The Use of Monetary Aggregate to Target Nominal GDP," Working Paper.

Feldstein, M. and J.H. Stock, (1994): "Measuring Money Growth When Financial Markets are Changing," Working Paper.

Friedman, M. and J. Schwartz, (1963): *A Monetary History of the United States 1867-1960*, Princeton: Princeton University Press.

Froot, K.A., D.S. Scharfstein, and J.C. Stein, (1992): "Risk Management: Coordinating Corporate Investment and Financing Policies," Working Paper.

Furfine, C. and J. Stehm, (1996): "Analyzing Alternative Daylight Credit Policies in Real-Time Gross Settlement Systems," *Working Paper*.

Giannini,C., (1994): "Confidence Costs and the Institutional Genesis of Central Banks," *Working Paper*.

Gilbert, R.A., ed. (1995): "Antitrust Issues and Payment Systems Networks," *Federal*

Reserve Bank of St. Louis Review, 77.

Glasner, D., (1989): *Free Banking and Monetary Reform*, Cambridge: Cambridge University Press.

Goodfriend, M. (1991) "Money, Credit, banking and Payments System Policy," *Federal Reserve Bank of Richmond Economic Review*, pp. 7-23.

Goodhart, C.A.E., (1969): *The New York Money Market and the Finance of Trade*, 1900-1913, Cambridge, MA: Harvard University Press.

Goodhart, C.A.E., (1988): *The Evolution of Central Banks*, Cambridge, MA: MIT Press.

Goodhart, C.A.E., (1991): *Money, Information, and Uncertainty*, Cambridge, MA: MIT Press.

Goodhart, C., T. Ito, and R. Payne, (1995): "One Day in June, 1993: A Study of the Working of Reuters 2000-2 Electronic Foreign Exchange Trading System," Working Paper, Parts I and II.

Gorton, G., (1985): "Clearinghouses and the Origin of Central Banking in the United States," *Journal of Economic History*, 45, 277-283.

Gorton, G., (1996): "Reputation Formation in Early Bank Note Markets," *Journal of Political Economy*, 104, 346-397.

Gorton, G. and Mullineaux, (1987): "The Joint Production of Confidence: Endogenous Regulation and Nineteenth Century Commercial-Bank Clearinghouses," *Journal of Money, Credit, and Banking*, 19, 457-468.

Gorton, G. and Rosen, R. (1995): "Banks and Derivatives," working paper, Wharton Financial Institutions Center.

Grant, J., (1992): *Money of the Mind: Borrowing and Lending in America from the Civil War to Michael Milken*, New York: Farrar Straus Giroux.

Grinblatt, M., (1994): "An Analytic Solution for Interest Rate Swap Spreads," Working Paper.

Hamouda, O.F. and J.N. Smithin, eds., (1988): *Keynes and Public Policy After Fifty Years - Volume II: Theories and Method*, New York: New York University Press.

Harris,L. (1981) *Monetary Theory,* New York: McGraw-Hill Book Company.

Harvey, C.R. and R.D. Huang, (1994): "The Impact of the Federal Reserve Bank's Open Market Operations," Working Paper.

Hayek, F. (1978) *The Denationalization of Money,* Hobart Paper.

Heise, A. (1992): "Commercial Banks in Macroeconomic Theory," *Journal of Post Keynesian Economics,* 14, 285-296.

Hendricks, D. (1994): "Netting Agreements and the Credit Exposures of OTC Derivatives Portfolios," *Federal Reserve Bank of New York Quarterly Review,* 19, 7-18.

Hicks, J., (1967): *Critical Essays in Monetary Theory,* Oxford: Clarendon Press.

Hoover, K.D., (1988): *The New Classical Macroeconomics - A Sceptical Inquiry,* Oxford: Basil Blackwell.

Hoover, K. D. (1988b): "Money, Prices and Income in the New Monetary Economics,"*Oxford Economic Papers,* 40, 150-167.

Howells, P. and I. Biefang-Frisancho Mariscal, (1992): "An Explanation for the Recent Behavior of Income and Transaction Velocities in the United Kingdom," *Journal of Post Keynesian Economics,* 14, 367-388.

Humphrey, D.B., (1984): *The U.S. Payments System: Costs, Pricing, Competition and Risk,* New York: NYU.

Kambhu, J., F. Keane, and C. Benadon, (1996): "Over-the-Counter Derivatives Markets: Interpretation of a Global Survey," *Federal Reserve Bank of New York Economic Policy Review,* April, 1-15.

Kashyap, A.N. and J.C. Stein, (1993): "Monetary Policy and Bank Lending," Working Paper.

Kasman, B., (1992): "A Comparison of Monetary Policy Operating Procedures in Six Industrial Countries," *Federal Reserve Bank of New York Quarterly Review,* 17, 5-24.

Keynes, J.M., (1950): *A Treatise on Money,* London: MacMillan and Co., Limited, vols. I and II.

King, R.G., (1983): "On the Economics of Private Money," *Journal of Monetary*

Economics," 12, 127-162.

Klein, B. (1974): "The Competitive Supply of Money," *Journal of Money, Credit and Banking*, 6.

Klein, R.A. and J. Lederman, eds.,(1996): *Derivatives Risk and Responsibility*, Chicago: Irwin.

Laidler, D.E.W., (1969): *The Demand for Money: Theories and Evidence*, Scranton, Pennsylvania: International Textbook Company.

Lavoie, M., (1992): *Foundations of Post-Keynesian Economic Analysis*, Brookfield, Vermont: Edward Elgar Publishing Company.

Li, H.(1996), "Pricing of Swaps with Default Risk," Working Paper.

Lloyd, C. (1986) *Explanation in Social History*, New York: Blackwell.

Lyons, R.K., (1993): "Tests of Microstructural Hypotheses in the Foreign Exchange Market," Working Paper.

Marquardt,J. (1987): "Financial Market Supervision: Some Conceptual Issues," Working Paper.

Mayer, M., (1995): "Seeking a Grip on the Payments System," Working Paper.

Mengle, D.L., (1995): "Regulatory Solutions to Payment System Risks: Lessons from Privately Negotiated Derivatives," *Journal of Financial Services Research*, 9, 381-391.

Merton, R.C. and Z. Bodie, (1995): "Financial Infrastructure and Public Policy: A Functional Perspective," Working Paper.

Merton, R.C. and Z. Bodie, (1995): " A Conceptual Framework for Analyzing the Financial Environment," Working Paper.

Moore, B.J.,(1988): *Horizontalists and Verticalists - The Macroeconomics of Credit Money*, Cambridge: Cambridge University Press.

Moser, J.T., (1994): "Origins of the Modern Exchange Clearinghouse: A History of Early Clearing and Settlement Methods at Futures Exchanges," Working Paper.

Mott, T., (1989): "A Post Keynesian Perspective on a 'Cashless Competitive Payments

System,'" *Journal of Post Keynesian Economics*, XI, 360-384.

Myers, M.G., (1931): *The New York Money Market- Volume I: Origins and Development*, New York: Columbia University Press.

Niehans, J. (1978): *The Theory of Money*, Baltimore: Johns Hopkins University Press.

O'Brien, R.,ed., (1994): *Finance and the International Economy*, New York: Oxford University Press.

Pan, Y., (1995): "Two Essays on Design and Valuation of Corparate Securities and One Essay on International Swaps," Ph.D. Dissertation, Columbia University.

Paolo, A.,(1994): "Studies on Central Bank Operations and Payment Mechanisms," Ph.D. Dissertation, Brown University.

Parkinson, P., A. Gilbert, E. Gollob, L. Hargraves, R. Mead, J. Stehm, and M.A. Taylor, (1992): "Clearance and Settlement in U.S. Securities Markets," Washington, DC: Board of Governors of the Federal Reserve System.

Perold, A., (1995): "The Payment System and Derivative Instruments," *Harvard Business School Working Paper.*

Pesek, B.P., (1988): *Microeconomics of Money and Banking and Other Essays*, New York: New York University Press.

Petersen, D.J., (1995): "Monetary Aggregates, Payments Technology, and Institutional Factors," *Federal Reserve Bank of Atlanta Economic Review*, Nov/Dec, 30-37.

Portes, R. and A.K. Swoboda, eds., (1987): *Threats to International Financial Stability*, Cambridge: Cambridge University Press.

Roberds, W. (1993): "The Rise of Electronic Payments Networks and the Future Role of the Fed with Regard to Payment Finality," *Economic Review*, 78, 1-22.

Roberds, W. (1995): "Financial Crises and The Payments System: Lessons from the National Banking Era," *Economic Review*, 80, 15-31.

Rogers, C., (1989): *Money, Interest, and Capital - A Study in the Foundations of Monetary Theory*, Cambridge: Cambridge University Press.

Rosenberg, A. (1985) *The Structure of Biological Science*, New York: Cambridge University

Press.

Rosenberg, A. (1992) *Economics – Mathematical Politics of Science of Diminshing Returns*, Chicago: University of Chicago Press.

Rousseas, S., (1992): *Post Keynesian Monetary Economics*, 2nd ed., Armonk, New York: M.E. Sharpe.

Saunders, A. and L.J. White, eds., (1986): *Technology and the Regulation of Financial Markets - Securities, Futures, and Banking*, Lexington, Massachusetts: Lexington Books.

Sechrest, L.J.,(1993): *Free Banking - Theory, History, and a Laissez-Faire Model*, Westport, Connecticut: Quorum Books.

Sober, E. (1988) *Reconstructing the Past: Parsimony, Evolution and Inference*, Cambridge: MIT Press.

Solomon, E.H., ed.,(1987): *Electronic Funds Transfers and Payments: The Public Policy Issues*, Boston: Kluwer-Nijhoff Publishing.

Sprague, O. (1910): *History of of Crises Under the National Banking System*, Washington, DC: GPO.

Stehm, J. (1992): "Clearance and Settlement of Mortgage-Backed Securities Through the Participants Trust Company," Working Paper.

Stigum, M., (1989): *The Repo and Reverse Markets*, Homewood, Illinois: Dow Jones-Irwin.

Subrahmanyam, G., (1993): *Empirical Definition of Money*, New York: Garland Publishing, Inc.

Sultan, J. (1995): "Volatility Spillover from Interest Rate Swaps," Working Paper.

Teggart, F. (1977) *Theory and Processes of History*, Berkeley: University of California Press.

Thompson, N., (1993): *Portfolio Theory and the Demand for Money*, New York: St. Martin's Press.

Timberlake, R.H., (1984): "The Central Banking Role of Clearinghouse Associations," *Journal of Money, Credit, and Banking*, 16, 1-15.

Tobin, J., (1980): *Asset Accumulation and Economic Activity - Reflections on Contemporary Macroeconomic Theory*, Chicago: University of Chicago Press.

Ungar, E., (1996): *Swap Literacy - A Comprehensible Guide*, Princeton: Bloomberg Press.

Wenninger, J. and D. Laster, (1995): "The Electronic Purse," *Federal Reserve Bank of New York Current Issues in Economics and Finance*, 1, 1-5.

White, E. N., (1983): *The Regulation and Reform of the American Banking System*, Princeton: Princeton University Press.

White, L.H., (1984): "Competitive Payments Systems and the Unit of Account," *American Economic Review*, 74, 699-712.

White, L. (1984b): *Free Banking in Britain: Thoery, Experieince, Debate, 1800-1845*, Cambridge: Cambridge University Press.

White, L.H., (1989): *Competition and Currency - Essays on Free Banking and Money*, New York: New York University Press.

Wilcox, J. and Hancokc, D. (1996) "Intraday management of Bank Reserves: The Effects of Caps and Fees," *Journal of Money, Credit and Banking*, 28, pp 870-908.

Wray, L.R.,(1992): "Commercial Banks, the Central Bank, and Endogenous Money," *Journal of Post Keynesian Economics*, 14, 297-310.

Tables and Figures

National Banking Era Crises

	1873	1884	1890	1893	1907	1914
Proximate Cause	Stock Market Crash & Closure	Stock Market Crash	Stock Market Crash	Stock Market Crash & Commercial Failures	Run on NYC Trusts	Outbreak of WW1
Loan Certificates Issue, NYC ($M)	26.6	24.9	16.6	41.5	101.0	NA
Loan Certificates Issue, Nationwide ($M)	NA	NA	NA	60-100	330	212
Bank Reserves, NYC ($M)	46.9	70.7	92.5	99.0	181.0	NA
Bank Reserves/ Monetary Base, Nationwide ($M)	230/783	347/1,189	478/1,366	529/1514	1,205/2,889	1,630/3,353
Suspension of payments?	Yes	No	No	Yes	Yes	No
Followed by recession?	Yes	No	No	Yes, severe	Yes, severe	No

Source: Roberds (1993)

Table: Features of Selected G-10 Payment Systems, 1994

Country and System Name	Settlement Type: Net, Gross, Real-Time Gross	Annual Number of Transactions ('000s)	Annual Dollar Value of Transactions (billions)	Ratio of Annual Transactions to Annual GDP
Belgium				
CH	N	15,886	10,091.69	44.3
Canada				
IIPS		2,215	11,638	20.7
France				
SAGITTAIRE	N	4,100	19,965	15.03
CH Paris	N	722,200	25,699	19.34
TBF	RTGS			
Germany				
EIL-ZV	RTGS	3,400	12,252	5.98
Platz	GS	30,900	6,457	3.15
Konv. Abrechnung	N	430,600	18,134	8.86
EAF	N	12,700	89,347	43.64
Italy				
Local Clearing	N	240,675	2,640	2.6
ME	N	2,084	11,150	11.0
SIPS	N	3,526	16,087	15.8
BISS	RTGS	43	68	0.1
Japan				
FEYCS	N	7,077	65,056	14.2
BOJ-NET	RTGS	3,854	398,363	86.7
Netherlands				
8007-S.W.I.F.T.	N	2.0	5,577	16.9
FA	N,RTGS	0.4	5,051	15.3
Sweden				
RIX	RTGS	84	5,176	26.3
Switzerland				
SIC	RTGS	88,717	24,344	93.4
United Kingdom				
CHAPS	N	11,649	38,400	37.5
TOWN	N	48	1,044	1.0
United States				

Fedwire	RTGS	72,048	211,202	32.6
CHIPS	N	45,598	295,444	41.1

Source: BIS (1995), as presented in Furfine and Stehm (1996).

CENTRAL BANK PARTICIPATION IN THE PAYMENTS SYSTEM

	BE	CA	FR	DE	IT	JP	NL	SE	CH	UK	US
Statutory responsibility for payments system		■O	■	■	O	O	■	■O	■		■
Settlement agent for interbank payments											
resulting from payment/clearing ops.	■	■	■	■	■	■	■	■	■	■	■
on a gross continuous basis			O	■	■	■	■	■	■		■
resulting from securities transactions	■		■	■	■	■	■	■		■	■
internal network available to banks	■		■	■		■	■	■			■
Involvement in payment clearing system											
setting/enforcing of rules	■		■	■O	■	■		■	■	■O	■
auditing systems	■		■		■	■		■	■		■
owns systems	■		■	■	■	■		■			■
operates systems	■		■	■	■O	■		■	■		■
Involvement in securities transfer system											
for gov't securities	■		■	■O	■	■		■O		■	■
other securities	■		■	■	■		■	■O		■	
Provision of daylight overdraft facilities			■	■O	■O	■O	■O	■	■O		■
quantitative limits			■	■	■	■	■		■		■
collateral required			■	■	■	■	■	■	■		■
Provision of standing credit facilities	■		■	■	■	■	■	■	■	O	■
quantitative limits	■			■	■	■	■	■			■
collateral required	■		■	■	■	■	■	■	■		■
Restrictions on banks' use of reserve holdings											
reserve requirements	O	■O	■	■	■	■	■	■	■	■O	■
averaging for required reserves		■	■	■	■O	■			■		■
Involvement in prudential supervision											
of individual banks			■	■	■	■	■	■O	■O	■	■
of other payement system participants					■	■					■O

Source: Borio and Van den Bergh (1993). ■=yes, O=note in source, blank=no.

RISK MANAGEMENT IN REAL-TIME GROSS SETTLEMENT SYSTEMS

Country	FR	DE	IT	JP	NL	SE	CH	US
System	TBF	CB Express	BISS	BOJ-NET	CB Current Account	RIX	SIC	Fedwire
Membership								
banks	■	■	■	■	■	■	■	■
others		■		■	■	■	■O	■O
Control on orders								
real-time monitoring	■	■O	■	■	■	■	■	■O
revocability				■O	■O		■	
Resolution of unrecovered orders								
rejection		■	■	■	■O			O
queueing to end of day	■						■	
Standing central banks credit facility								
available	■	■O	■O		■O	■O	■O	■
ceiling	■		■		■			■
collateral: full		■	■O		■		■	
collateral: partial	■					■		O
priced	O	O	O		O		O	■O
Intraday interbank credit market				■				

Source: Borio and Van den Bergh (1993). *■=yes, O=note in source, blank=no.*

RISK MANAGEMENT IN NET SETTLEMENT SYSTEMS

Country	BE	BE	CA	FR	FR	FR	FR	DE	IT	IT	IT	JP	JP	NL	UK	UK	US
System	CEC	Manual	ACSS	Clearing house	SAGIT-TAIRE	Ordin-ateur de compens ation	SIT	Daily Clearing	National Clearing	ME	SIPS	Zengin	FEYSS	BCH-SWIFT	Town-clearing	CHAPS	CHIPS
Membership Criteria																	
type of institution	■	■	■	■	■	■	■	■	■	■	■	■	■	■	■	■	■
other			■		■	■	■		■						■	■	
Control of net balances																	
real-time monitoring							■		■	■	■	■	■			■	■
bilateral debit caps							■						■			■	■
multilateral debit caps									■							■	■
Resolution of settlement failures																	
no rules															■	■O	
conditional orders: unwind	■	■	■	■	■	■	■	■	■		O	O		■			
unconditional orders:																	
loss-sharing												■	■O				■
collateral												■					■
central bank guarentee												■					

Source: Borio and Van den Bergh (1993).. *■=yes, O=note in source, blank=no.*

New York Clearing House Clearings (1854-1899)

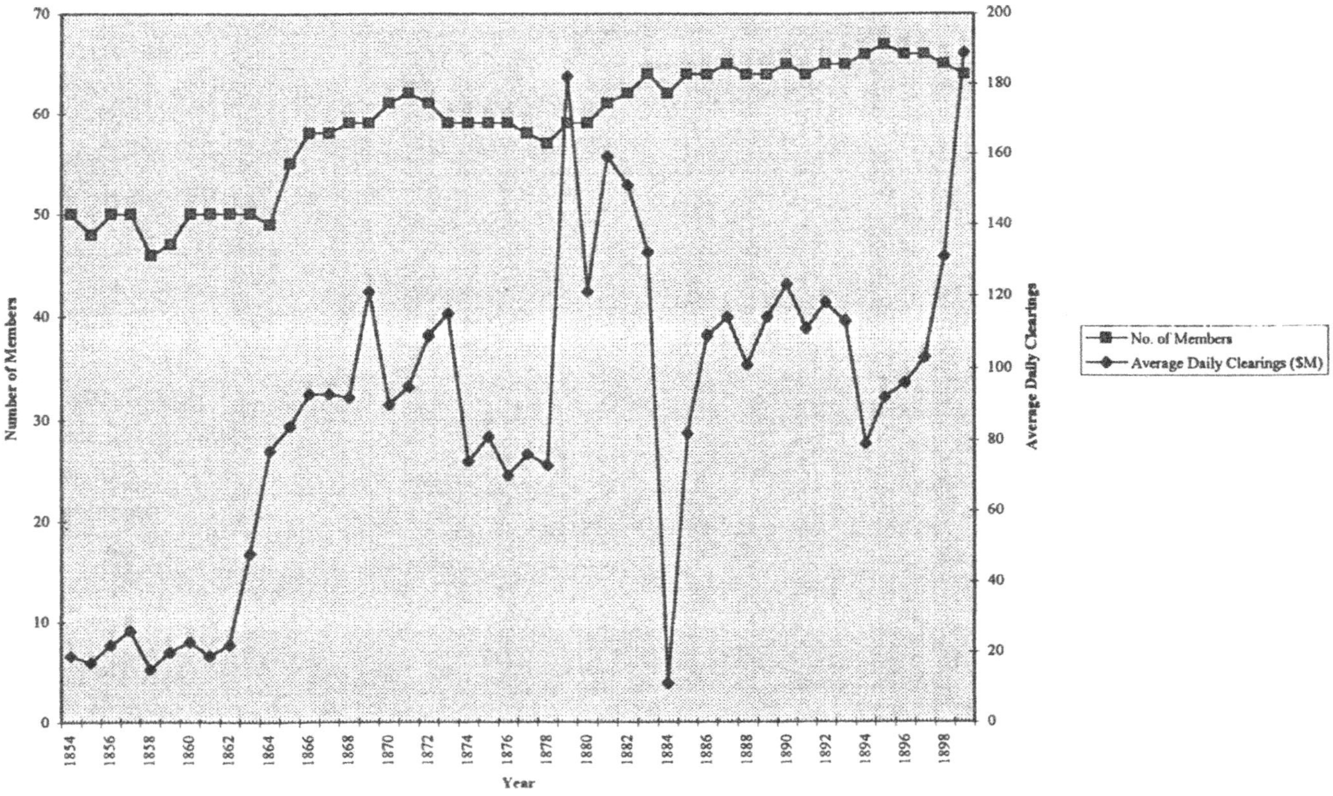

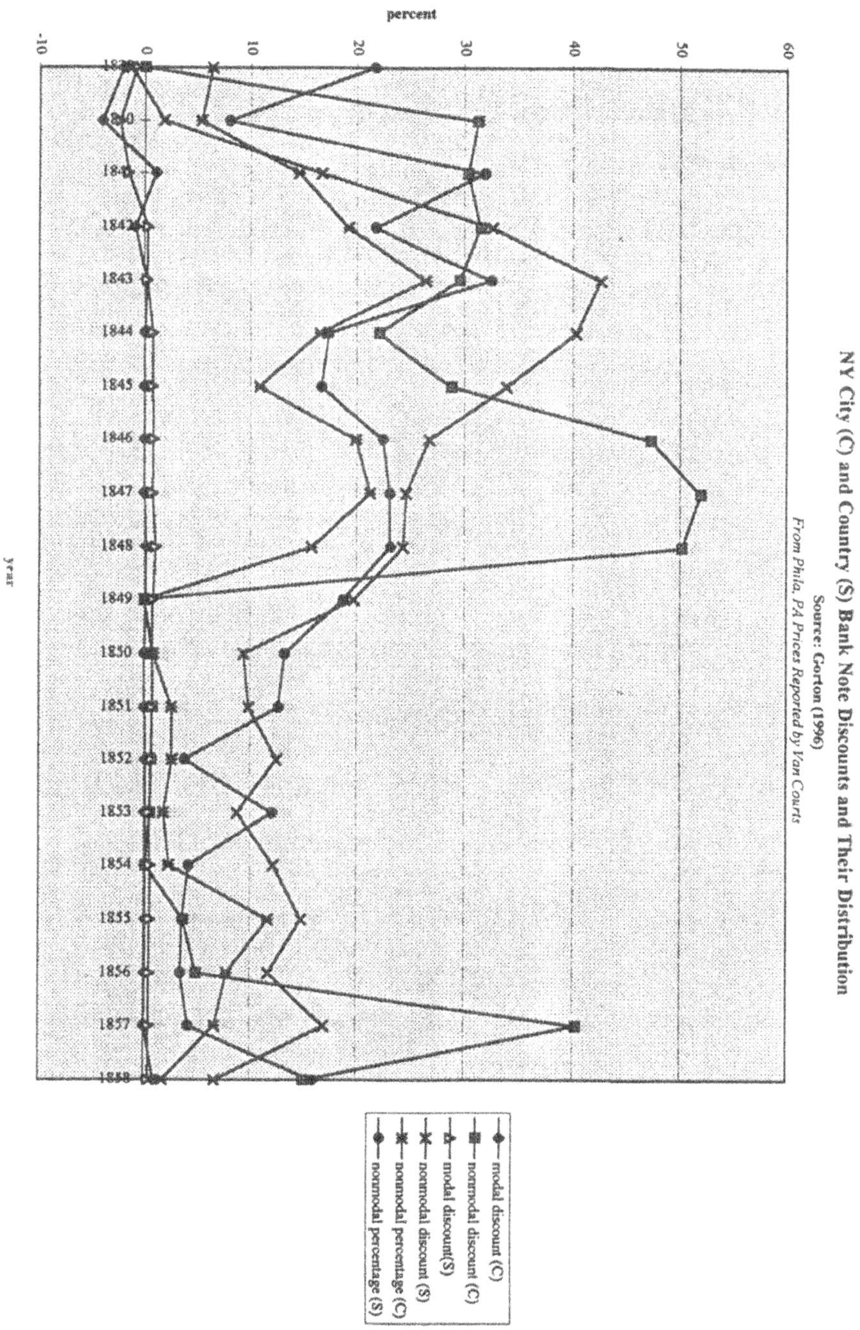
NY City (C) and Country (S) Bank Note Discounts and Their Distribution
Source: Gorton (1996)
From Phila, PA Prices Reported by Van Courts
percent
year
modal discount (C)
nonmodal discount (C)
modal discount(S)
nonmodal discount (S)
nonmodal percentage (C)
nonmodal percentage (S)

Graph 1

Derivatives, Notional Amount

Insured Commercial banks

$ Trillions

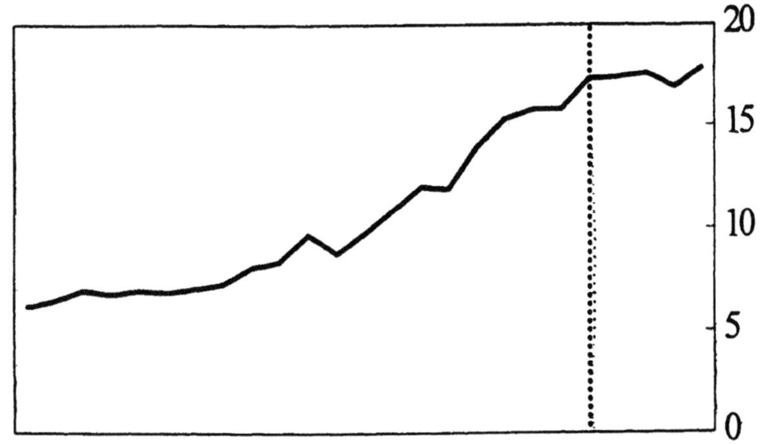

1	2	3	4	1	2	3	4	1	2	3	4	1	2	3	4	1	2	3	4	1	2	3	4	1
6.2	6.5	7.0	6.8	7.0	6.9	7.1	7.3	8.1	8.4	9.7	8.8	9.8	10.9	12.0	11.9	13.9	15.3	15.8	15.8	17.3	17.4	17.6	16.9	17.8

1990 1991 1992 1993 1994 1995 1996

Note: Dotted line indicates that beginning in 1Q95, spot foreign exchange was not included in the definition of total derivatives.

Source: Call Reports

OCC

Graph 4

Nine Banks With Most Derivatives Dominate

All Commercial Banks: First Quarter 1996 Data Are Preliminary

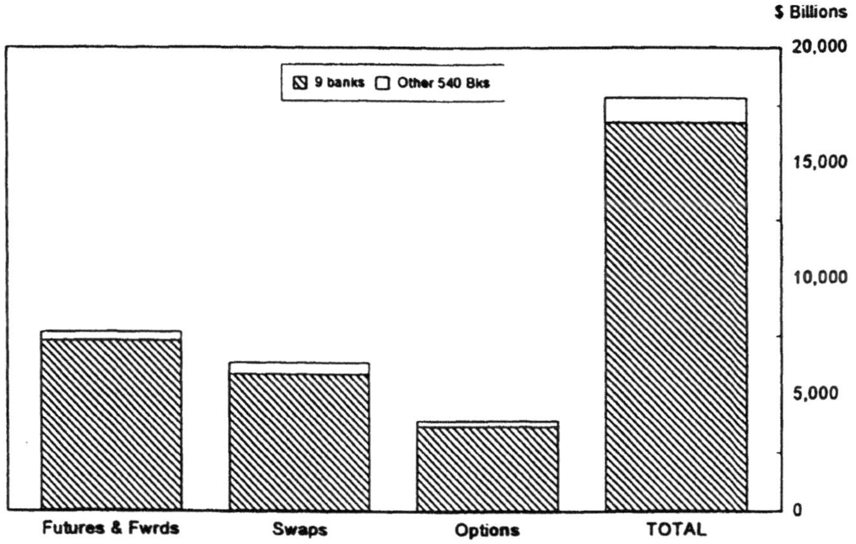

Concentration of Derivative Contracts, Q1 1996 ($ Billions)*

	($) 9 Banks	(%) Tot Derivs	($) 540 Banks	(%) Tot Derivs	($) All Banks	(%) Tot Derivs
Futures & Fwrds	7,278	40.8	375	2.1	7,653	42.9
Swaps	5,836	32.7	500	2.8	6,336	35.5
Options	3,625	20.3	233	1.3	3,858	21.6
TOTAL	16,738	93.8	1,108	6.2	17,847	100.0

in billions of dollars; notional value of futures, total exchange traded options, total over the counter options, total forwards, and total swaps. Note that first quarter 1996 data do not include spot fx in the total notional amount of derivatives.

ata Source: Call Reports

OCC

A Unified Approach to Performance Attribution

Thomas K. Philips
Paradigm Asset Management

D. Ho and T. Schneeweis (eds.), Applications in Finance, Investments, and Banking, 159–196.

I. Introduction

In this paper, we develop a unified accounting based performance attribution methodology for equity portfolios and asset allocation strategies. Within this framework, we decompose the returns generated by a manager into an index return plus a number of component returns, the components being determined by the manager's mandate. For example, in attributing the returns of a domestic equity portfolio, we determine the fraction of the manager's excess return that arises from sector selection, stock selection and an interaction effect that we call sector/stock selection.

In early work, Dietz (1966) and Fama (1972) examine various aspects of performance measurement for managed portfolios. Dietz's primary focus in on the accurate measurement of total returns at the aggregate fund level, while Fama is the first to develop a decomposition-based methodology for performance attribution. Brinson, Hood and Beebower (1986) and Brinson, Singer, and Beebower (1991) expand on Fama's ideas and develop an accounting-based methodology for performance attribution in which they attribute excess returns to timing, security selection and an interaction term that they generally ignore. They focus on the asset allocation problem, for which this interaction term tends to be small. As we shall see, this need not be true when attributing returns from equity portfolios. In a related paper, Brinson and Fachler (1985) propose a methodology for international performance attribution. More recently, Ankrim (1992) has proposed a risk adjusted accounting decomposition that takes into account both the sector exposures and the Capital Asset Pricing Model (CAPM) ß of the stocks in the portfolio. This method has the advantage of offering a risk adjusted breakdown of the portfolio's return, but required accepting the relationship between ß and return implied by the CAPM. As Fama and French (1992a, 1992b) have shown, however, this relationship is a tenuous one, and has not held up well over the past 5 decades.

All of the above mentioned papers have two factors in common:

1. Returns are decomposed in an additive fashion.
2. Returns are attributed for a single period.

An alternative multiplicative attribution methodology is described in a paper by Allen (1991). Though additive and multiplicative decompositions work equally well (in a mathematical sense), an additive decomposition is more readily understood and interpreted. For this reason, our decomposition is an additive one. We also develop a methodology to attribute the returns of a portfolio over multiple periods. The methodology is general, and is applicable to any single period additive attribution, including those described in the above referenced work by Brinson *et al.* and Fama.

The remainder of this paper is organized as follows. In Section II we formulate the problem in mathematical terms, and state all the assumptions made in our analysis. In Section III, we examine domestic asset allocation in detail. Section IV deals with domestic equity portfolios, while Section V deals with international equity portfolios. In Section VI, we examine global asset allocation. Both unhedged and hedged portfolios are considered in sections V and VI.

The complexity of the material increases as we go from Section III to VI, and we suggest that the reader work through these sections in a linear sequence. At the start of each section, all the special terms used in that section are defined. Immediately following the mathematical development, a simple numerical example is presented to clarify the methodology. In Sections VII and VIII, we relax the simplifying assumptions made in the earlier sections. In Section VII we discuss the problem of portfolio rebalancing and show how to account for intramonth cash flows. Section VIII we examine multiperiod performance attribution. In Section IX we discuss a number of practical problems that arise in the implementation of any performance attribution methodology. Finally, in Section X, we present our conclusions.

II. Problem Formulation

We begin by stating the simplifying assumptions that will be in force through Sections II through VI:

1. The attribution analysis is carried out for a single period.
2. The portfolio is not rebalanced during this period.

3. There are no cash flows in to or out of the portfolio in this period.
4. The value of the portfolio is positive (though any given asset class/country/sector may have a net short position).

Assumptions 1 to 3 greatly simplify the analysis, and are relaxed in Sections VII and VIII, where we discuss the cash flow problem and propose a methodology for multiperiod performance attribution. Assumption 4 simply ensures that the return of the portfolio is a well-defined number. Under these simplifying assumptions, the following equation relates the total return of a portfolio for a single period to the weights and returns from each of the asset classes (or countries or sectors) in the portfolio for the same period.

$$R_{Portfolio} = \sum_{1 \le i \le N} w_i r_i \tag{2}$$

where w_i is the portfolio's <u>beginning of period</u> weight in the ith asset class (country/sector), r_i is the return from the ith asset class (country/sector) during the period, and N is the number of distinct classes (countries/sectors) that the portfolio can be invested in. In words, it states that the total return from a portfolio over some period is given by the summation over all asset classes (countries/sectors) of the beginning of month weight in that asset class (country/sector) multiplied by the return from that asset class (country/sector) over that period. A virtually identical equation holds for the benchmark to which the portfolio is to be compared.

$$R_{Benchmark} = \sum_{1 \le i \le N} w_i^0 r_i^0 \tag{3}$$

where w_i^0 is the benchmark's beginning of period weight in the ith asset class (country/sector), r_i^0 is the index or benchmark return from the ith asset class (country/sector) during the period, and N is the number of distinct asset classes (countries/sectors) that the benchmark in invested in.

With no loss of generality, we assume that the portfolio is always invested in a subset of the asset classes (countries/sectors) that the benchmark is invested in. If the portfolio is invested in asset classes that are not included in the benchmark, we simply modify the benchmark to include these asset classes with a beginning of period weight of 0. The total value of a portfolio is the sum of the individual asset class (country/sector) holdings, so that

$$\sum_{1\leq i\leq N} w_j = \sum_{1\leq i\leq N} w_j^o = 1. \tag{3}$$

The difference between equations (1) and (2) is the value added by the portfolio manager, and it is this difference that we attribute to various selection skills. Formally we write

$$R_{Manager} = R_{Benchmark} + \sum_j \textit{Excess return\_from the } j^{th} \textit{ selection skill}, \tag{4}$$

where the various selection skills are chosen to suit the manager's mandate. Equations (1) through (4) are the key equations in our methodology.

III. Domestic Asset Allocation

Domestic asset allocators are assumed to vary the exposure of their portfolio to various asset classes, and to remain indexed within each asset class. We consider two cases--in the first, indexation is perfect, i.e. within each asset class the asset allocator's index fund realizes exactly the same return as the index that is used to define the benchmark. In the second, it is imperfect; i.e. the return from the asset allocator's index portfolios differ from the returns of the benchmark's index portfolios. This could happen, for example, if the index funds were created by an approach other than full replication.

Case 1: Perfect Indexation

	Manager	Benchmark
Beginning of period weight in asset class I	w_I	w^o_i
Return for the period from asset class I	r_I	r^o_i
Return for the period from portfolio	$\sum_{1\le i\le N} w_i r^o_i$	$\sum_{1\le i\le N} w^o_i r^o_i$

We can rewrite the manager's returns as

$$R_{\text{Manager}} = \sum_{1\le i\le N} w_i r^o_i$$

$$= \sum_{1\le i\le N} w^o_i r^o_i + \sum_{1\le i\le N} (w_i - w^o_i) r^o_i$$

$$= R_{\text{Benchmark}} + \sum_{1\le i\le N} \Delta w_i r^o_i \qquad (5)$$

where we have defined $\Delta w_i = w_i - w^o_i$ to be the manager's differential weighting in the ith asset class. On comparing equations (5) and (4), we see that the second term on the right hand side of (5) is the manager's excess return from asset allocation.

Example:

	Manager	Benchmark
Beginning of month weight in stocks	.5	.6
Beginning of month weight in bonds	.5	.4
Return for the month from stocks	10%	10%
Return for the month from bonds	5%	5%
Return for the month from portfolio	7.5%	7.5%
Manager's excess return from asset allocation	-.1x10%+.1x5%=-.5%.	

Case 2: Imperfect Indexation

	Manager	Benchmark
Beginning of period weight in asset class i	w_i	w_i^{o}
Return for the period from asset class i	r_i	r_i^{o}
Return for the period from portfolio	$\underset{1\le i\le N}{S} w_i r_i$	$\underset{1\le i\le N}{S} w_i^{o} r_i^{o}$

We now rewrite the manager's return as

$$R_{Manager} = \underset{1\le i\le N}{S} w_i r_i$$

$$= \underset{1\le i\le N}{S} w_i^{o} r_i^{o} + \underset{1\le i\le N}{S} (w_i - w_i^{o}) r_i^{o} + \underset{1\le i\le N}{S} w_i (r_i - r_i^{o})$$

$$= R_{Benchmark} + \underset{1\le i\le N}{S} \Delta w_i r_i^{o} + \underset{1\le i\le N}{S} w_i \Delta r_i$$

where Δw_i is the manager's differential weighting in the ith asset class, and $\Delta r_i = r_i - r_i^{o}$ is the manager's excess return (or indexation error) from the ith asset class. Comparing equations (6) and (5), we see that the second term on the right hand side remains unchanged—it's the manager's excess return from asset allocation. The third term is the manager's excess return from his implementation of the various index portfolios.

Example:

	Manager	Benchmark
Beginning of month weight in stocks	.5	.6
Beginning of month weight in stocks	.5	.4
Return for the month from stocks	9%	10%
Return for the month from bonds	5%	5%
Return for the month from portfolio	7%	8%
Manager's excess return from asset allocation	-.1x10%+.1x5%=-.5%	
Manager's excess return from index implementation	.5x-1%+.5x0%=-.5%	

In this example we clearly see the effect of imperfect indexation: the manager looses an additional 50 basis points because of the underperformance of his equity index fund.

IV. Domestic Equity Management

To attribute returns of a domestic equity manager, we measure the manager's exposure to and excess return from each of a number of sectors that constitute the benchmark. Traditionally, the benchmark is decomposed into a number of economic (or industry) sectors, and the manager's returns are attributed to stock selection and (economic) sector selection. However, it is not necessary to decompose the benchmark in this way. One could, in the spirit of Fama and French [8,9], decompose the benchmark into Small Cap Value, Small Cap Growth, Large Cap Value and Large Cap Growth sectors, and the attribution would still apply. Our analysis is general, and the choice of decomposition is left to the user. In Section IX, we present some practical considerations on the choice of a decomposition.

	Manager	Benchmark
Beginning of period weight in sector i	w_i	w_i^B
Return from the period for sector i	r_i	r_i^B
Return for the period from portfolio	$\sum_{1\le i\le N} w_i r_i$	$\sum_{1\le i\le N} w_i^B r_i^B$

The manager's return can now be decomposed as follows:

$$
\begin{aligned}
R_{\text{Manager}} &= \sum_{1\le i\le N} w_i r_i \\
&= \sum_{1\le i\le N} w_i^B r_i^B + \sum_{1\le i\le N} (w_i - w_i^B) r_i^B + \sum_{1\le i\le N} w_i^B (r_i - r_i^B) + \sum_{1\le i\le N} (w_i - w_i^B)(r_i - r_i^B) \\
&= R_{\text{Benchmark}} + \sum_{1\le i\le N} \Delta w_i r_i^B + \sum_{1\le i\le N} w_i^B \Delta r_i + \sum_{1\le i\le N} \Delta w_i \Delta r_i \qquad (7)
\end{aligned}
$$

where Δw_i is the manager's differential weighting in the ith sector, and Δr_i is his excess return from the ith sector.

The second term in equation (7), which weights the sector returns of the benchmark by the difference in sector weights, is the manager's excess return from sector selection. The third term, which weights the manager's excess returns in each sector by the corresponding weight of the benchmark portfolio, is the manager's excess return from stock selection, and the fourth term is an interaction of the two that we call sector/stock selection. It is a measure of the excess return that the manager realizes by overweighting sectors in which he has good stock selection skills. The sum of the last two terms in equation (7) is exactly equal to the last term in equation (6). Equation (7) decomposes the manager's excess return from implementation skills into an excess return from stock selection and an excess return from sector/stock selection.

Stated somewhat differently, the excess return from selection is a measure of the manager's ability to pick sectors that will do well in absolute terms, the excess return from stock selection is a measure of the manager's ability to add value across all sectors, and the excess return from sector/stock selection is a measure of the manager's ability to pick sectors in which he can add value. It is possible for a manager to outperform the benchmark in every sector and yet have a negative return from sector/stock selection, as the next example shows.

Example

	Manager	Benchmark
Beginning of year weight in Small Cap Value	.25	.1
Beginning of year weight in Small Cap Growth	.25	.1
Beginning of year weight in Large Cap Value	.25	.4
Beginning of year weight in Large Cap Growth	.25	.4
Return for the year from the Small Cap Value	30%	10%
Return for the year from the Small Cap Growth	30%	10%
Return for the year from the Large Cap Value	50%	20%
Return for the year from the Large Cap Growth	50%	20%
Return for the year from portfolio	40%	18%
Manager's excess return from sector selection		2[.15x10%-.15x20%]=-3%
Manager's excess return from stock selection		2[.1x20%-.4x30%]=28%
Manager's excess return from sector/stock selection		2[.15x20%-.15x30%]=-3%

The manager lost 3% from his sector selection--he was underweighted in the large cap sectors which outperformed the small cap sectors. He gained 28% from stock selection--notice that he outperformed the market in every single sector. Finally, he lost 3% from sector/stock selection, as he was underweighted in the large cap sectors where he realized his largest excess returns.

In practice, we concern ourselves mostly with the sector and stock selection skills that a manager displays. We use the sector/stock selection component as an elementary control variable--a manager who gets a large fraction of his excess returns from sector/stock selection is likely to have a better understanding of the sectors in which he can realize excess returns than a manager who realizes a small fraction of his excess returns in this way. Similarly, a manager whose sector/stock selection component is consistently negative is likely to have very poor risk control, or a poorly thought-out investment process. In either case, this warrants a closer examination by the plan sponsor.

V. International Equity Management

Case I. Managed Portfolio and Benchmark Unhedged

The attribution process for an international equity manager who uses no currency hedging instruments (such as options, futures and forwards), and who is measured against an unhedged benchmark, is virtually identical to that for a domestic equity manager. In the place of sector, stock and sector/stock selection skills, we attribute the manager's returns to country, stock and country/stock selection skills. Note the absence of a currency selection component. As no active currency decisions are made in such a portfolio, there can be no excess return from currency selection. In the second half of this section, we show that a currency selection component appears with the introduction of currency hedging instruments.

We measure all returns in US dollar terms. Local currency returns are not usually realizable to foreign investors (except perhaps if the investment was realized via a swap), and there is little point in measuring an excess return that is hypothetical. The decision to invest in a foreign country's equity market carries with it an implicit decision to buy an equal amount of foreign exchange risk, and it is the combination of the two that is finally realized by the dollar denominated investment account.

	Manager	Benchmark
Beginning of period weight in country I	w_i	w_i^0
Return for the period from country i (in US $ terms)	r_i	r_i^0
Return for the period from portfolio	$\sum_{1\le i\le N} w_i r_i$	$\sum_{1\le i\le N} w_i^0 r_i^0$

The manager's return is now decomposed as

$$R_{\text{Manager}} = \sum_{1 \le i \le N} w_i r_i$$

$$= \sum_{1 \le i \le N} w_i^B r_i^B + \sum_{1 \le i \le N} (w_i - w_i^B) r_i^B + \sum_{1 \le i \le N} w_i^B (r_i - r_i^B) + \sum_{1 \le i \le N} (w_i - w_i^B)(r_i - r_i^B)$$

$$= R_{\text{Benchmark}} + \sum_{1 \le i \le N} \Delta w_i r_i^B + \sum_{1 \le i \le N} w_i^B \Delta r_i + \sum_{1 \le i \le N} w_i \Delta r_i \qquad (8)$$

Equations (7) and (8) are clearly analogous: the second term in (8) is the manager's excess return from country selection, the third term is his excess return from stock selection, and the fourth term is his excess return from country/stock selection. As in the case of domestic equity attribution, the second term is a measure of the manager's ability to pick countries that do well in absolute terms, the third term is a measure of his ability to pick stocks, and the fourth term is a measure of his ability to pick countries in which he can add value.

Example

	Manager	Benchmark
Beginning of quarter weighting in Germany	.5	.4
Beginning of quarter weighting in France	.5	.6
Return for the quarter from Germany	10%	5%
Return for the quarter from France	5%	10%
Return for the quarter from portfolio	7.5%	8%
Excess return from country selection		.1x5%-.1x10%=-.5%
Excess return from stock selection		.4x5%-.6x5%=-1%.
Excess return from country/stock selection		.1x5%+(-.1)x(-5%)=1%

Case II. Managed portfolio and/or Benchmark contains currency hedging instruments

We next consider the more difficult problem of attributing the returns of a portfolio that contains currency hedging instruments. The following observation underlies our methodology: portfolio containing equities and currency hedging instruments (such as options, forwards, and futures) may be thought of as a linear combination of two portfolios--one containing unhedged equities and the other containing all the currency hedging instruments. An attribution analysis can be run on the returns from the two portfolios separately, and the results can then be combined to attribute the returns from the entire portfolio.

	Manager	Benchmark
Beginning of period equity weight in country I	w_I	w_I^o
Equity return from country i (in US $ terms)	r_i	r_I^o
Beginning of period currency portfolio weight in country I	x_I	x_I^o
Return from currency portfolio from country I	c_I	c_I^o

Three observations about the currency weights are in order

1. The currency weight in a country is the aggregate weight of all the currency hedging instruments denominated in that country's currency.
2. As currency hedging instruments are usually bought on margin (or on no margin at all, as in the case of forward contracts), we define the weight of a currency position as the ration of the market value of the position to the total cash value of the entire portfolio.
3. Forward contracts are counted only once--on the short side. For example, a forward contract that called for the delivery of Deutschmarks against Sterling would be counted in the German portion of the portfolio, but would be ignored in the UK. Counting the hedge in both countries double counts the forward contract, leading to incorrect results. The following examples will clarify this.

Example 1.

A \$100 million portfolio is invested in \$90 million worth of German equities and \$50 million worth of French Franc call options at 20% margin. Then $w_{Germany} = .9$, and $x_{France} = .5$.

Example 2.

A \$200 million portfolio is invested in \$100 million worth of German equities, \$100 million dollars worth of Deutschmarks, and \$50 million worth of forwards contracts for the delivery of Deutschmarks against Sterling. Then $w_{Germany} = .5$ and $x_{Germany} = .75$.

Example 3.

A fully hedged EAFE index fund holds \$100 million worth of equities. The hedges are implemented via one month forward contracts that sell the corresponding currency forward against the US dollar. Then $x_i = x_{♀} = w_i = w_{♀}$ for all the EAFE countries.

We next define the return from a currency portfolio. At the start of every period, we mark all the securities in the portfolio to market in US dollar terms. At the end of the period, we mark these securities to market again. The return is given by

$$c_i = 100x[\frac{\text{Change in market value of currency portfolio in country } i \text{ in U.S. \$ terms}}{\text{Initial market value of currency portfolio in country } i \text{ in U.S. \$ term}} \qquad (9)$$

The next three examples clarify the computation of returns on currency portfolio.

Example 4.

A French currency portfolio holds US \$1 million worth of French Francs as cash. The beginning of year exchange rate was 6FF per US dollar. The end of year exchange rate was 5FF/US dollar. The return on the portfolio for the year is 20%.

Example 5.

A French currency portfolio holds US $1 million worth of French Francs as cash and an option to buy US $1 million worth of French Francs at 10 FF per US dollar at the end of the year. The beginning of year exchange rate is 6FF per US dollar, and the end of year exchange rate is 5FF per US dollar. The option was priced at US $100,000 at the beginning of the year, and was bought on 10% margin. The value of the option at the end of the year when it expires is $\$1,000,000x(\frac{10}{5}-1) = \$1,000,000$. The return on the option is 900%. Note that the margin on the option is irrelevant to the return--it will be accounted for by an increase in the currency weight. The return on the portfolio is given by $\frac{10}{11}x20\% + \frac{1}{11}x900\% = 100\%$.

Example 6.

A French currency portfolio holds US $1 million worth of French Francs as cash and a forward contract to buy US $1 million worth of French Francs at 10 FF per US dollar at the end of the year. The beginning of year exchange rate is 6FF per US dollar, and the end of year exchange rate is 5 FF per US dollar. It is easily seen that the profit realized on the forward contract is US $1,000,000, so that the return from the portfolio over the year is given by

$\frac{1}{2}x20\% + \frac{1}{2}x100\% = 60\%$.

The presence of currency hedging instruments requires us to rewrite equations (1) and (2) so as to include the returns from the currency portfolio. The return of the managed portfolio is now given by

$$R_{Manager} = \sum_{1 \le i \le N} w_i r_i + \sum_{1 \le i \le N} x_i c_i \tag{1'}$$

and that of the benchmark by

$$R_{Benchmark} = \sum_{1 \le i \le N} w_i^o r_i^o + \sum_{1 \le i \le N} x_i^o c_i^o.$$

(2')

To allow for the purchase of derivative instruments, we modify equation (3) to

$$\sum_{1 \le i \le N} w_i \le 1,$$

(3a')

and

$$\sum_{1 \le i \le N} w_i^o \le 1.$$

(3b')

The sum of the country weights in the managed portfolio does not necessarily equal the sum of the country weights in the benchmark. The sum of the currency weights must be non-negative for both the portfolio and the benchmark. This is expressed as

$$\sum_{1 \le i \le N} x_i \le 0,$$

(3c')

and

$$\sum_{1\le i\le N} x_i^o \geq 0.$$

(3d')

Equations (1') to (3') along with equations (4) and (5) form the basis of our analysis of international equity managers and asset allocators. The international equity manager's return can now be broken down as

$$R_{\text{Manager}} = \sum_{1\le i\le N} w_i r_i + \sum_{1\le i\le N} x_o c_i$$

$$= \sum_{1\le i\le N} w_i^o r_i^o + \sum_{1\le i\le N} (w_i - w_i^o) r_i^o + \sum_{1\le i\le N} w_i^o (r_i - r_i^o) + \sum_{1\le i\le N} (w_i - w_i^o)(r_i - r_i^o)$$

$$+ \sum_{1\le i\le N} x_i^o c_i^o + \sum_{1\le i\le N} (x_i - x_i^o) c_i^o + \sum_{1\le i\le N} x_i^o (c_i - c_i^o) + \sum_{1\le i\le N} (x_i - x_i^o)(c_i - c_i^o)$$

$$= R_{\text{Benchmark}} + \sum_{1\le i\le N} \Delta w_i r_i^o + \sum_{1\le i\le N} w_i^o \Delta r_i + \sum_{1\le i\le N} \Delta w_i \Delta r_i$$

$$+ \sum_{1\le i\le N} \Delta x_i c_i^o + \sum_{1\le i\le N} x_i^o \Delta c_i + \sum_{1\le i\le N} \Delta x_i \Delta c_i. \tag{10}$$

The first term in equation (10) is the return of the benchmark portfolio, and is equal to the sum of the returns of the benchmark equity portfolio and the benchmark currency portfolio. For example, if the benchmark was the hedged EAFE index, the equity component of its return would be the US dollar return from an unhedged EAFE portfolio, and the currency component would be the US dollar return from all the forward contracts specified in the definition of the index. The next three terms are identical to those in equation (8)--they are the country selections, stock selections, and country/stock selections components respectively.

The fourth, fifth, and sixth terms reflect the performance of the currency portfolio relative to the benchmark currency portfolio. The fourth term measures the effect of the manager's overweighting in certain countries, and is therefore his excess return from currency selection. The fifth term measures how well his currency portfolio did against the benchmark portfolio in each of the countries, and by analogy to stock selections, we call this the currency management component. Finally, we have the cross product of currency selection and currency management, which we call currency selection/management.

By analogy to the analysis of the domestic equity manager, the excess returns form country and currency selection are a measure of the manager's ability to pick countries and currencies that perform well in absolute terms, the excess returns from stock selection and currency management are a measure of his ability to add value in the various countries and currencies, and the excess returns from country/stock selection and currency selection/management are a measure of his ability to pick countries and currencies in which he can realize the greatest excess returns.

While this may seem to be a large number of components to attribute returns to, in almost all cases of interest the last two terms in equation (10) disappear, leaving us with just four terms--country selection, stock selection, country/stock selection and currency selection. The reason for the disappearance of the last two terms is simple--these terms exist only when $c_i{}^1c_i^{?}$ for at least one value of i. If the benchmark is an unhedged one, we can redefine it to include a currency portfolio with $x_i^{?}=0$ and $c_i^{?}=c_i$ for $1\leq i \leq N$. This forces the second and third terms to 0. If the benchmark is hedged, we find that managers almost always hedge their portfolios in the same way as the benchmark does; i.e. if the benchmark is hedged with one month forwards, the managed portfolio also tends to be hedged with one month forwards. managers then vary their exposure to a currency to implement currency decisions, so that $c_i^{?}=c_i$ for all i, and $x_i^{?1}x_i$ for one or more values of i. Again, the last two terms disappear.

We conclude this section with two simple examples. In the first, a managed portfolio is compared to an unhedged benchmark. A dummy currency portfolio is added to the benchmark so as to force the currency management and currency selection/management terms to 0. In the second, a managed portfolio is compared to a hedged benchmark. Both the portfolio and the benchmark implement their hedges using one month forward contracts.

Example 1.

	Manager	Benchmark
Beginning of month weight in German equities	1.0	1.0
Return for the month from German equities	5%	10%
Beginning of month weight in Deutschmark calls	.5	0
Return for the month from Deutschmark calls	20%	20%
Return for the month from portfolio	15%	10%
Excess return from country selection		0x10%=0%
Excess return from stock selection		1x-5%=-5%
Excess return from country/stock selection		0x-5%=0%
Excess return from currency selection		.5x20%=10%
Excess return from currency management		0x0%=0%
Excess return from currency selection/management		.5x0%=0%

Example 2

	Manager	Benchmark
Beginning of month weight in German equities	.6	.6
Beginning of month weight in French equities	.4	.5
Return for the month from German equities	6%	6%
Return for the month from French equities	5%	6%
Beginning of month weight in Deutschmark forwards	.4	.5
Beginning of month weight in French Franc forwards	0	.5
Return for the month from Deutschmark forwards	2%	2%
Return for the month from French Franc forwards	-4%	-4%
Return for the month from portfolio	6.4%	5%
Excess return from country selection		.1x6%-.1x6%=0%
Excess return from stock selection		.5x0%+.5x(-1%)=-.5%
Excess return from country/stock selection		.1x0%-.1x(-1%)=.1%
Excess return from currency selection		-.1x2%-(.5)x(-4%)=1.8%
Excess return from currency management		2x.5%x0%=0%
Excess return from currency selection/management		-1x0%-.5%x0%=0%

VI. Global Asset Allocation

A global asset allocator may perform asset allocation in one of many ways. Our analysis is focused on three different asset allocation methodologies.

1. The manager chooses between asset classes by varying the exposure of the portfolio to the asset classes that are used to define the benchmark. Within each asset class, the portfolio is indexed. For example, the manager might vary the exposure of the portfolio

to global equity and global fixed income. Such a manager can be treated as a domestic asset allocator, with the domestic asset classes being replaced by global ones. If the benchmark is hedged, a currency portfolio can be added, as is done for an international equity manager.

2. The manager varies the exposure of his portfolio to a set of countries, and within each country be chooses the same mix of assets as the benchmark. Such a manager can be treated as an international equity manager, and the analysis of the previous section applies, with a small change in terminology. His excess return from country selection is now called his excess return from asset allocation, and the sum of his excess returns from stock selection and country/stock selection is now called his excess return from index implementation. In the special case when $r_i = r_i^{\circ}$, then only the asset allocation term remains.

3. The manager both selects countries and varies the exposure of the portfolio to asset classes within each country. This calls for a slightly different analysis, which we next present. We analyze only the case when both the benchmark and the managed portfolio are unhedged, as the attribution for the currency component developed in the last section carries over unchanged.

	Manager	Benchmark
Beginning of period weight in country i	w_i	w_i°
Weight in asset class j in country i	a_{ij}	a_{ij}°
Number of asset classes in each country	M	M
Return for the period from asset class j in country i	r_{ij}	r_{ij}°
Return for the period from portfolio	$\sum_{1 \le i \le N} w_i \sum_{1 \le i \le N} a_{ij} r_{ij}$	$\sum_{1 \le i \le N} w_i \sum_{1 \le i \le N} a_{ij}^{\circ} r_{ij}^{\circ}$

The manager's return may now be decomposed as

$$R_{\text{Manager}} = \sum_{1 \le i \le N} w_i \sum_{1 \le i \le N} a_{ij} r_{ij}$$

$$= \sum_{1 \le i \le N} w_i^B \sum_{1 \le i \le N} a_{ij}^B r_{ij} + \sum_{1 \le i \le N} (w_i - w_i^B) \sum_{1 \le i \le N} a_{ij}^B r_{ij}$$

$$+ \sum_{1 \le i \le N} w_i \sum_{1 \le i \le N} \left(a_{ij}^B (r_{ij} - r_i^B) + (a_{ij} - a_{ij}^B) r_{ij}\right]$$

$$= R_{Benchmark} + \sum_{1 \le i \le N} \Delta w_i r_i^B + \sum_{1 \le i \le N} w_i \Delta r_i, \qquad (11)$$

where $r_i^B = \sum_{1 \le i \le N} a_{ij}^B r_{ij}$ is the return on the benchmark portfolio in the ith country,

Δw_i is the manager's overweighting in the ith country, and $\Delta r_i \; \sum_{1 \le i \le N} a_{ij}^B (r_{ij} - r_i^B) +$

$(a_{ij} - a_{ij}^B) r_{ij}$ is the manager's excess return in the ith country. By analogy to equation (6), the second term on the right hand side is the manager's excess return from asset allocation, and the third term is his excess return from index portfolio management. We next work a simple example to illustrate these concepts.

	Manager	Benchmark
Beginning of year weight in France	.6	.5
Beginning of year weight in Germany	.4	.5
Beginning of year weight in French equities	.7	.6
Beginning of year weight in French fixed income	.3	.4
Beginning of year weight in German equities	.5	.6
Beginning of year weight in German fixed income	.5	.4
Return for the year from French equities	10%	9%
Return for the year from French fixed income	6%	6%
Return for the year from German equities	8%	8%
Return for the year from German fixed income	5%	4%
Return for the year in France	8.8%	7.8%
Return for the year in Germany	6.5%	6.4%
Return for the year from portfolio	7.88%	7.1%
Excess return in France		1%
Excess return in Germany		.1%
Excess return from asset allocation		.1x7.8%-.1x6.4%=.14%

VII. Cash Flows and Rebalancing--Problems and Solutions

In this section we relax some of the restrictions imposed in Section II, and specifically, now allow intra-period cash flows into or out of portfolio. Possible reasons for such a cash flow include:

1. The rebalancing of the portfolio, leasing to a cash flow into some asset classes and out of others,

2. A mid period contribution to the portfolio by the plan sponsor,
3. The reinvestment of dividends or other distributions from the portfolio.

The correct way to deal with these cash flows is to break the period up into a number of smaller sub-periods, with all cash flows occurring at the boundaries between sub-periods. A multi-period attribution can then be carried out for the portfolio as described in Section VIII. Unfortunately, it is often difficult to obtain data for periods shorter than a month, and cash flows often occur in the mid-month. We therefore modify our attribution so as to approximately reflect the effect of the cash flows. Our approximation is chosen so that in the absence of cash flows, the attribution reduced to the exact attributions presented in Sections III to VI. The three key problems that we have to contend with in the presence of cash flows are:

1. The return from each asset class is no longer given by the ratio of the value of the assets at the end of the period to the value of the assets at the beginning of the period.
2. The weight in each asset class is no longer a well defined quantity, and
3. The return of the portfolio is no longer given by equation (1).

The first problem is dealt with by using the *time weighted return* for each asset class in the attribution. The second and the third problem are dealt with by the following device. We rewrite equation (1) as

$$1 + R_{\text{Portfolio}} = \sum_{1 \le i \le N} w'_i (1 + r_i), \qquad (1'')$$

where w'_i is an *effective weight* in the ith asset class, and r_i is the *time weighted return* from the ith asset class. We then compare $1+R_{\text{Benchmark}}$ and attribute the difference to various selection skills, as was done before. The computation of time weighted returns is tedious, as it requires access to portfolio data on a daily basis, and is best performed by the custodian for the investment account. Before we describe the computation of the effective weights, we set forth some notation.

Time weighted return from asset class i in period t	r_{it}
Portfolio weight in asset class i at the start of period t	w_{it}
Portfolio weight in asset class i at the end of period t	e_{it}
Time weighted return for the entire portfolio in period t	$R_{Portfolio,t}$
Effective weight of asset class i at the start of period t	$\hat{w}_{it}$

In the absence of cash flows, it is easy to see that

$$e_{it} = \frac{w_{it}(1+r_{it})}{1+R_{Portfolio,t}} \tag{12}$$

so that

$$w_{it} = \frac{e_{it}(1+R_{Portfolio,t})}{1+r_{it}} \tag{13}$$

We use equation (13) to define the effective weight in the presence of cash flows as

$$\hat{w}_{it} = \frac{e_{it}(1+R_{Portfolio,t})}{1+r_{it}}. \tag{14}$$

This definition has two consequences.

1. In general, $\sum_{1 \le i \le N} \hat{w}_{it} \neq 1$.

2. By the definition of the effective weights,

$$\sum_{1 \le i \le N} \hat{w}_{it}(1 + r_{it}) = 1 + R_{Portfolio,t} \cdot \tag{15}$$

Equations (14) and (15) are central to our method for attributing the performance of portfolios with intra month cash flows. We rewrite equation (4) as

$$1 + R_{Manager} = 1 + R_{Benchmark} + \sum_{j} \textit{Excess return from the } j^{th} \textit{ selection skill} \tag{4''}$$

On substituting equations (2) and (15) into equation (4") and expanding, we see that the only term in the attribution that changes its basic form is the term that measures the excess return from asset allocation (or sector or country selection). This is now given by $\sum_{1 \le i \le N} (\hat{w}_{it} - w_{it}^{o})(1 + r_{it}^{o})$ instead of $\sum_{1 \le i \le I} (w_{it} - w_{it}^{o}) r_{it}^{o}$. The change, however, is less dramatic than it would appear.

Observe that for any set of weights $\{w_{it}\}$ that sum to 1,

$$\sum_{1 \le i \le N} (w_{it} - w_{it}^{o}) r_{it}^{o} = \sum_{1 \le i \le N} (w_{it} - w_{it}^{o})(1 + r_{it}^{o}) \ , \tag{16}$$

so that in the absence of any cash flows, starting out with equations (4) and (4") leads to exactly the same numerical results. Our decision to express returns as percentages in earlier sections is a pragmatic one. Investors are more likely to express return as a percentage than to express them in factor form. We close this section with two numerical examples. In the first, we attribute the returns of a domestic asset allocator. In the second, we attribute the returns of an international equity manager. In both examples, note that the sum of the various excess return is exactly equal to the managers time weighted excess return.

Example 1: Domestic Asset Allocator:

	Manager	Benchmark
Beginning of month weight in stocks	.5	.6
Beginning of month weight in bonds	.5	.4
End of month weight in stocks	.6	.6111
End of month weight in bonds	.4	.3899
Time weighted return for the month from stocks	10%	10%
Time weighted return for the month from bonds	5%	5%
Time weighted return for the month from portfolio	8.5%	8%
Effective weight in stocks	.59182	.6
Effective weight in bonds	.41333	.4
Excess return from asset allocation		[-.0081x1.1+.01333x1.05] x100%=.5%

Example 2: International Equity Manager:

	Manager	Benchmark
Beginning of quarter weighting in Germany	.5	.4
Beginning of quarter weighting in France	.5	.6
End of quarter weighting in Germany	.6	.3888888
End of quarter weighting in France	.4	.6111111
Time weighted return for the quarter from Germany	10%	5%
Time weighted return for the quarter from France	5%	10%
Return for the quarter from portfolio	7.5%	8%
Effective weight in Germany	.58636	.4
Effective weight in France	.40952	.6
Excess return from country selection=		[.18636x1.05-.19048x1.1]x100%=-.5%
Excess return from stock selection=		.4x5%-.6x5%=-1%
Excess return from country/stock selection=		.18636x5%+(-.19048)x(-5%)=1.884%

VIII. Multiperiod Performance Attribution

We next address the problem of multiperiod performance attribution, or how to combine a set of subperiod (typically monthly) attributions into a full period (often annual) attribution. For portfolios that are infrequently rebalanced, and for which the cash flows at each rebalancing are small, the methodology developed in Section VII can be readily adapted as follows.

1. Discard all the subperiod attributions.
2. Compute the time weighted return from each asset class and for the entire portfolio for the period.
3. Compute a set of effective weights, using the end of period weights and these compounded returns, following the method developed in Section VII.
4. Perform the attribution with these weights and returns as shows in Section VII.

Unfortunately this does not work well with most actively managed portfolios, for which turnover can easily exceed 100% per annum. For such portfolios we propose a different method. As usual, we start off with some notation.

Portfolio return in the tth subperiod	$R_{Portfolio,t}$
Benchmark return in the tth subperiod	$R_{Benchmark,t}$
Manager's excess return from the jth selection skill in the tth subperiod	d_{jt}
Number of selection skills that the manager's returns are attributed tc	M
Number of subperiods	T
Portfolio return for the entire period	$R_{Portfolio}$
Benchmark return for the entire period	$R_{Benchmark}$
Manager's excess return from the jth selection skill for the entire perio	Δ_j
Manager's excess return for the tth subperiod	$d_t = \sum_{1 \le i \le N} d_{jt}$

In each subperiod we have

$$R_{Portfolio,t}=R_{Benchmark,t}+d_t$$

and compounding the returns for the entire period gives

$$
\begin{aligned}
1+R_{Portfolio} &= \prod_{1\le t\le T}(1+R_{Portfolio,t}) \\
&= \prod_{1\le t\le T}(1+R_{Benchmark,t}+\delta_t) \\
&= \prod_{1\le t\le T}(1+R_{Benchmark,t})\prod_{1\le t\le T}\Big(1+\sum_{1\le j\le M}\frac{\delta_{jt}}{1+R_{Benchmark,t}}\Big) \\
&= (1+R_{Benchmark})\prod_{1\le t\le T}\Big(1+\sum_{1\le j\le M}\frac{\delta_{jt}}{1+R_{Benchmark,t}}\Big)
\end{aligned}
\tag{17}
$$

Equation (17) expresses the portfolio return for the entire period as the product of the benchmark return for the period and a set of terms containing the weighted sums of the various excess returns in each subperiod. For example, if we were attributing the returns of a domestic equity manager, the first term in the set would contain the weighted sum of the excess returns from sector selection, stock selection and sector/stock selection for the first subperiod. On multiplying the terms, we see that a large number of cross product terms exist. A typical cross product term might involve the excess return from sector selection from one subperiod, the excess return from stock selection in another, and the excess return from sector/stock selection in yet a third. These terms arise because we multiply a set of additive decompositions to get equation (17). Dealing with these cross products in a satisfactory manner is the central problem of multiperiod performance attribution.

The solution we propose is to allocate to any given skill only those products that are composed exclusively of subperiod excess returns from that skill. All the remaining terms are attributed to a component that we call the ***temporal interaction***. For example, the product of the excess return from country selection in one subperiod and the excess return from country selection in another subperiod is attributed to the temporal interaction. The temporal interaction, which is typically small, is completely unrelated to the skills of the manager, and arises only because we multiply a set of additive subperiod attributions together to compute an additive full period attribution. In evaluating the performance of a money manager, we focus primarily on his excess returns from the various selection skills appropriate to his mandate. We examine the temporal interaction only if it seems unusually large, as this is almost always indicative of a data error.

The following identity now proves useful:

$$\prod 1 \le t \le T(1+x_t+y_t) = 1+[\prod 1 \le t \le T(1+x_t)-1]+[\prod 1 \le t \le T(1+y_t)-1]+ \text{ Cross Product Terms.} \tag{18}$$

On substituting equation (18) into equation (17) and gathering terms we get

$$\begin{aligned} R_{Portfolio} &= R_{Benchmark} \\ &+(1+R_{Benchmark})x(\prod_{1\le t\le T}(1+\frac{\delta_1 t}{1+R_{Benchmark,t}})-1) \\ &+\dots \\ &+(1+R_{Benchmark})x(\prod_{1\le t\le T}(1+\frac{\delta_{Mt}}{1+R_{Benchmark,t}})-1) \\ &+(1+R_{Benchmark})x\text{Cross product terms} \\ &= R_{Benchmark}+\Delta_1+\dots+\Delta_M \ +\text{Temporal Interaction} \end{aligned} \tag{19}$$

where $\Delta_i = (1+R_{Benchmark})x(\prod_{1\le t\le T}(1+\frac{\delta_i t}{1+R_{Benchmark,t}})-1)$, and the temporal interaction is given by $R_{Portfolio} - R_{Benchmark} - \Delta_1 - \cdots - \Delta_M$.

Equation (19) gives us our desired relationship between the full period excess returns from a particular skill and the sub period excess returns from that skill. The following example, in which we compound two monthly attributions of a domestic equity manager to get a two month attribution, illustrates the use of the methodology.

<u>Example:</u>

Benchmark return in January	10%
Manager's return in January	11%
Manager's excess return from sector selection in January	1%
Manager's excess return from stock selection in January	-1%
Manager's excess return from sector/stock selection in January	1%
Benchmark return in February	5%
Manager's return in February	6%
Manager's excess return from sector selection in February	2%
Manager's excess return from stock selection in February	-1%
Manager's excess return from sector/stock selection in February	0%
Benchmark return for two months	[1.1x1.05-1]x100%=15.5%
Manager's return for two months	[1.11x1.06-1]x100%=17.66%
Manager's excess returns for two months	2.16%

$$\textit{Excess return from sector selection } 1.155x[(1+.\frac{01}{1.1})(1+.\frac{02}{1.05})-1]x100\% = 3.27\%$$

$$\textit{Excess return from stock selection } 1.155x[(1-.\frac{01}{1.1})(1-.\frac{01}{1.05})-1]x100\% = 2.14\%$$

$$\textit{Excess return from cty.stk. selection } 1.155x[(1+.\frac{01}{1.1})(1+\frac{0}{1.05})-1]x100\% = 1.05\%$$

$$\textit{Temporal Interaction } 2.16\% - [3.27\% - 2.14\% + 1.05\%] = .02\%$$

In this example the temporal interaction is negligibly small at 2 basis points. In attributing the returns from portfolios over periods randing from 1 to 5 years, we find that the temporal interaction is typically on the order of 10 to 15 basis points, and can safely be ignored.

In Figures I through IV we show the results of applying this multiperiod attribution methodology to two different money managers. The first is a domestic tactical asset allocator who varies his portfolio's exposure to stocks, bonds and cash in response to changes in his forecasted returns from these markets. The second is an international equity manager whose benchmark is the Morgan Stanley Europe Index with 13 countries. The manager's names have been changed to conceal their identity. The numbers used in the first example are derived from a simulation performed by the manager, while those in the second example are real returns from a portfolio that was managed for the IBM Retirement Fund. Each example has two plots associated with it. On the first plot (Figures I and III) we display the monthly excess returns of the managed portfolio, defined to be the difference between the return of the managed portfolio and its benchmark (a 50/50 S&P 500/Ranging Brothers Aggregate split in the case of the domestic asset allocator, and the Morgan Stanley Europe 13 Index in the case of the international equity manager), the cumulative excess return of the portfolio, defined to be the difference in the cumulative or compounded returns of the portfolio and the benchmark since the inception of the portfolio, and the 12 month moving average of the monthly excess return. The monthly excess return and its 12 month moving average are plotted on a scale of -400 basis points to +400 basis points. A fixed scale greatly simplifies the comparison of two or more portfolios, and we find that this particular scale allows the satisfactory display of the excess returns of almost all our managed portfolios. The scale of the plot of the cumulative excess return is shown on the right side and is not fixed, because the range of cumulative returns is so large that a fixed scale proves impractical. If the manager is able to add value, one would expect to see a positive bias to the sequence of excess returns and its 12 month moving average, and a positive slope and endpoint for the cumulative excess return. The slope of the cumulative excess return plot is easily estimated visually and gives us a quick estimate of the manager's current performance.

At the bottom of the chart we present two tables of summary statistics for the portfolio. At the bottom right hand corner, the results of a multiperiod attribution are presented, with all of the excess returns being annualized. Notice that the temporal interaction term is small in both cases. To the left of this table a table of overall performance statistics is presented. At the top of the table, we place the annualized excess return, followed by the annualized tracking error (defined to be Ö12xthe monthly standard deviation of the excess returns), and the information ratio (defined to be the ratio of the annualized excess return to the annualized tracking error. An information ratio of .5 is considered good, and a manager who can realize an information ratio of 1 or higher for extended periods of time must be considered outstanding. The second set of numbers (those relating to the CAPM or linear model) is estimated from the linear regression

$$(R_p - R_f) = a + ß x (R_I - R_f) e \qquad (20)$$

where R_p is the return on the portfolio, R_I is the return on the index, and R_f is the risk free rate of return, which we take to be the monthly return on the 91 day T=Bill. For a detailed explanation of this method of performance evaluation we refer the interested reader to the classic papers by Jensen (1968, 1969). The probability that a is positive is a byproduct of this regression, and its derivation can be found in any standard textbook on regression such as Weisberg (1985).

On the second plot (Figures II and IV) we display time series of the excess returns due to each of the selection terms, and some summary statistics for these selection terms in small boxes to the right of the plots. The mean and the standard deviation are self explanatory, and the probability that the excess return from a given selection skill is positive is derived by assuming that the excess returns are normally distributed. The probability that the true mean of the excess return is positive is then given by $\Phi(\frac{\textit{Annualized Excess Return}}{\textit{Annualized Standard Deviation}} x \sqrt{\frac{N}{12}})$, where $\Phi(x) = \frac{1}{\sqrt{2x}} \int_x^{\infty} exp[-y^2/2]dy$, 20 and N is the length of the measurement interval in months.

The wealth of information on these charts might seem a bit intimidating at first sight, but we have not had any objections from users on this score. In fact, most users prefer to see all the information presented and to then focus on those factors which they deem the most important.

IX. Problems That Arise in Practice

The key problems we have faced in implementing the attribution methodology described in this paper are

1. The choice of an appropriate benchmark, and of its decomposition into sectors, and
2. The acquisition and timely updating of the data required for the attribution.

The Choice of a Benchmark:

The benchmark used must satisfy two key criteria:

1. If should be appropriate to the manager's mandate and the plan sponsors requirements

2. It must admit a decomposition into sectors that is reflective of the manager's investment process and for which sector returns are readily computed.

For domestic and global asset allocators, we suggest that the plan sponsor define a custom benchmark by combining a set of indices such as the S&P 500 and the Shearson Ranging Government Corporate Index. Returns for these indices are readily available, and the weights are fixed by the plan sponsor.

For domestic equity portfolios, we suggest the use of the S&P 500 or the Russell 3000 can be decomposed into Value, Growth, and Small Cap sectors. BARRA defines Growth, Value and Small Cap decompositions for the Russell 3000. In addition to defining these decompositions, they also maintain the appropriate indices on a timely basis. Many money managers find such a decomposition to be reflective of their investment process. It is also possible to break up the benchmark into a set of economic sectors, but there is little consensus on what the appropriate decomposition ought to be, or to which sector a company ought to be assigned. Furthermore, once a decomposition has been decided on, it is still necessary to define and maintain a set of sector indices. Finally, if the portfolio is managed externally, the composition of the benchmark needs to be transmitted to the manager every month, so that he can compute his sector weights and returns.

For international equity portfolios, we suggest the use of one of the many available indices, such as the Morgan Stanley Capital International or the Salomon-Russell indices, the choice being dictated by the manager's mandate. We decompose these indices by country, as weights and returns for each of the countries are readily available. Furthermore, small cap stocks that do not belong to the benchmark are readily classified by country.

The Acquisition of Data:

The results of any attribution are strongly dependent on the quality of the input data. The most common sources of data error that we have encountered in implementing this methodology are:

1. Random errors made by the portfolio manager or the custodian in communicating portfolio and benchmark results,
2. Systematic errors in computation, especially in the computation of time weighted returns when there are large cash flows into or our of the portfolio, and
3. Pricing errors caused by the benchmark and the portfolio being priced at different times or in different geographic locations. This problem is particularly acute with international equity portfolios, where differences in exchange rate and closing prices can cause errors of over 100 basis points in a month.

Constant vigilance is really the only way to combat the first problem. A check for abnormally large or small returns and a test to ensure that all the sector weights add up to 1 will catch a large fraction of such errors. If possible, obtain information directly from the custodian for the account, as the custodian routinely reconciles any discrepancies in the data with the manager.

Systematic errors in computation and errors caused by differential pricing are much harder to detect. In particular, we find that most money managers and many custodians compute internal rates of return instead of time weighted returns. In the absence of cash flows, no error is incurred by this approximation. In the presence of cash flows, however, the two may differ markedly. The long run average of such errors is small, but in any given month they can cause the manager's computed return to differ from the custodian's computed return by a large amount, often in excess of one hundred basis points.

No complete solution to these problems exists. Their effect can, however, by minimized by the use of a single source of data, preferably the custodian. As an attribution concerns itself with the difference between the manager's return and the benchmark's return, systematic errors in the custodian's methodology and pricing will tend to cancel each other out. If the custodian does not have the necessary data, all the data ought to be supplied by the manager. A certain amount of data scrubbing and comparison with published benchmarks is now in order, but this is a small price to pay for a substantial increase in accuracy.

X. Conclusion

We have described a performance attribution methodology that can be used to analyze the performance of domestic and international equity managers and asset allocators. In addition, we have described methods to deal with cash flows in to and out of the portfolio, and to perform multiperiod attributions. These methods are general and can be applied to any additive single period performance attribution methodology.

This methodology has been in use for nearly two year, and has proved useful. It has given us insights into the investment process, and has helped identify a number of problems. As with any analytic tool, the blind use of such an analysis can sometimes mislead. With a little care, though, it can give many insights into the nature of a manager's skills, facilitate the choice of a manager and the definition of his mandate, and help monitor the manager's performance on an ongoing basis.

Acknowledgements

It is a pleasure to acknowledge the assistance provided by Randolph Nelson, David Stein and the referees. Their thorough reading of earlier drafts of this manuscript helped excise many errors, and greatly improved the presentation. Any errors that remain are mine alone.

References

Allen, G., (1991) "Performance Attribution for Global Equity Portfolios," *Journal of Portfolio Management*, Fall.

Ankrim, E.M., (1992) "Risk Adjusted Performance Attribution," *Financial Analysts Journal*, March-April, pp. 74-82.

Brinson, G.P., Hood, E.R., and Beebower, G.L., (1986) "Determinants of Portfolio Performance," *Financial Analysts Journal*, July-August, pp. 39-44.

Brinson, G.P., and Fachler, N., (1985) "Measuring Non-U.S. Equity Portfolio Performance, *Journal of Portfolio Management*, Spring.

Brinson, G.P., Singer, B.D., and Beebower, G.L., (1991), "Determinants of Portfolio Performance II: An Update," *Financial Analysts Journal*, May-June, pp. 40-48.

Dietz, O., (1966) *Pension Funds: Measuring Investment Performance*, New York: The Free Press.

Fama E. (1972) "Components of Investment Performance," *Journal of Finance*, Vol. 27, No.3, pp. 551-567.

Fama, E.F., and French, K.R., (1992) "The Cross-Section of Expected Stock Returns," *Journal of Finance*, Vol. 47, No. 2, pp. 427-465.

Fama, E.F., and French, K.R., (1992) "The Economic Fundamentals of Size and Book to Market," Preprint, March.

Jensen, M., (1968) "The Performance of Mutual Funds in the Period 1945-1964," *Journal of Finance*, Vol. 23, No. 2, pp. 389-416.

Jensen, M., (1969) "Risk, the Pricing of Capital Assets, and the Evaluation of Investment Portfolios," *Journal of Business*, Vol. 42, No. 2, pp. 167-247.

Weisberg, S., (1985) *Applied Linear Regression*, 2nd Ed., New York: John Wiley and Sons..

VOLATILITY

Ronald C. Heynen
Banque Paribas

Harry M. Kat
Bank of America

D. Ho and T. Schneeweis (eds.), Applications in Finance, Investments, and Banking, 197–255.

INTRODUCTION

In this chapter we provide an overview of the many volatility predictors that were suggested over time. We first discuss volatility predictors based on historical price and return data. Afterwards, we turn to predictors based on other sources of information. We concentrate on stock return volatility. The methods discussed are, however, equally valid for other assets. Although all predictors are discussed in isolation, it is important that a combination of individual forecasts may sometimes outperform any of its constituents. "The reason that a combined forecast may be preferable is that neither constituent forecast is using all of the data in the available information set in an optimum fashion".[1] In the discussion the terms "estimation", "forecasting" and "prediction" are used interchangeably to emphasize the fact that we see volatility not just as a parameter of some probabilistic model which has to be estimated, but much more as a real-world variable the value of which must be predicted or forecasted.

An accurate prediction of capital asset return volatility is of great importance in many applications of modern investment technology. Future volatility is an important input for static hedging, portfolio selection and margining problems, where volatility is typically used as an explicit measure of risk. Future volatility is also an important input for option hedging strategies and pricing models derived using the Black and Scholes

---

[1]Granger (1980, p. 160).

(1973) paradigm. The importance of an accurate volatility prediction for the hedging of ordinary and exotic options was discussed extensively in Kat (1993a, 1993b). Kat used stochastic simulation methods to study the distribution of the hedging errors that may arise when delta-hedging the risks from writing ordinary, averaging and lookback call options on the S&P 500 with an initial time to maturity of one year. His results clearly show that more accurate volatility predictions can substantially improve the hedging efficiency of dynamic trading strategies, even in imperfect markets where transaction costs are non-zero and volatility is unknown and changing.

ESTIMATION FROM HISTORICAL RETURNS

CONSTANT VOLATILITY

The simplest approach to predicting volatility is to assume that the return over any interval j, which in practice has to be adjusted for things such as dividends, split-ups, etc., is normally distributed with both mean and variance proportional to the length of that interval t_j *i.e.* that

$$R_j \sim N[\mu t_j, \sigma^2 t_j],$$

where $R_j = C_j - C_{j-1}$ denotes the return over interval j and C_j is the natural logarithm of the stock price at the closing of interval j. When returns are assumed to be serially independent, the "classical" approach to estimate s^2 is to use the natural estimator of the variance of return per unit of time (years, months, weeks, days, hours) given by

$$v_{CC}^2 = \frac{1}{n-1} \sum_{j=1}^{n} \frac{(R_j - mt_j)^2}{t_j},$$

(1)

where $m = 1/n \sum (R_j / t_j)$ and n denotes the number of disjoint time intervals, not necessary of equal length, used to calculate the return data. We will refer to the above predictor as the "random walk predictor". As usual, assuming that the above probabilistic model is correct, we should try to calculate the above estimate from as much data as possible to reduce sampling error. When using a large set of daily close-to-close returns, the assumption that m=0 has a negligible effect on the estimate v_{CC}^2. Under that approximation, (1) can be rewritten as

$$v_{CC}^2 = \frac{1}{n}\sum_{j=1}^{n}\frac{(R_j)^2}{t_j}. \tag{2}$$

It is well-known that the square root of the estimator of the stock return's variance is not an unbiased estimator of its standard deviation. For relatively large sample sizes, however, the difference is not worth worrying about. In what follows we concentrate on return variance.

Another point concerns the length of the time interval between successive close-to-close returns. When working with daily close-to-close data, the length of the differencing interval is not uniquely fixed because of differences between weekdays, weekends, holidays and weekend-holidays and varies from 24 hours for a normal trading day to 72 hours for a weekend to even 96 hours for a weekend-holiday. Fortunately, stock return volatility during non-trading days is relatively low. French and Roll (1986) for example, found that in the U.S. the variance of the close-to-close return over a weekend was only 10.7% higher than the variance of the close-to-close return over a normal trading day. For practical purposes therefore, one does not make a large mistake when treating all close-to-close periods as being of the same length.

The classical approach considers only closing prices and excludes all other publicly available information. Assuming the above probabilistic setting is correct, there are, however, numerous ways to improve on the estimator's statistical efficiency by incorporating additional information. One of them is Parkinson's (1980) "extreme value method". Assuming that the stock trades continuously and that stock returns are normally distributed with a zero mean, Parkinson used daily high and low prices to estimate the daily stock return's variance as

$$v_{HL}^2 = \frac{1}{4n\ln 2}\sum_{j=1}^{n}(H_j - L_j)^2, \qquad (3)$$

where H_j and L_j are the natural logarithms of the stock price's high and low respectively over day j. Under the assumptions made, this estimator is about 5.2 times as efficient as the random walk estimator (2). This is no surprise, since high and low prices contain information about all realizations of the underlying process over an interval, whereas the classical approach uses only one: the closing price. The problem with the above estimator is that (by assumption) it skips over non-trading periods and therefore tends to provide a downward biased estimate of 24-hour volatility. Correcting for this bias requires the availability of opening and closing prices. Let O_j denote the natural logarithm of the stock's opening price on day j. Assuming that continuous trading takes place only during a fraction $(1-f)$ of the day and that during trading as well as non-trading hours the stock return has a zero mean, Garman and Klass (1980) modified the previous estimator as

$$v_{HLOC}^2 = \frac{1}{n}\sum_{j=1}^{n}\left[0.12\frac{(O_j - C_{j-1})^2}{f} + 0.88\frac{V_j^2}{(1-f)}\right], \quad 0 < f < 1, \tag{4}$$

where

$$V_j^2 = 0.511(H_j - L_j)^2 - 0.383(C_j - O_j)^2 - 0.019[(C_j - O_j)(H_j + L_j - 2O_j) - 2(H_j - O_j)(L_j - O_j)]. \tag{5}$$

The coefficients in this and the previous formula derive from the moment generating function of the variables involved. Theoretically the above estimator's efficiency is about 8.4 times higher than the random walk estimator's efficiency.

At this stage a number of points are worth noting:

- First, since Garman and Klass considered not the entire joint distribution of high, low and closing prices, but only its first few moments, the above estimator can still be improved upon by considering higher moments. Ball and Torous (1984) derived such a maximum likelihood estimator, based on daily high, low and closing prices. Using stochastic simulation they showed their estimator to perform more efficiently than both estimators (3) and (4). Also, the Parkinson and Garman and Klass estimators will be biased if used in the case where $\mu \neq 0$. Alternative estimators which solve the latter problem can be found in Rogers and Satchell (1991) and Kunitomo (1992).

- Second, even during trading hours the price process can not be monitored continuously. These discontinuities cause the extreme value estimators to be biased downwards, since the observed high and low may understate, respectively overstate the true high and low during the day. Also, as is clear from Stoll and Whaley (1990), the opening (closing) price may be realized some time after (before) the opening (closing) of the exchange. Note that both points are especially relevant for stocks with relatively low trading continuity.

- Third, throughout it has been assumed that stock returns are normally distributed. Research, however, has shown that the observed distribution of stock returns differs slightly from the assumed normal distribution, the most striking difference being the former's substantial excess kurtosis. Since an estimator which is optimal for one distribution is not necessarily almost optimal for a very similar distribution, Geske and Torous (1991) suggested a more robust estimator which, in case of slight deviations from normality, is significantly more efficient than the random walk estimator given by (1). Monte Carlo simulations confirmed this proposition and showed that when stock returns are not exactly normally distributed, the random walk estimator may be upwardly biased.

- Fourth, and related to the previous point, the actual behaviour of stock prices is far more complex than assumed. As mentioned before, prices behave differently over trading and non-trading periods. Also, opening and closing prices are often subject to short-term disturbances, such as adjustments for margin considerations and/or overnight positioning, which may reduce instead of increase the reliability of estimates partially based on opening and/or closing prices. In reality, extreme values typically occur within a few minutes of the opening or closing.

- Fifth, we did not yet consider the influence of the market's microstructure, which can be expected to be stronger the higher the sampling frequency of the data. Volatility estimators using high frequency data may become biased or inefficient as a result of the prevalence of minimum price changes (typically one-eighth of a dollar for listed stocks in the U.S.). With respect to the effect of this form of rounding in observed prices, Marsh and Rosenfeld (1986) concluded that it does not bias the traditional estimator of volatility, but reduces its efficiency, and that it both biases and reduces the efficiency of the extreme value estimator. Working with another model of discreteness, Cho and Frees (1988) on the other hand showed that the random walk estimator overestimates true volatility in most cases. The same conclusion can be drawn from Ball (1988).

- Sixth, another microstructural bias stems from the bid-ask spread. Generally, we have to rely on transactions data consisting of bid as well as ask prices without being able to tell the difference between them. When subsequent trades alternately tend to take place on the bid and the ask, this creates the illusion of volatility where there actually is none. Especially with high-frequent transactions data, this "bid-ask bounce" causes an upward bias in the volatility estimates. Choi and Shastri (1989), assuming independence between transaction types and price changes, wrote the variance of observed transactions return as the sum of the true return variance and the so-called "spread induced variance". They showed that the latter is a decreasing function of the conditional probability of successive transactions being of the same type and an increasing function of the percentage bid-ask spread. Assuming a positive relationship between the spread and volatility, this implies that the magnitude by which the variance of observed transaction returns overestimates true variance is an increasing function of the true variance itself. Fortunately, Glosten (1987) showed that the upward bias in the standard variance estimator (when applied to transactions data) can theoreticaly be eliminated by adding twice the first-order serial covariance of successive transaction returns to the initial estimate. As discussed in Roll (1984), in an efficient market the former is theoretically equal to minus the square of one-half the realized bid-ask spread.

- Seventh, when working with index returns it is important that indices are generally calculated from last transaction prices instead of mid-quote prices. The resulting lagging effect may lead to a deviation of observed volatility from true volatility. On the other hand, as long as the number of stocks trading at the bid is more or less equal to the number of stocks trading at the ask, bid-ask bounce is diversified away. With widespread buying or selling, however, bid-ask bounce may become a problem even for index returns.

The general message of the above remarks is that what we are really looking for is a good forecast of the stock return's future variability. In doing so, we should not concentrate on theoretical unbiasedness and efficiency too much, since these characteristics only have meaning in the assumed probabilistic setting, which may be misspecified in the first place.

When empirically evaluating the performance of different volatility predictors one first has to determine actual, *i.e.* realized, volatility. Although other definitions are possible, the latter is typically calculated using formula (1). Having determined actual volatility, one can go several ways to evaluate the forecast efficiency of a specific volatility predictor. The most popular method is to regress realized volatility on its prediction and interpret the coefficient of determination of this regression as a measure of forecast efficiency. However, although a given volatility predictor may yield a higher R^2 and as such have the highest information content, it is not necessarily better in terms of rationality, *i.e.* it is not necessarily less biased. To obtain an idea of the rationality of a forecast one therefore has to test whether the intercept and the slope of the above regression differ from zero and one respectively. Note, however, that from a practical point of view forecast efficiency may be more important than rationality. Another approach to evaluate volatility predictions is to compare realized and predicted volatility directly by calculating well-known statistics like the mean error, mean squared error, mean absolute error and mean absolute percentage error. This provides essentially the same information as the above regression approach. Finally, it is important that most empirical studies on relative forecast efficiency concentrate on only one forecast horizon of given length, typically a week, a month, or a quarter. Given the fact that, as will be discussed shortly, volatility is not constant, a study of forecast efficiency over other horizons might lead to different conclusions. Moreover, a predictor which works well for one asset may prove to be suboptimal for another.

Beckers (1983), using a regression approach, compared the predictive ability of the random walk and Parkinson's extreme value estimator over a one quarter period on data for 208 individual stocks over the period 1973-1980. He found that the high-low estimator provided no real improvement over the traditional close-to-close estimator. This result emphasizes that empirical questions can not be answered satisfactory by theory alone but only by empirical research. Additional empirical results concerning the efficiency of the high-low estimator can be found in Wiggins (1991).

CHANGING VOLATILITY

Until now we have assumed that volatility is constant. However, this is certainly not the case in reality. During the 1857-1987 period for example, estimates of the standard deviation of monthly stock returns derived from daily S&P 500 returns varied from as low as two to as high as twenty percent with substantial changes occurring over relatively short periods of time. "Tests whether these differences could be attributed to estimation error strongly reject the hypothesis of a constant variance."[2] We therefore now turn to techniques which explicitly allow for deterministically or stochastically changing volatility. When volatility is constant, the horizon over which volatility is predicted is of no real concern. We can calculate a volatility prediction for any arbitrary interval of length t_1 by multiplying any other prediction over an interval t_2 by simply multiplying the latter by the square root of t_1 / t_2. However, when volatility is allowed to change over time, the forecast horizon becomes an important factor. In that case return variance is no longer proportional to the length of the forecast horizon. Empirical research, for example, has shown that high (low) volatilities tend to decline (rise). As a result, annualized[3] short-term volatility can be substantially higher or lower than longer-term annualized volatility.

A very simple way to deal with changing volatility would be to stick to the constant volatility estimators which we discussed previously while at the same time letting the sample period vary with the forecast horizon. By using a small sample when forecasting volatility over a short period of time, and increasing the sample size when the length of the forecasting horizon increases, we might pick up some of volatility's

---

[2]Schwert (1989, p. 1115).

[3]As with interest rates, volatility is usually expressed on an annual basis, where, as with interest rates, annualization takes place assuming that volatility remains unchanged.

systematic behaviour. As a matter of fact, one rule of thumb which is well-known among market makers in options is to match the sampling period to the remaining lifetime of the option contract being valued. Moreover, many data vendors provide their customers with volatility predictions calculated from 30-day and 90-day samples.

A less ad-hoc way to deal with changing volatility is to model the time series behaviour of volatility explicitly. An obvious approach is to use a two-stage method[4] by first calculating a series of, for example, monthly sample variances using equation (1) and subsequently estimating standard ARIMA time series models for this time series monthly estimates. Examples of this approach can be found in Poterba and Summers (1986) and French, Schwert and Stambaugh (1987). Implicitly this approach assumes that volatility is constant within a month and only becomes variable for longer horizons. Furthermore, the method essentially reduces the available amount of information, which results in an increase in the variability of the volatility forecasts calculated from the estimated ARIMA model. Additionally, as noted by Chou (1988), the corresponding parameter estimates are extremely sensitive to the chosen sampling frequency for which the time series of volatility estimates is calculated.

A third approach to modeling changing volatility is to do so not in isolation, but as part of a more sophisticated and explicit model of stock return behaviour. To find an appropriate representation of the actual behaviour of stock return volatility over time,

---

[4]See Pagan (1984, 1986) for a general discussion.

we should first study the actual behaviour of stock returns themselves. Something we should have done before assuming anything whatsoever in the first place. Summarizing the conclusions of numerous authors, it has become clear that an acceptable model of high frequency stock (index) returns should be able to generate the following stylized facts: (1) symmetry, (2) substantial excess kurtosis in comparison to the normal distribution, (3) changing and mean reverting volatility, (4) low autocorrelation, and (5) substantial positive autocorrelation between squared and absolute returns which declines slowly as the time lag increases. Moreover, there are several well established statistical anomalies in stock return data, such as a particularly high return in January and a particularly low return on Mondays. Although we are primarily interested in (3), it stands to reason that the other points may prove useful in leading us to the best possible representation.

A very popular group of return models which incorporate changing volatility and which are at the same time able to generate many of the above stylized facts, is formed by the class of ARCH-type models, where the acronym stands for AutoRegressive Conditional Heteroskedasticity. Research into the latter started with Engle (1982), who introduced the linear ARCH(p) model in which the conditional variance was written as a linear function of the first p past squared innovations. Later Bollerslev (1986) generalized the model by allowing the current conditional variance to be a function of the first q past conditional variances as well, a model known as linear

GARCH (*p,q*). Engle and Bollerslev (1986) introduced the IGARCH (*p,q*) model, where multistep variance forecasts do not approach the unconditional variance. Engle, Lilien and Robins (1987) were the first to allow the conditional variance to affect the mean in their ARCH-M (*p*) model. Although most authors assume the conditional error distribution to be a normal distribution, extensions to the Student-*t* distribution can be found in the GARCH (*p,q*)-*t* model of Engle and Bollerslev (1986) and Bollerslev (1987). Finally, Nelson (1991) introduced the EGARCH (*p,q*) model, where variance does not only depend on the magnitude but also on the sign of past errors, which is in line with empirical evidence.[5] Multivariate extensions of most of these models are relatively easy to construct. An extensive overview of recent theoretical and empirical research in this field can be found in Bollerslev, Chou and Kroner (1992).

Without spending time on technicalities, which can be found in the references, the general form of a GARCH *(p,q)* process for returns with a constant mean is

$$R_t | \Omega_{t-1} \rightarrow F(\mu, \sigma_t^2),$$

$$\varepsilon_t = R_t - \mu,$$

[5]See, for example, Christie (1982) or Nelson (1991).

where F (μ, σ_t^2) is the conditional return distribution and W_{t-1} is the information set available at time *t-1*. The latter is generally assumed to consist of the set of past returns only. To ensure a well defined process all the parameters are restricted to be non-negative. The equation for the conditional variance can be rewritten as

$$\varepsilon_t^2 = \alpha_0 + \sum_{i=1}^{\max(p,q)} (\alpha_i + \beta_i)\varepsilon_{t-i}^2 - \sum_{j=1}^{q} \beta_j(\varepsilon_{t-j}^2 - \sigma_{t-j}^2) + (\varepsilon_t^2 - \sigma_t^2), \tag{5}$$

which shows that the GARCH (*p*,*q*) model is similar to an ARMA model in squared residuals of orders max(*p*,*q*) and *q*, with serially uncorrelated but heteroscedastic innovations (ε_t^2 - σ_t^2). For *q*=0, (5) reduces to an ARCH (*p*) process, while repeated substitution shows that under certain conditions the general GARCH model is just an infinite order ARCH model with exponentially decaying weights for larger lags. As a result, a low order GARCH model may have properties similar to a high order ARCH model. Although the unconditional variance of the process is constant, the conditional variance is time dependent. More specifically, there is a tendency for extreme values to be followed by other extreme values, but, since there is no role for the sign of past residual returns in the model, of unpredictable sign. As a result squared returns and absolute returns are positively autocorrelated even when returns themselves are uncorrelated.

Until now the most popular choice for F has been the normal distribution function, while the order set mostly used is simply (1,1). The latter GARCH(1,1) specification appears to be an adequate representation of many financial time series. This reduces (5) to

$$R_t | \{ R_{t-i}, i > 0 \} \rightarrow N(\mu, \sigma_t^2), \tag{7}$$

$$\sigma_t^2 = \alpha_0 + \alpha_1 \varepsilon_{t-1}^2 + \beta_1 \sigma_{t-1}^2,$$

where $\varepsilon_t = R_t - \mu_t$. By rewriting (7) it becomes clear that the conditional variance exceeds the unconditional variance when recent shocks are large in comparison to the latter, and the other way around

$$\sigma_t^2 = \sigma_u^2 + \alpha_1 \sum_{i=0}^{\infty} \beta^i \left(\varepsilon_{t-1-i}^2 - \sigma_u^2 \right),$$

where σ_u^2 is the model's unconditional variance, which is given by $\alpha_0 / (1 - (\alpha_1 + \beta_1))$. From (7) it can be derived that the minimal MSE forecast of the conditional variance s steps ahead is given by

$$E_t [\sigma_{t+s}^2] = \sigma_u^2 + (\alpha_1 + \beta_1)^{s-1} (\sigma_{t+1}^2 - \sigma_u^2)$$

which shows that as the forecast horizon increases, current information becomes less important and the latter forecast converges to the unconditional variance. This means that we can interpret $\alpha_1 + \beta_1$ as a measure of the speed by which shocks to volatility decay. When $\alpha_1 + \beta_1$ approaches 1 from below, the effect of past volatility shocks increases, which may cause volatility to deviate from its long-term mean for a very large number of periods into the future. Empirical research suggests that for many speculative return series this is indeed the case. It can be shown that although the conditional error distribution is normal, the unconditional error distribution is somewhat leptokurtic. This, of course, results from the autocorrelation in the squared residuals. Conditionally standardized Student-*t* distributed errors can be used to provide a second source of unconditional leptokurticism, an idea which was first applied in Bollerslev (1987). Other alternatives used or suggested are the generalized error distribution, the normal-Poisson mixture distribution and the normal-lognormal mixture distribution. Maximum likelihood estimates of the GARCH model's parameters can be obtained by numerical maximization of the log-likelihood function using the Berndt, Hall, Hall and Hausman (1974) algorithm (a modified scoring algorithm) with numerical first order derivatives. Problems like local optima have not been reported.

One-day ahead volatility forecasts can be calculated directly from the explicit specification of the model's conditional variance. More-than-one-day forecasts, which we need for the execution of dynamic trading strategies for example, can be generated by repeated substitution. From the GARCH(1,1) model, the time *t* forecast of the variance of the stock return over the next τ days can be calculated as

$$\sigma_{\tau}^{2} = \tau\sigma_{u}^{2} + \left[\sigma_{t+1}^{2} - \sigma_{u}^{2}\right]\sum_{j=1}^{\tau}(\alpha_1 + \beta_1)^{j-1}, \qquad (8)$$

where σ^2_{t+1} is the next-day forecast and $\sigma_u{}^2$ denotes the model's unconditional variance, which, as mentioned before, is given by $\alpha_0 / (1 - (\alpha_1 + \beta_1))$. With $(\alpha_1 + \beta_1) < 1$, equation (8) implies that as the number of periods increases forecasted volatility reverts to the model's unconditional mean volatility. From a volatility prediction point of view the GARCH model is well suited for real-time application. Forecast updates are readily available, either based on the old parameter estimates or re-estimations (partly) based on new observations. Furthermore, one might consider calculating confidence bounds around the volatility forecasts obtained from (8). Although similar in idea, this would, at least theoretically, imply a substantial improvement over the unconditional "volatility cone" approach developed by Burghardt and Lane (1990), which is discussed extensively in section 5.

As an alternative to the GARCH(1,1) model one might choose for Nelson's (1991) EGARCH(1,1) model, where in comparison to the GARCH model the variance equation is replaced by

$$\ln\sigma_t^2 = \alpha_0 + \beta_1 \ln\sigma_{t-1}^2 + \beta_2 \psi_{t-1} + \beta_3(|\psi_{t-1}| - E|\psi_{t-1}|), \tag{9}$$

where $y_t = \varepsilon_t / \sigma_t$ and for a normal conditional distribution $E|y_{t-1}| = (2/p)^{1/2}$. Contrary to the GARCH model, there are no restrictions on the model's parameters necessary to ensure non-negativity of the conditional variances. Instead of making the conditional variance a positive linear combination of positive random variables, the EGARCH model ensures nonnegativity by working with the logarithm of the conditional variance. The above specification of the variance equation links the conditional variance not only to the absolute magnitude of the lagged scaled residual in relation to its mean, but also to the actual sign of this innovation. It is the latter term which allows the conditional variance to respond asymmetrically to changes in the stock price. For selected parameter values there will be a negative relationship between stock returns and volatility, which would be in line with empirical evidence. The GARCH model does not capture this relationship because it links the conditional variance to past squared innovations, implying that there is no role for the sign of past residual returns in the model.

Maximum likelihood estimates of the EGARCH model's parameters may again be obtained by numerical maximization of the log-likelihood function. As with the GARCH model, we may calculate volatility forecasts one day ahead directly from the explicit specification of the model's conditional variance. Volatility forecasts for a period of more than one day can be obtained from the above equation, with implicit products,[6]

$$\sigma_\tau^2 = \sigma_{t+1}^2 + \sum_{k=2}^{\tau} \sigma_t^2 \beta_1^k \exp\left[\beta_1^{k-1}\left(\beta_2 \psi_t + \beta_3(|\psi_t| - \sqrt{2/\pi})\right)\right]$$

$$\exp\left[(\beta_0 - \beta_3\sqrt{2/\pi})\frac{1-\beta_1^k}{1-\beta_1} + \beta_3\beta_1^{k-1}\sqrt{2/\pi} + \frac{1}{2}(\beta_2^2 + \beta_3^2)\frac{1-\beta_1^{2(k-1)}}{1-\beta_1^2}\right]$$

$$\prod_{m\ 0}^{k-2}[F_m(\beta_1,\beta_2,\beta_3) + F_m(\beta_1,-\beta_2,\beta_3)],$$

$$F_m(\beta_1,\beta_2,\beta_3) = \exp[\beta_1^{2m}\beta_2\beta_3]N[\beta_1^m(\beta_2+\beta_3)]$$

[6]See Heynen et al. (1994).

where $N[x]$ denotes the standard normal cumulative distribution function with upper limit of integration x. Although the above equation is substantially more complex than its GARCH(1,1) equivalent, it can again be shown to exhibit clear mean-reversion. As the length of the forecast horizon increases, forecasted variance tends towards the models' unconditional next-day variance, which is given by

$$\sigma_u^2 = \exp\left[\frac{\beta_0 - \beta_3\sqrt{2/\pi}}{1-\beta_1} + \frac{(\beta_2^2+\beta_3^2)}{2(1-\beta_1^2)}\right]\prod_{m=0}^{\infty}[F_m(\beta_1,\beta_2,\beta_3) + F_m(\beta_1,-\beta_2,\beta_3)]. \tag{10}$$

When choosing between different models one should be aware of the danger of "data-snooping", *i.e.* reading too much into regularities which are specific to the sample data which is under examination. In other words, one must distinguish between the model which best summarizes a given data-set on the one hand and the model which best forecasts out-of-sample data on the other. It is perfectly well possible for a single model to fit a given data set very well and at the same time to provide very disappointing out-of-sample forecasts and the other way around. Dimson and Marsh (1990), studying quarterly volatility estimates, suggested that especially more sophisticated volatility forecasting models tend to suffer from this deficiency. From the work of Akgiray (1989) and Pagan and Schwert (1990), however, it appears that this line of criticism does not apply to the family of ARCH models. Akgiray (1989, p. 78), working with daily data on the value-weighted CRSP index over the period 1963-1986, concluded, using various error statistics, that in out-of-sample predicting monthly volatility "GARCH forecasts constitute substantial improvement over the traditional forecasts." The regression results in Day and Lewis (1990) on weekly S&P 100 volatilities over the period 1983-1989 suggest that there is little difference in forecast efficiency between GARCH and EGARCH forecasts. In interpreting these results, however, one should be aware of the fact that the latter conclusions are based on a single short-term forecast horizon. Moreover, as goes for all empirical results, they may not be valid for other assets.

We studied the differences between the random walk predictor (1) and the GARCH(1,1) predictor (8) in forecasting S&P 500 volatility over non-overlapping forecast horizons ranging from 5 to 100 trading days. Both models were estimated on daily return data over the period 1980-1987.[7] Forecast evaluation was done over the period 1988-1992 using the median error (Me), the median squared error (Mse), the median absolute error (Mae) and the median absolute percentage error (Mape). Since predictor (2) is based on the assumption that volatility is constant, it yields the same

[7]Actually, instead of the original S&P 500 return series, estimation was done on the residuals of an AR(1) specification of the S&P 500 returns. This procedure was used to eliminate possible first-order autocorrelation in the original series.

forecast for every period. Regression of realized volatility on its prediction is therefore not possible. To facilitate comparison, before calculating the above statistics all errors were expressed on an annual basis and multiplied by 100. The evaluation results can be found in table 1.

	S&P 500 Index Volatility Forecast Efficiency							
	Random Walk				GARCH (1,1)			
Horizon	Me	Mse	Mae	Mape	Me	Mse	Mae	Mape
5	5.21	0.35	5.92	42.98	2.23	0.16	4.01	27.93
10	4.78	0.31	5.59	37.48	2.23	0.12	3.49	24.25
15	4.65	0.29	5.4	38.24	2.16	0.12	3.46	26.09
20	4.36	0.27	5.21	33.46	2.18	0.08	2.9	22.04
25	4.96	0.27	5.23	38.78	2.25	0.08	2.74	19.84
30	5.42	0.3	5.47	42.56	2.76	0.11	3.32	25.5
35	3.67	0.2	4.48	30.63	1.82	0.08	2.85	21.91
40	3.23	0.17	4.09	29.09	2.55	0.09	2.94	21.01
45	3.69	0.21	4.61	27.67	2.49	0.14	3.77	27.07
50	4.03	0.23	4.8	30.72	2.87	0.14	3.68	22.9
55	3.86	0.15	3.89	27.03	2.14	0.08	2.81	15.74
60	3.99	0.18	4.24	28.24	2.48	0.1	3.27	17.82
65	4.06	0.2	4.47	28.88	2	0.09	2.96	16.35
70	4.26	0.18	4.26	30.68	2.66	0.07	2.72	19.16
75	4.34	0.21	4.57	31.45	3.31	0.15	3.94	24.65
80	2.79	0.24	4.87	21.27	3.24	0.12	3.43	21.1
85	3.33	0.2	4.42	22.51	1.97	0.06	2.53	13.44
90	3	0.15	3.83	21.92	2.49	0.1	3.05	18.15
95	2.79	0.13	3.56	18.16	1.76	0.1	3.15	15.59
100	3.55	0.13	3.55	24.32	2.98	0.09	2.98	20.39

From table 1 we see that both predictors tend to produce more accurate forecasts as the forecast horizon becomes longer. More important, we see that, irrespective of the forecast horizon, the GARCH predictor is more efficient than the random walk predictor. This difference in forecast efficiency is most pronounced for shorter horizons. This is plausible. The GARCH predictor allows for and takes account of changes in volatility around the unconditional mean volatility, while the random walk predictor does not. When the GARCH(1,1) model fits the data better than the random walk model (as it does), this shows up most clearly in the quality of the short-term forecasts.

Apart from the ARCH-type models, there are a number of other types of models which might provide an adequate (or even better) description of stock return behaviour and which might therefore also be used to forecast volatility. De Gooijer (1989), for example, found that over the period 1977-1978 the daily stock returns of a number of individual stocks were adequately modeled by a bilinear model.[8] As discussed in Franses (1991), bilinear models may generate return series which are very similar to those generated by ARCH-type models. As a result successful discrimination may be difficult. For brevity, we do not elaborate on these matters any further and limit ourselves to ARCH-type models on which there is nowadays a rich theoretical as well as empirical body of literature available.

All techniques discussed so far are parametric in nature. It is still very much an open question whether non-parametric forecasts or combinations of parametric and non-parametric forecasts will yield significant improvements in forecasting power. A

[8]See De Gooijer and Kumar (1992) for details.

first step in this direction can be found in Pagan and Schwert (1990), who studied the performance of non-parametric kernel and flexible Fourier forecasts over the periods 1900-1925 and 1926-1937.

In the above ARCH-type models return variance changes as a deterministic function of past returns. To change this, one might consider adding a stochastic error term to the variance equation. Stochastic variance models like this can be found in the option pricing models of, for example, Hull and White (1987), Scott (1987, 1991), Wiggins (1987), Chesney and Scott (1989) and Melino and Turnbull (1990). The general approach in these papers is to value options on assets with mean reverting stochastic volatility by treating volatility as one of the state variables and assuming that there is no risk premium for bearing volatility risk or, equivalently, that volatility is uncorrelated with aggregate consumption. The prices obtained in this way generally strongly depend on the level of correlation between the stock price and volatility and the extent to which the option is in-the-money or out-of-the-money. When the former correlation is positive the Black and Scholes (1973) model (with volatility equal to its initial value) tends to underprice out-of-the-money options and to overprice in-the-money options. When there is negative correlation the reverse is true.

Among the volatility models that gained most popularity in the option pricing literature is the continuous time stochastic volatility model of Hull and White (1987), given by

$$d\ln\sigma_t^2 = (\gamma_0 + \gamma_1 \ln\sigma_t^2)dt + \theta\, dW_t,$$

where W_t is a Wiener process. In comparison to the Black and Scholes (1973) model, introducing the above volatility process doubles the number of sources of risk in the economy. From a theoretical point of view this means that, unless we introduce additional assets which can be used to hedge the additional source of risk, like options, we are now confronted with an incomplete market. In order to make empirical parameter estimates, discrete time observations will have to be used. Therefore, it is necessary to specify a discrete time version of the stochastic volatility model. A natural candidate is given by the AR(1) specification.

Nelson (1990) showed that an attractive alternative to the discrete time AR(1) approximation which in the continuous time limit also converges to the specified continuous time version is given by the EGARCH(1,1) model. However, Dassios (1992) proved that although both the EGARCH(1,1) model and the previously specified AR(1) model converge in the continuous time limit to the Hull and White (1987) model, the AR(1) model converges at a more rapid rate.

Unlike the (E)GARCH model, for the stochastic volatility model it is not possible to specify an analytic expression for the loglikelihood. Although it is possible to use simulation methods to compute maximum likelihood parameter estimates, these methods have the disadvantage to be computationally very elaborate. A more attractive approach to obtain maximum likelihood parameter estimates is provided by the

Kalman filter technique. A third alternative would be the use of generalized method of moments, as is done, for example, in Melino and Turnbull (1990). Ruiz (1993), however, showed that for the kind of parameter values likely to arise in practice, maximum likelihood estimation using the Kalman filter is more efficient than generalized method of moments estimation.

For a given set of parameters estimates, the more-than-one-day volatility forecast from the discrete time stochastic volatility model is given by[9]

$$\sigma_\tau^2 = \sigma_u^2 \sum_{k\,1}^{\tau} (\sigma_t^2)^{\beta_1^k} \exp\left(\frac{-\beta_0 \beta_1^k}{1-\beta_1}\right) \exp\left(-\frac{1}{2}\frac{\sigma_\eta^2 \beta_1^{2k}}{1-\beta_1^2}\right),$$

where the unconditional next-day variance $\sigma_u{}^2$ is given by

$$\sigma_u^2 = \exp\left(\frac{\beta_0}{1-\beta_1}\right) \exp\left(\tfrac{1}{2}\right).$$

Again, the long-term volatility forecast tends towards the unconditional volatility σ_u, whereas the short-term volatility prediction tends towards the short-term volatility σ_t.

---

[9]See Heynen and Kat (1994).

Implied Volatility

Until now we have concentrated on the use of historical stock prices in forecasting volatility. There are, however, numerous other sources of information which can be used. One of these is the set of historical and current option prices, which can be used to calculate what is known as "implied volatility". The implied volatility of an option is that value of volatility which, when used as an input to an option pricing model, produces a theoretical value equal to the option's market price. It is a transformation of the asset's price,[10] which intuitively can be interpreted as the market's opinion on volatility,

The Calculation of Implied Volatility

For European call options on a non-dividend paying stock, implied volatility is typically calculated from the well-known Black and Scholes (1973) option pricing formula. Insertion of the stock price *S*, the option's exercise price *X*, its remaining time to maturity *T-t*, the interest rate *r* and the market value of the option itself in the Black and Scholes formula gives (if it exists) a unique volatility figure, since the partial derivative of the call price with respect to volatility is positive and monotonic. This procedure is illustrated by the following example. The Black and Scholes formula is given by

$$c = SN(d_1) - X e^{-r(T-t)} N(d_2),$$

[10]In practice, option traders often price options in terms of volatility instead of dollars.

where

$$d_1 = \frac{\ln(S / X) + (r + \sigma^2 / 2)(T - t)}{\sigma\sqrt{T - t}},$$

$$d_2 = d_1 - \sigma\sqrt{T - t},$$

and $N(x)$ is the standard normal cumulative probability density function. Suppose that the market price of a call on an underlying stock is \$1.875, the stock price is \$21, the option's exercise price is \$20, the interest rate is 10% and the option's remaining time to maturity is 3 months. The option's implied volatility then, is defined as the value of s for which, when the above values are inserted in the Black and Scholes formula, the option's price is equal to \$1.875.

Because the Black and Scholes formula can not be inverted with respect to the variable σ, no explicit formula for the implied volatility exists. Fortunately, there are a number of numerical approximation procedures available to calculate the implied volatility for given values of c, S, $T-t$, X and r with any desired accuracy. In the appendix we discuss some of these numerical approximation procedures. The most popular method is the so-called Newton-Raphson technique, which typically locates the implied volatility with high accuracy within a few iteration steps. For the above example the Newton-Raphson technique gives in three iteration steps an accurate approximation for the implied volatility of \$0.235 (23.5% annually).

The Black and Scholes formula is only valid for European options on non-dividend paying stocks. When the underlying stock does pay dividends, the Black and Scholes formula has to be corrected for these dividends by lowering the stock price with the discounted value of all future dividends paid during the life of the option. When the relevant option is American-style instead of European-style we need another model. In this case one can use the binomial model developed by Cox, Ross and Rubinstein (1979), which can easily be adapted to value American call options on dividend paying stocks. This model, with an application to S&P 100 index options, is discussed in Harvey and Whaley (1991). Using this model, implied volatilities can be calculated using the bisection method which is discussed in the appendix.

The Black and Scholes model is based on the assumption that the volatility of the underlying stock return is known and constant during the relevant option's lifetime. However, in general implied volatilities calculated from option market prices are biased in the sense that implied volatilities will typically be different for options with different exercise prices and times to maturities. The presence of these biases can be interpreted as evidence that the assumption of constant underlying asset return volatility is not correct. Biases in calculated implied volatilities can, however, also be the result of measurement errors in the Black and Scholes input parameters. It can be shown that the parameter with respect to which the calculation of implied volatility is most sensitive is the call price itself. Concerning the influence of measurement errors, three points should be noted.

- First, there is the problem of the non-linearity of the Black and Scholes formula. As a result of this non-linearity, an unbiased estimate of the call price will in general not produce an unbiased estimate for the implied volatility.[11] Possible price measurement errors, caused by the bid-ask spread or the presence of tick rules, may create additional biases since they are filtered through a non-linear formula. Fortunately, as shown by Feinstein (1989a), for an at-the-money option the Black and Scholes formula is well approximated by a function that is linear in terms of volatility. This implies that for at-the money option prices unbiased estimates of the option price turn into unbiased estimates for the implied volatility. This means that an estimate of implied volatility is best obtained from at-the-money options. Additionally, the latter contracts are often the most liquid as well as the most sensitive to volatility, which makes them especially good candidates to extract the market's knowledge on volatility from.

---

[11]See Butler and Schachter (1986).

- Second, we have the problem of non-simultaneity. One should take care that the prices of both the option and the underlying stock are observed at the same moment in time. If this is not the case, implied volatility calculations may be seriously distorted. We might therefore consider using an average value over a number of consecutive observations, whether it be daily or transactions data. This approach may also be used to deal with the effects of other microstructural constraints, like the bid-ask spread and tick rules. Using transactions data on individual stocks, Brenner and Galai (1981) showed that there may be significant differences between the implied volatility based on the last transaction price of the day and the average implied volatility for that same day. A similar conclusion for S&P 100 index options was reached by Harvey and Whaley (1991).

- Third, since many market makers in index options generally hedge their inventory positions with futures contracts, index options tend to trade off the index futures instead of the index itself. The most important reason for this is the fact that it is often easier as well as cheaper to trade futures than it is to trade the underlying index. As a result, futures mispricing also shows up in option prices, leading to a distorted implied volatility estimate. We might solve this problem by using Black's (1976) model to calculate implied volatility from the futures price instead of the underlying asset's cash price. As an alternative we could also limit our calculations to those moments when the futures seem fairly priced. Another reason to calculate implied volatility from options on index futures instead of options on the index itself is the fact that the futures contract is being traded as a single instrument while the index is not. The futures price can therefore be expected to reflect new information quicker than the index itself, since the latter is based on last transaction prices instead of bid-ask prices.

THE TERM STRUCTURE OF IMPLIED VOLATILITIES

As mentioned, the Black and Scholes formula is based on the assumption that volatility is constant. If this assumption were true, implied volatilities for the same underlying asset would not differ across different exercise prices and time to maturities. In practice, however, this is not the case and one is confronted with "mispricings" in comparison to Black and Scholes prices. Implied volatilities vary across times to maturities, thereby implying the existence of what is sometimes called a "term structure of implied volatilities". This means that one has to be very careful in interpreting implied volatility estimates. Implied volatility calculated from a given option price only provides information about volatility over that option's remaining time to maturity as seen from the moment the calculation was made. Hull and White (1987) developed an option pricing model for the case that the underlying asset return volatility is stochastic. Building on this model, Feinstein (1989b) showed that given the assumption that options are correctly valued by the Hull and White (1987) model, the implied volatility calculated from an at-the-money option via the Black and Scholes formula should be an unbiased estimate of the best volatility forecast available over the remaining time to maturity of the option. Since the time to maturity of most actively traded options is relatively short, it will generally not be possible to predict volatility using implied volatility over periods longer than three to six months without making additional assumptions.

When traders are confronted with consecutive buy and sell orders, the hedging of the inventory position becomes a complicated dynamic process where knowledge of the behaviour of implied volatilities is of great importance. The relation between short and longer term implied volatilities is of particular interest when hedging long term options using short term options. Heynen et al. (1994) developed different models for the dynamics of the term structure of implied volatilities for Dutch EOE index options. They found that the relationship between short and longer term near-the-money implied volatilities was best described by the term structure relationship which is implied by an EGARCH(1,1) process for the underlying index return. From this process the term structure of implied volatilities can be derived as,[12]

$$[\ln \sigma^2_{imp}(t,T_1) - \ln \sigma^2_u] = \frac{T_2}{T_1}\frac{(1-\beta_1^{T_1})}{(1-\beta_1^{T_2})}[\ln \sigma^2_{imp}(t,T_2) - \ln \sigma^2_u] \tag{11}$$

[12]In order to derive relation (11) additional information is needed about how options are priced in the presence of conditional heteroskedasticity. See, for example, Duan (1993).

where $\sigma^{imp}(t,T_1)$ is the near-the-money (±7.5% in- or out-of-the-money) implied volatility of an option with time to maturity T_1, σ^{u} is the unconditional or long term volatility which is specified by equation (10) and b_1 is taken from (9). From the formula it can be inferred that longer term near-the-money implied volatilities tend to regress to the long term volatility level of the underlying EGARCH(1,1) process. From the fact that the EGARCH(1,1) process is very successful in adequately describing asset return volatility, it may be expected that relation (11) can also be applied to other option price series. Relation (11) can also be useful for the pricing of near-the-money long term options relative to short term options.

THE SMILE EFFECT

Implied volatilities calculated from option market prices will typically be different for options with different exercise prices. The most prominent example of such exercise price implied volatility bias, is the so-called "smile effect," *i.e.* the tendency that for a specific time to maturity in-the-money and out-of-the-money implied volatilities are larger than at-the-money implied volatilities. For index options this was observed by Sheikh (1991), Canina and Figlewski (1993) and Heynen (1994). Taylor and Xu (1994) observed the same phenomenon for currency options. As was mentioned earlier, knowledge of these implied volatility biases is especially useful for obtaining correct hedge ratios. In this context, the stability of these biases through time is of particular interest. Furthermore, if these biases are not stable, it becomes important what underlying economic factors cause this instability.

Sheikh (1991), who studied the transaction prices of call options on the S&P 100 from July 1983 to December 1985, observed significant smile patterns in two of the three subperiods in his sample. He suggested that the observed biases corresponded to the biases that can be expected to arise when option prices are properly described by the stochastic volatility model of Hull and White (1987). Sheikh's results were confirmed by Canina and Figlewski (1993), who studied the closing prices of call options on the S&P 100 index from March 1983 to March 1987. They also observed smile patterns, with deep-in-the-money calls having much higher implied volatilities than at-the-money calls. However, they showed that a substantial amount of the upward bias in deep-in-the-money implied volatilities resulted from the removal from their sample of call prices that violated the Merton (1973) lower arbitrage boundary. Taylor and Xu (1994), who studied the smile effect observed for currency options traded at the Philadelphia Stock Exchange from November 1984 to January 1992, attempted to explain the observed bias using the Hull and White (1987) model. They constructed a theoretical quadratic series expansion of the smile effect and compared this model with the observed patterns. Although the observations supported the theoretical predictions, the observed smile patterns were approximately twice as large as those implied by the theoretical model. Finally, Heynen (1994) studied implied volatility patterns in transactions prices and quotes of calls on the Dutch EOE index over the period from January 1989 to October 1989. He observed significant smile patterns for short as well as long times to maturity. Heynen tested the hypothesis that the observed bias can be explained by a certain class of alternative option valuation models. The latter hypothesis was rejected for the whole sample under consideration, as the observed bias for long term options was too persistent in comparison to what would have been expected from theoretical considerations. Heynen developed an alternative explanation by studying the additional costs that are involved in hedging options in the presence of stochastic volatility. From this study he derived theoretical upper and lower no-arbitrage boundaries between which observed transaction prices should fall with high probability. It was shown that for different times to maturity there is a striking similarity between the shape of the observed smile patterns and the shape of these calculated upper boundaries. Further analysis showed that for the option class under consideration there is a net demand for in-the-money and out-of-the-money options for short as well as longer times to maturity. This supports the result that observed transaction prices tend to settle at the calculated upper boundary.

From the above it can be concluded that the observed exercise price bias in implied volatilities cannot always be explained by a more sophisticated option valuation model. The observation of varying asset return volatility on the one hand and the presence of market imperfections such as transaction costs and discontinuous trading on the other hand, imply that a no-arbitrage option price is not uniquely defined. At best one can specify price intervals between which transactions will occur with high probability. It is the study of these price intervals which can help us develop knowledge about observed implied volatility biases.

THE FORECAST PERFORMANCE OF IMPLIED VOLATILITY

The conjecture that implied volatility can be used as a forecast of the volatility over the remaining time to maturity of the option it was calculated from has also been established empirically. Comparing the forecast efficiency of at-the-money implied volatilities from call options on S&P 500 futures over the period 1983-1988 with that of the random walk estimator using the mean squared and the mean absolute error, Feinstein (1989b, p. 34) found that implied volatility "emerged as the more efficient forecast measure." As was to be expected, over longer and medium term horizons, averaging the implied volatilities from at-the-money options yielded an even better predictor. Both observations can also be found in a much earlier study on individual stock return volatility over the period 1975-1977 by Beckers (1978), who, using regression analysis, noted that "the implicit standard deviation is a better predictor of future stock price volatility than past standard deviations."[13] Interestingly, the opposite conclusion was reached by Canina and Figlewski (1993) who, studying implied

[13]Beckers (1978, p. 28).

volatilities from S&P 100 calls over the period 1983-1987, found that "implied volatility is a less accurate forecast than historical volatility."[14] Clearly, these results deserve further study. As to the characteristics of implied volatility as a rational forecast, most studies found that high (low) volatility forecasts are generally too high (low). This implies that it is possible to improve these forecasts by multiplying them with a factor less than one and then adding a constant. The actual forces behind this phenomenon, however, are still an unsolved issue. A regression comparison of the efficiency of implied volatilities from S&P 100 calls over the period 1983-1989 and GARCH and EGARCH volatility forecasts can be found in Day and Lewis (1990). From their results it may be concluded that the efficiency of these three predictors is more or less similar.

Those who think that the implied volatilities from options which are not at-the-money also contain valuable information may consider calculating the implied volatility for all options of a given maturity on a given underlying value and consolidate these into a single volatility forecast. This approach may also be used to diversify noise believed to be present in all implied volatilities. The easiest way to do this is to compute their weighted average

$$\sigma_{imp} = \sum_{j=1}^{J} \left(\frac{w_j}{\sum_j w_j} \right) \sigma_{imp}(X_j),$$

[14]Canina and Figlewski (1993, p. 672).

where w_j is the weight that is given to call j and J is the total number of available calls with a given time to maturity on the underlying stock. $\sigma^{imp}(X_j)$ is the implied volatility of an option with exercise price X_j. Apart from weighting equally, as in Schmalensee and Trippi (1978) and Patell and Wolfson (1979), the weights may be chosen equal to, for example, the partial deriviatives of the theoretical Black and Scholes price with respect to volatility. This emphasizes at-the-money options at the cost of out-of-the-money and in-the-money options. This weighting scheme was first used by Latane and Rendleman (1976). On the other hand, Chiras and Manaster (1978) used an average, weighted by the elasticity of the option's price with respect to volatility. As shown by Day and Lewis (1988) the latter weighting scheme gives more weight to out-of-the-money options.[15] Another technique is to minimize the weighted sum of the (squared, absolute or relative) deviations between the option's market values and their corresponding Black and Scholes values as a function of the implied volatility. More specifically, one searches for the single volatility estimate across all options of a given maturity on a given underlying asset value, which minimizes the weighted sum of the deviations of the market values from their corresponding theoretical values based on that volatility. Implicitly this may give more weight to at-the-money options, since these option prices are specifically sensitive to volatility. Examples of this approach can

---

[15]Some theoretical background for these weighting schemes can be found in Rahman and Kryzanowski (1986).

be found in Beckers (1978) and Whaley (1982). Day and Lewis (1988) extended this procedure by weighting each observation in proportion to the day's total trading volume as a percentage of the total trading volume of its expiration series. Their results show that this places the largest weight on those options which are either at-the-money or one strike price out-of-the-money. In addition, the scheme in a way minimizes the extent to which the results are affected by non-synchronous trading or the bid-ask spread by giving little weight to thinly traded options.

Beckers (1978) studied the efficiency of various of the implied volatility predictors discussed previously, using regression analysis and individual stock option data from 1975-1976. He concluded that the implied volatility of a single at-the-money option "had more predictive power than any weighting scheme could give."[16] The same result can also be found in Feinstein (1989b, p. 43), who concluded that "averaging among the multiple contracts with different strike prices appeared to offer little advantage over relying on at-the-money call options." This means that when it comes to using implied volatility for the prediction of future volatility, the most efficient longer term forecast will be an intertemporal average of a number of consecutive at-the-money implieds, while for shorter horizons, since in that case forecast interval mismatch may overrule any other errors, one should use the implied volatility of a single at-the-money call option as predictor.

---

[16]Beckers (1978, p. 19).

Apart from the fact that implied volatilities from different options on the same stock often differ across expiration dates and exercise prices, research has discovered some other characteristics as well. Merville and Pieptea (1989) showed the existence of a common marketwide volatility factor, giving rise to relatively high correlation among implied stock volatilities. A similar result for cash volatilities can be found in Schwert and Seguin (1990). Merville and Pieptea (1989) and Stein (1989) also showed that implied volatilities tend to regress to their mean. Again, the same phenomenon can also be found in cash volatilities and is in line with the information-based volatility model developed by Bookstaber and Pomerantz (1989). A third well-known observed regularity is the inverse relation between changes in stock prices and changes in their corresponding volatilities, which can, for example, be found in Christie (1982) and Brenner and Galai (1981). This effect forms the basis of the EGARCH model which was discussed previously. As part of his option pricing service, Fischer Black developed a volatility prediction rule, which is described in detail in Cox and Rubinstein (1985), which combines the previously discussed observations. The performance of this predictor was studied by Beckers (1978) on individual stock option data over the period 1975-1977. This study showed that in terms of R^2, Black's predictor outperformed all the volatility measures we discussed previously. This should not come as too much of a surprise, since it uses valuable additional information. More recent tests of Black's prediction rule are, as far as we know, not available.

THE IMPLIED VOLATILITY CONE.

In section 3 we mentioned that in an efficient options market the implied volatility of an at-the-money option can intuitively be interpreted as the market's forecast of the average volatility over the remaining time to maturity of the option. This market forecast can be compared with a volatility forecast based on historical stock returns. If one assumes that a forecast based on historical stock returns outperforms the market's forecast, then the difference between both forecasts can be interpreted as over- or undervaluation of the option. More specifically, if the implied volatility is significantly higher (lower) than the volatility forecast based on historical returns this implies that the option is overvalued (undervalued). In the case of overvaluation (undervaluation) this can be considered as a sell (buy) signal.[17]

In order to make a comparison between implied volatilities and volatility forecasts based on historical returns, the significance of these volatility forecasts has to be determined. This can be done by estimating historical volatilities over different time intervals (for example 1-month, 3-month, 6-month, 1-year and 2-year volatilities) during a period preceding the period over which we want to compare volatility forecasts with implied volatilities. By doing so, we obtain insight in the degree in which, for example, 1-month or 9-month volatility has varied historically. This variation determines the

---

[17]Most of this section is based on Burghardt and Lane (1990).

significance interval of volatility forecasts in a future period. Through comparison of the implied volatilities in this future period with the estimated significance interval one can then make a statement about possible over- or undervaluation of the option considered.

APPENDIX

NUMERICAL PROCEDURES TO COMPUTE IMPLIED VOLATILITY

In this appendix we discuss two numerical procedures to calculate the implied volatility of an European call or put option. The first method is a trial-and-error procedure. The second method is the so-called Newton-Raphson procedure. The advantage of the Newton-Raphson method over the trial-and-error procedure is that generally the correct value can be found with only a few iteration steps.

The Bisection Method. This method can be illustrated by the following example. Given the Black and Scholes valuation formula for European calls,

$$c = SN(d_1) - X e^{-r(T-t)} N(d_2)$$

where

$$d_1 = \frac{\ln(S / X) + (r + \sigma^2 / 2)(T - t)}{\sigma\sqrt{T - t}}$$

$$d_2 = d_1 - \sigma\sqrt{T - t}$$

and c=1.875, S=21, X=20, r=0.1 and T-t=0.25, we must determine the value for σ for which the Black and Scholes price is equal to \$1.875. For a starting value of σ=0.20, the Black and Scholes price is equal to 1.76. Because this value is too low and because the Black and Scholes formula is an increasing function of σ, we proceed with a higher value for σ. With σ=0.30\$ we have c=2.10. From this result it can be concluded that the correct value for σ is between 0.20 and 0.30. This procedure can be repeated using the trial σ=0.25. In this case the value for c is also too high, from which can be inferred that the true value for σ must be between 0.20 and 0.25. Every time the procedure is repeated the interval which contains the correct value for σ is halved such that σ can be determined with any desired accuracy. For the above example the implied volatility is 0.235 (23.5% annually). For European puts the same method can be used. In this case, of course, the Black and Scholes formula for European puts has to used. For European calls and puts on stocks which pay one or more dividends during the remaining time to maturity of the option, the bisection method can also be used. In that case, however, one should correct the Black and Scholes formula for dividends by subtracting the discounted value of all future dividend payments before expiration from the value of the stock price. For American calls and puts on dividend paying stocks no closed-form formulas exist. In that case the implied volatility should be calculated from the binomial Cox, Ross and Rubinstein (1979) model.

The Newton-Raphson Method. The Newton-Raphsonmethod is an iterative procedure with which an accurate estimate for the implied volatility can be calculated in only a few iteration steps. The Newton-Raphson method uses the first order partial derivative of the Black and Scholes price with respect to volatility. The iteration scheme is given by,

$$\sigma_{i+1} = \sigma_i - \frac{c(\sigma_i)}{c'(\sigma_i)}$$

In this iteration scheme σ_i and σ_{i+1} denote respectively the given value and the subsequently calculated value for the estimation of the implied volatility, c is the market price of the option, $c(\sigma_i)$ is the Black and Scholes price given σ_i . $c'(\sigma_i)$ is the first order partial derivative with respect to σ ($\partial c/\partial s$) calculated given σ_i . Given a starting value for σ, using the above scheme one can calculate an estimate for the implied volatility with increasing accuracy. The rate of convergence for this procedure is determined by the choice of the starting value σ_0 . A common choice is given by σ_0=0.20 which guarantees convergence to the correct implied volatility in two or three iteration steps. For European calls and puts the first order partial derivative of the Black and Scholes price with respect to the variable σ (this derivative is sometimes also referred to as the "vega" of the option) is given by

$$\partial c / \partial \sigma = S\sqrt{T-t}\,\frac{1}{\sqrt{2\pi}}e^{-d_1^2/2}.$$

where d_1 is given by

$$d_1 = \frac{\ln(S/X) + (r + \sigma^2/2)(T-t)}{\sigma\sqrt{T-t}}.$$

The iteration scheme can also be used for European calls and puts on dividend paying stocks. In this case, however, the Black and Scholes formula and vega have to be corrected for dividends. For American calls and puts the above method cannot be applied because there are no analytic formulas available. In this case one has to use the bisection method or a variant on the Newton-Raphson method, the so-called Newton chord, or "secant', method. For this method the previous iteration scheme can be used, where the partial derivative is replaced by the differential quotient of the theoretical option price with respect to s. For the Newton chord method the iteration scheme is given by

$$\sigma_{i+1} = \sigma_i - c(\sigma_i)\frac{\sigma_{i-1} - \sigma_i}{c(\sigma_{i-1}) - (\sigma_i)}.$$

For this method two starting values for s are required. It should be noted that for each subsequent iteration step only one theoretical option price for s_i has to be calculated, whereas for the Newton-Raphson procedure the theoretical option price as well as the first order partial derivative for σ^i have to be calculated. So, the Newton chord method *may* be computationally more efficient than the Newton-Raphson method and has the advantage that it can also be applied in those cases where no analytic formula is available; the actual improvement in efficiency over the generic Newton-Raphson approach is not, however, guarenteed, since the chord method converges with order 1.6 whilst standard Newton-Raphson converges quadratically for all but the most pathological of cases.

REFERENCES

Akgiray, V. (1989) "Conditional Heteroskedasticity in Time Series of Stock Returns: Evidence and Forecasts," *Journal of Business 62*, pp. 55-80.

Ball, C.A. (1988) Estimation Bias Induced by Discrete Security Prices, *Journal of Finance 43*, pp. 841-865.

Ball, C.A. and W.N. Torous (1984) "The Maximum Likelihood Estimation of Security Price Volatility: Theory, Evidence and Application to Option Pricing," *Journal of Business 57*, pp. 97-112.

Beckers, C.E. (1978) "Variance Prediction: An Empirical Study, University of California Berkeley, Graduate School of Business Administration, Research Program in Finance Working Paper No. 83.

Beckers, C.E. (1983) Variances of Security Price Returns Based on High, Low, and Closing Prices," *Journal of Business 56*, pp. 97-112.

Berndt, E.K., B.H. Hall, R.E. Hall and J.A. Hausman (1974) "Estimation Inference in Nonlinear Structural Models, " *Annals of Economic and Social Measurement 4*, pp. 653-665.

Black, F. (1976) "The Pricing of Commodity Contracts," *Journal of Financial Economics 3*, pp. 167-179.

Black, F. and M.S. Scholes (1973) "The Pricing of Options and Corporate Liabilities," *Journal of Political Economy, 3*, pp. 637-654.

Bollerslev, T. (1986) "Generalized Autoregressive Conditional Heteroskedasticity," *Journal of Econometrics 31*, pp. 307-327.

Bollerslev, T. (1987) "A Conditionally Heteroskedastic Time Series Model for Speculative Prices and Rates of Return," *Review of Economics and Statistics 59*, pp. 542-547.

Bollerslev, T., R.Y. Chou and K.F. Kroner (1992) "ARCH Modeling in Finance: A Review of the Theory and Empirical Evidence," *Journal of Econometrics 52*, pp. 5-60.

Bookstaber, R.M. and S. Pomerantz (1989) "An Information-Based Model of Market Volatility," *Financial Analysts Journal, November-December*, pp. 37-46.

Brenner, M. and D. Galai (1981) "The Properties of the Estimated Risk of Common Stocks Implied by Option Prices, University of California, Berkeley, Graduate School of Business Administration, Research Program in Finance, Working Paper No. 112.

Burghardt, G. and M. Lane (1990) "How to Tell if Options are Cheap," *Journal of Portfolio Management, Winter*, pp. 72-78.

Butler, J.S. and B. Schachter (1986) "Unbiased Estimation of the Black-Scholes Formula," *Journal of Financial Economics 15*, pp. 341-357.

Canina, L. and S. Figlewski (1993) "The Information Content of Implied Volatility," *Review of Financial Studies, Vol. 6, No. 3*, pp. 659-681.

Chesney, M. and L.O. Scott (1989) "Pricing European Currency Options: A Comparison of the Modified Black-Scholes Model and a Random Variance Model," *Journal of Financial and Quantitative Analysis 24*, pp. 267-284.

Chiras, D.P. and S. Manaster (1978) "The Informational Content of Option Prices and a Test of Market Efficiency," *Journal of Financial Economics 6*, pp. 213-234.

Cho, D.C. and E.W. Frees (1988) "Estimating the Volatility of Discrete Stock Prices," *Journal of Finance 43*, pp. 451-466.

Choi, J.Y. and K. Shastri (1989) "Bid-Ask Spreads and Volatility Estimates," *Journal of Banking and Finance 13*, pp. 207-219.

Chou, R.Y. (1988) "Volatility Persistence and Stock Valuations: Some Empirical Evidence Using GARCH," *Journal of Applied Econometrics 3*, pp. 279-294.

Christie, A.A. (1982) "The Stochastic Behaviour of Common Stock Variances," *Journal of Financial Economics 10*, pp.407-432.

Cox, J.C. and M. Rubinstein (1985) *Options Markets*, Prentice-Hall.

Cox, J.C., S.A. Ross and M. Rubinstein (1979) "Option Pricing: A Simplified Approach," *Journal of Financial Economics 7*, pp. 229-263.

Dassios, A. (1992). "Asymtotic Approximations to Stochastic Variance Models," Discussion Paper London School of Economics.

Day, T.E. and C.M. Lewis (1988) "The Behaviour of the Volatility Implicit in the Prices of Stock Index Options," *Journal of Financial Economics 22*, pp. 103-122.

Day, T.E. and C.M. Lewis (1990) "Stock Market Volatility and the Information Content of Stock Index Options," *Journal of Econometrics 52*, pp. 267-287.

De Gooijer, J.G. (1989) "Testing Non-Linearities in World Stock Market Prices," *Economics Letters 31*, pp. 31-35.

De Gooijer, J.G. and K. Kumar (1992) "Some Recent Developments in Non-Linear Time Series Modelling, Testing and Forecasting," *International Journal of Forecasting 8*, pp. 135-156.

Dimson, E. and P. Marsh (1990) "Volatility Forecasting without Data-Snooping," *Journal of Banking and Finance 14*, pp. 399-421.

Duan, J.C. (1993) "The GARCH Option Pricing Model," forthcoming in *Mathematical Finance*.

Engle, R.F. (1982) "Autoregressive Conditional Heteroscedasticity with Estimates of the Variance of United Kingdom Inflation," *Econometrica 50*, pp. 987-1007.

Engle, R.F. and T. Bollerslev (1986) "Modelling the Persistence of Conditional Variances," *Econometric Reviews 5*, pp. 1-50.

Engle, R.F., D.M. Lilien and R.P. Robins (1987) "Estimating Time Varying Risk Premia in the Term Structure: the ARCH-M Model," *Econometrica 55*, pp. 391-407.

Feinstein, S. (1989a) "The Black-Scholes Formula is Nearly Linear in σ for at-the-money Options; Therefore Implied Volatilities from at-the-money Options are Virtually Unbiased," Working Paper, Boston University.

Feinstein, S. (1989b) "The Hull and White Implied Volatility: A Theoretical and Empirical Investigation of a Volatility Forecast Implied by the Hull and White Stochastic Volatility Option Pricing Model," Working Paper Boston University.

Franses, P.H. (1991) "Some Similarities Between GARCH and Bilinear Time Series Models," Working Paper Erasmus University Roterdam.

French, K.R. and R. Roll (1986) "Stock Return Variances: The Arrival of Information and the Reaction of Traders," *Journal of Financial Economics 17*, pp. 5-26.

French, K.R., G.W. Schwert and R.F. Stambaugh (1987) "Expected Stock Returns and Volatility," *Journal of Financial Economics 19*, pp. 3-29.

Garman, M.B. and M.J. Klass (1980) "On the Estimation of Security Price Volatilities from Historical Data," *Journal of Business 53*, pp. 67-78.

Geske, R. and W. Torous (1991) "Volatility Estimation for Option Pricing and Risk Control," Paper presented at the 2nd International Conference of the Centre for Research in Finance, IMI Group, Rome.

Granger, C.W.J. (1980) *Forecasting in Business and Economics*, Academic Press.

Harvey, C.R. and R.E. Whaley (1991) "S&P 100 Index Option Volatility," *The Journal of Finance 4*, pp.1551-1561.

Heynen, R.C. (1994 "An Empirical Investigation of Observed Smile Patterns," forthcoming in *The Review of Futures Markets*.

Heynen, R.C. and H.M. Kat (1994) "Volatility Prediction: A Comparison of the Stochastic Volatility, GARCH(1,1) and EGARCH(1,1) Model," Paper presented at the 14th AMEX Options and Derivatives Colloquium, New York.

Heynen, R.C., A. Kemna and T. Vorst (1994) "Analysis of the Term Structure of Implied Volatilities," *Journal of Financial and Quantitative Analysis*.

Hull, J.C. and A. White (1987) "The Pricing of Options on Assets with Stochastic Volatilities," *Journal of Finance 42*, pp. 281-300.

Kat, H.M. (1993a) "Replicating Ordinary Call Options in an Imperfect Market: A Stochastic Simulation Study," Paper presented at the 13th AMEX Options and Derivatives Colloquium, New York.

Kat, H.M. (1993b) "Hedging Lookback and Asian Options," Working Paper MeesPierson Derivatives.

Kunitomo, N. (1992) "Improving the Parkinson Method of Estimating Security Price Volatilities," *Journal of Business 65*, pp. 295-302.

Latane, H. and R. Rendleman (1976) "Standard Deviations of Stock Price Ratios Implied in Option Prices," *Journal of Finance 31*, pp. 369-381.

Marsh, T.A. and E.R. Rosenfeld (1986) "Non-Trading, Market Making, and Estimates of Stock Price Volatility," *Journal of Financial Economics 15*, pp. 359-372.

Melino, A. and S.M. Turnbull (1990) "Pricing Foreign Currency Options with Stochastic Volatility," *Journal of Econometrics* 45, pp. 239-265.

Merton, R.C. (1973) "Theory of Rational Option Pricing," *Bell Journal of Economics and Management Science* 4, pp. 141-183.

Merville, L.J. and D.R. Pieptea (1989) "Stock-Price Volatility, Mean-Reverting Diffusion, and Noise," *Journal of Financial Economics 24*, pp. 193-214.

Nelson, D.B. (1990) "ARCH Models as Diffusions Approximations," *Journal of Econometrics* 45, 7-38.

Nelson, D.B. (1991) "Conditional Heteroskedasticity in Asset Returns: A New Approach," *Econometrica* 59, pp. 347-370.

Pagan, A.R. (1984) "Econometric Issues in the Analysis of Regressions with Generated Regressors," *International Economic Review* 25, pp. 221-247.

Pagan, A.R. (1986) "Two Stage and Related Estimators and Their Applications," *Review of Economic Studies* 53, pp. 517-538.

Pagan, A.R. and G.W Schwert (1990) "Alternative Models for Conditional Stock Volatility," *Journal of Econometrics* 45, pp. 267-290.

Parkinson, M. (1980) "The Extreme Value Method for Estimating the Variance of the Rate of Return," *Journal of Business 53*, pp. 61-65.

Patell, J.M. and M.A. Wolfson (1979) "Anticipated Information Releases Reflected in Call Option Prices," *Journal of Accounting and Economics 1*, pp. 117-140.

Poterba, J. and L. Summers (1986) "The Persistence of Volatility and Stock Market Fluctuations," *American Economic Review 76*, pp. 1142-1151.

Rahman, A. and L. Kryzanowski (1986) "Alternative Specifications of the Errors in the Black-Scholes Option Pricing Model and Various Implied Variance Formulas," *Economics Letters 21*, pp. 61-65.

Rogers, L.C.G. and S.E. Satchell (1991) "Estimating Variance from High, Low and Closing Prices," *Annals of Applied Probability 1*, pp. 504-512.

Roll, R. (1984) "A Simple Implicit Measure of the Effective Bid-Ask Spread in an Efficient Market," *Journal of Finance 39*, pp. 1127-1139.

Ruiz, E. (1993) "Quasi-Maximum Likelihood Estimation of Stochastic Volatility Models," Working Paper, London School of Economics.

Schmalensee, R. and R.R. Trippi (1978) "Common Stock Volatility Expectations Implied by Option Premia," *Journal of Finance 33*, pp. 129-147.

Schwert, G.W. (1989) "Why Does Stock Market Volatility Change Over Time ?," *Journal of Finance 44*, pp. 1115-1153.

Schwert, G.W. and P.J. Seguin (1990) "Heteroskedasticity in Stock Returns," *Journal of Finance 45*, pp. 1129-1155.

Scott, L.O. (1987) "Option Pricing when the Variance Changes Randomly: Theory, Estimation and an Application," *Journal of Financial and Quantitative Analysis 22*, pp. 419-438.

Scott, L.O. (1991) "Random-Variance Option Pricing: Empirical Tests of the Model and Delta-Sigma Hedging, in: F.J. Fabozzi (ed.)," *Advances in Futures and Options Research, Vol 5*, JAI Press, pp. 113-135.

Sheikh, A.M. (1991) "Transactions Data Tests of S&P 100 Call Option Pricing," *Journal of Financial and Quantitative Analysis* 4, pp. 459-475.

Stein, J. (1989) "Overreactions in the Options Market," *Journal of Finance* 44, pp. 1011-1023.

Stoll, H.R. and R.E. Whaley (1990) "Stock Market Structure and Volatility," *Review of Financial Studies* 3, pp. 37-71.

Taylor, S.J. and X. Xu (1994) "The Magnitude of Implied Volatility Smiles: Theory and Empirical Evidence for Exchange Rates, forthcoming in" *The Review of Futures Markets.*

Whaley, R.E. (1982) "Valuation of American Call Options on Dividend-Paying Stocks: Empirical Tests," *Journal of Financial Economics* 10, pp. 29-58.

Wiggins, J.B. (1987) "Option Values under Stochastic Volatility: Theory and Empirical Estimates," *Journal of Financial Economics* 19, pp. 351-372.

Wiggins, J.B. (1991) "Empirical Tests of the Bias and Efficiency of the Extreme Value Variance Estimator for Common Stocks," *Journal of Business* 64, pp. 417-432.

Diversifying Earnings Forecast Errors via Composites of Market-based, Analyst and Time-Series Predictions

Pieter T. Elgers*, May H. Lo** and Dennis Murray***

*University of Massachussetts at Amherst
**Western New England College
***University of Colorado at Denver

D. Ho and T. Schneeweis (eds.), Applications in Finance, Investments, and Banking, 257–284.

I. Introduction

Accuracy in predicting earnings is a fundamental concern in investment analysis. The substantial resources devoted to the production and dissemination of earnings forecasts evidence the reliance by investors upon earnings expectations for purposes of portfolio management.[1] Analytical research in finance has established the relevance of earnings to security valuation, and empirical research has shown that shifts in earnings expectations are associated with revisions in security prices.

Measures of earnings expectations that are available at a common date for a large number of publicly traded firms are generally limited to three sources: time-series, financial analyst, and market-based forecasts. Various studies have evaluated the relative predictive accuracy of the more broadly-based forecasts (i.e., financial analyst and market-based) compared to forecasts based solely on patterns in prior earnings (time-series forecasts). Generally, the broadly-based forecasts provide more accurate predictions, at least for firms of larger size (Brown *et al.* (1987), Collins *et al.* (1987)). Recently, research has been directed to the potential complementarity, rather than the substitutability, of alternative forecast sources. Generally, these studies report that simple linear composites of forecasts are more accurate than the individual forecasts used in their construction (Lobo and Nair (1990), Guerard (1989), Conroy and Harris(1987)).[2]

The present study adds several new dimensions to research on the potential benefits of composite forecasting. First, the study broadens the array of forecast sources considered for inclusion in composite forecasts. All prior research has evaluated composites of financial

---

[1]For example, Value Line develops earnings predictions over various intervals for a broad cross-section of firms, and IBES provides periodic reports of the current forecasts of a number of individual analysts, as well as summary statistics.

[2]Contrary evidence is offered in Chatfield *et al.* (1990) for a sample of electric utility firms. A composite of financial analyst and time series forecasts was found in that study to be less accurate than the financial analyst forecasts.

analyst and time-series forecasts.[3] Recent research, however, indicates that market expectations of future earnings may be inferred from the anticipatory behavior of security prices, and that such "market-based" forecasts improve upon time-series forecasts for all but the smallest firms (Collins *et al.* (1987)). The present study provides the first attempt to incorporate such market-based forecasts in the building of composite predictions.

As a second departure from earlier studies, composite forecasts are developed separately for firms in differing size groups. Firm size appears to be associated with the economic incentives for information production by investment analysts. For example, analyst following is positively related to firm size. Moreover, the association between earnings changes and contemporary security price changes is greater for smaller firms, while the association between earnings changes and anticipatory (prior year) security price changes is greater for larger firms (Freeman (1987), Collins and Kothari (1989)). This evidence suggests that the informativeness of analyst forecasts and of market-based forecasts is likely to vary with firm size, and the potential benefits from incorporating these broadly-based forecast sources in composite earnings predictions may be greater for larger firms. Also, the relative weights assigned to individual forecast sources in the production of composite forecasts are likely to vary with firm size, because the weights depend upon the relative errors of the individual forecasts. In addition, firm size is related to the historical stability of the earnings series (larger, more diversified firms have less volatile earnings); this factor affects both the inherent predictability of earnings and the potential benefits from a pooling of errors through composite forecasts.

The analysis extends over a longer time period (fourteen years, from 1976 through 1989) and a larger cross-section of firms than do previous studies. The larger number of cases allows separate analysis within size groups, discussed above. Further, a variety of statistical tests are permitted that rely upon the intertemporal rather than the cross-sectional distributions of the forecast errors. This avoids the troublesome issue of cross-sectional dependencies that might

---

[3]Lobo and Nair (1990) examine composites of several different analyst forecasts and multiple time series models. Market-based forecasts, which were not considered in that study, are likely to be less redundant than multiple forecasts from a single source, and thus may offer a greater potential for reduction of errors that are not systematic across forecast sources.

otherwise confound attempts at statistical inference, and also provides assurance that the results are not time-specific.

The empirical results of this study strongly support the usefulness of composite forecasts. The extent of correlation among the errors from the simple forecast sources is sufficiently weak so that substantial error reductions result from combining forecasts. Relative prior error (RPE) weights are found to be superior to regression weights in forming composite forecasts, owing to temporal instability in the covariance structure of forecast errors. Among the simple forecasts, market-based predictions are generally more accurate for smaller firms, and analyst forecasts are more accurate for larger firms. Composite forecasts are superior to the simple forecasts in all size groups.

The remaining discussion proceeds as follows. Part 1 provides additional background concerning the rationale for composite forecasting, the sources and measurement of the simple forecasts, and the properties of alternative weighting schemes. Part 2 describes the statistical methodology and contains the empirical results. Part 3 summarizes the findings and offers directions for further study.

II. Additional Background Rationale for Composite Forecasting

The construction of composite forecasts has aptly been characterized as an application of portfolio risk diversification techniques to the reduction of earnings prediction errors (Conroy and Harris (1987), Lobo and Nair (1990)). If alternative simple forecasts are unbiased, of equal error variance, and are less than perfectly positively correlated, then <u>any</u> convex combination of the simple forecasts will enable a reduction of forecast error. As a practical matter, however, alternative forecast sources have unequal error variances and some degree of bias. Consequently, composite forecasts may either reduce or increase the forecast error, depending upon the degree of correlation among the simple forecasts.

Exhibit 1 illustrates the potential effects on forecast error variance (mean square error, or MSE) resulting from composites of two simple forecasts, F and A. The illustration assumes that A has a high MSE relative to F. Three levels of correlation among the forecast errors are considered. Line FA shows the MSEs resulting from composites of F and A if the errors are perfectly positively correlated, and in this case no composite should be formed, i.e. F is the optimal predictor. Line FBA shows the MSE possibilities if F and A are perfectly negatively correlated, and in this case prediction errors can be eliminated entirely with a composite at point B. Perfect correlation, either positive or negative, is unlikely to exist in practical cases. Line FCDA shows the MSEs that result if the forecast errors are uncorrelated. In this case, point C identifies the minimum-variance composite, and some composites (i.e. those to the right of point D) increase prediction errors above those from simple forecast F.

Because the optimal weights shown in Exhibit 1 depend upon the covariances among prediction errors from alternative forecast sources, practical benefits from composite forecasting depend upon reliable information about these covariances at the start of the forecast period. It is a simple matter to develop *ex post* optimal weights, based upon historical data. Whether such weights are useful for *ex ante* construction of composite forecasts depends upon the stability of the covariance structure over the forecast horizon. Unstable covariances (and the resulting instabilities in optimal weights) might otherwise increase the error variance of composite forecasts above that available from a simple low error forecast (e.g., to the right of point D in Exhibit 1). The empirical section of this paper will provide evidence on the stability of optimum forecast weights over time.

Sources and measurement of simple forecasts: Three simple forecasts are included in the present study: (1) time-series forecasts, employing a random-walk-with-drift model; (2) market-based forecasts, inferred from anticipatory changes in share prices; and (3) financial analyst forecasts, measured as the mean consensus forecasts published monthly by IBES (Institutional Brokers Estimate Series). This section provides details about the measurement of each of these simple forecasts.

(1) *Random-walk-with-drift-forecasts (RWDF)*: this time-series forecast predicts that the change in earnings during the forecast year will equal the average change (or "drift") during a relevant past period:

$$RWDF_{j,t+1} = D_j / EPS_{j,t} \tag{1}$$

where $EPS_{j,t}$ is per share earnings for firm j in period t, and D_j is the average change in earnings over a representative number of past periods (five years, in the present study).

The RWDF performs well when compared to other univariate time-series based predictions. A number of prior studies utilizing Box-Jenkins analysis have failed to discover useful patterns in past series of annual earnings that can be used to develop predictions that are superior to simple random walk or random-walk-with-drift predictions (Collins and Hopwood (1980), Watts and Leftwich (1977)).

(2) *Market-based forecasts (MBFs)*: the relationship between percentage earnings changes and anticipatory changes in security prices was measured by estimating the following cross-sectional model in each of the thirteen years 1976-1988:

$$\%\Delta EPS_{j,t} = \beta_{0,t} + \beta_{1,t} SAR_{j,t-1} + \beta_{2,t} PE_{j,t-1} + \mu_{j,t} \tag{2}$$

where $\%\Delta EPS_{j,t}$ = percentage change in earnings, firm j in period t;

$SAR_{j,t}$ = size-adjusted security returns, year ending March 31 of the earnings year;

$PE_{j,t-1}$ = ratio of price at the end of March of the earnings year, to prior-year EPS (before extraordinary items); and

$m_{j,t}$ = disturbance term, with $E(m_{j,t}) = 0$ (no independence assumptions are made concerning m_{jt}).

The parameter estimates from this model were then used to predict earnings growth in year t+1 as:

$$MBF_{j,t+1} = \hat{\beta}_{0,t} + \hat{\beta}_{1,t} SAR_{j,t} + \hat{\beta}_{2,t} PE_{j,t} \quad (3)$$

This model includes two separate market-based measures relevant to earnings expectations. The rationale for predicting earnings based upon prior movements in security returns (SAR_{jt} in expression 3, above) was first proposed by Beaver *et al.* (1980). They reasoned that many economic events (e.g. product innovation, capital spending) may be reflected in security prices prior to the period in which they affect earnings. If so, then security returns might be a useful leading indicator for earnings changes. Consistent with information efficiency in the security market, these anticipatory security returns would be expected to reflect solely those components of security returns that are associated with changes in expected future cash flows. With respect to the second market-based variable (PE_{jt} in expression 3 above), Beaver and Morse (1978) have shown that price-earnings multiples are highly associated with next-period earnings growth, due in large part to transitory components in current earnings. To the extent that security prices behave "as if" the market is informed about transitory earnings components, these components will have minimal effects upon securities prices. Consequently, firms with negative (positive) transitory earnings components should have relatively high (low) price-earnings ratios and higher (lower) percentage earnings changes in the ensuing period. This implies that the information in price-earnings ratios may complement the information in anticipatory security returns, in predicting earnings changes.

(3) Financial analyst forecasts (FAFs) earnings per share forecasts are obtained from the IBES Consensus Tapes in each forecast year, and the forecasted change in earnings is:

$$FAF_{j,t+1} = ((IBES_{j,t+1} - EPS_{j,t}) / EPS_{j,t}) \quad (4)$$

where $IBES_{j,t+1}$ is the consensus forecasted earnings per share for year t+1, in the report issued in March of year t+1.

The decision to use the $March_{t+1}$ IBES report in measuring the financial analyst forecasts, as well as the decision to measure security returns and price-earnings multiples through $March_{t+1}$ in constructing the market-based forecasts, were dictated by the need to avoid timing advantages for any of the three forecast sources. Actual earnings for period t are used in constructing the time-series forecast described above. Accordingly, both the market-based and the financial analyst forecasts should also be conditioned upon knowledge of actual earnings for period t.[4]

Several features distinguish these three forecast sources. First, in comparison to time-series forecasts, both market-based and analyst forecasts potentially are based upon a much broader information set. Because the economic incentives for information production should vary across firms in a similar fashion for analysts as for investors, both market-based and analysts' forecasts are expected to be of higher quality for larger firms. The degree of redundancy between these two forecast sources, and hence the potential for composites to improve forecast accuracy, depends both upon the extent to which analysts exploit the earnings-relevant information in security returns and the degree to which analysts' forecasts reflect information not yet impounded in security returns.

Second, although analysts' forecasts are direct predictions of earnings, both the time-series and the market-based predictions require that the researcher specify the transformation of other variables (e.g. past realizations of the earnings series; security returns and prices in earlier periods) into earnings expectations. For example, a market-based prediction model, as in expression (3) above, specifies a mapping of earlier-period security returns and price-earnings multiples into forecasts of earnings changes in the forecast period. Deficiencies in either the functional form (assumed to be linear additive, in expression 3) or the parameters of this mapping would diminish the usefulness of market-based predictions. The same issue underlies attempts to evaluate time-series predictions of earnings.

As a third point of contrast, unlike time-series forecasts, both the consensus financial analyst forecasts and the market-based forecasts may be characterized as composites. The IBES

---

[4]This procedure does not impart a timing advantage to the FAFs or the MBFs because, by construction, the time-series model is updated only when additional realizations of the earnings

consensus forecast for an individual firm is an equally-weighted composite of the contemporary forecasts of up to forty separate financial analysts.[5] Likewise, security prices reflect a "market consensus" based upon transactions among many rivalrous buyers and sellers, and earnings-relevant information that is impounded in security prices is a composite of many individuals' earnings expectations.

Weighting schemes in constructing composite forecasts: The composite forecasts evaluated in this study consist of linear combinations of the FAF, MBF and RWDF predictions. A critical element in the formation of the linear combinations is the weighting scheme, since it is the scheme that determines the relative importance of each simple forecast in calculating the composite. This study employs two widely-used weighting schemes, regression and relative prior error (RPE), to be described below. Both approaches use weights estimated at the start of each forecast period, based upon information available from period periods. These approaches assume that the weights remain sufficiently stable through time so that estimation errors do not substantially impair the usefulness of the composite forecasts.

In order to construct the RPE forecasts, the weights assigned in a given period to each simple forecast are inversely related to the relative mean square error arising from the previous period's application of that simple forecasting technique. That is, the weight assigned to a simple forecast is a positive function of its past success. The RPE forecast takes the form:

$$RPE_{t+1} = W_F \; FAF_{t+1} + W_M \; MBF_{t+1} + W_R \; RWDF_{t+1} \qquad (5)$$

where W_F, W_M and W_R refer to the weights given to the financial analyst, market-based and random-walk-with-drift forecasts, respectively; and W_F, for example, is calculated as:

$$W_F = \sum_{j=1}^{N} (e^2_{M,j} + e^2_{R,j}) / \sum_{j=1}^{N} (e^2_{F,j} + e^2_{M,j} + e^2_{R,j}) (k-1) \qquad (6)$$

---

series become available.

where N equals the number of firms in an assumedly homogeneous error group in the estimation period, K is the number of simple forecasts in the composite, and the e^2's refer to the squared errors arising from applying a particular model in the estimation period. The weights are recalculated each year based upon the errors generated by the simple model in the previous year.

In order to construct the regression forecasts, the following regression is estimated in each year:

$$\%\Delta EPS_t = \beta_0 + \beta_1 FAF_t + \beta_2 MBF_t + \beta_3 RWDF_t + \mu_t \qquad (7)$$

The coefficients from this regression are applied to FAF_{t+1}, MBF_{t+1}, and $RWDF_{t+1}$ to generate the regression-based forecast, RBF_{t+1}, for year t+1. The coefficients in expression (7) are re-estimated each year.

Estimation of both the RPE weights and the regression coefficients was done within size groups. The sample firms were divided into three equal-size groups each year, based upon the market value of common equity at the start of the estimation year. Within group estimation of the weights and coefficients was done because of the expectation, discussed earlier, that the error variances from the different simple forecasts were likely to be associated with firm size. Evidence supporting this assumption will be reported in the empirical results to follow.

Measure of forecast accuracy: the relative performance of the simple and composite forecasts was measured by the mean square error (MSE) of the predicted percentage change in earnings. The MSE metric was selected for two reasons. First, MSE has been used as a gauge of earnings prediction accuracy in much of the research that the current study attempts to extend (Lobo and Nair (1990), Walz and Walz(1989), Guerard(1989)). Second, both the RPE and the regression criteria for weighting the single source forecasts rest upon a minimum -MSE criterion. It appears inconsistent to use one criterion for the setting of composite weights, and a

---

[5]The number of analysts following an individual firm varies between one and forty during the latest year (1989) included in this study. The average number of analysts per firm has increased

second criterion for the evaluation of the success of the weighting schemes. Because MSE as an accuracy metric is sensitive to outlying observations, all of the forecasted percentage earnings changes were winsorized at ±100 percent (i.e., extreme values were reset to these upper and lower limits).[6]

III. Empirical Results

Sample selection and descriptive statistics: the study employs all firm-year observations available from 1990 editions of the Industrial Annual Compustat and CRSP tapes, meeting the following criteria: (a) March forecast of earnings available on the IBES consensus tape; (b) calendar fiscal year end; (c) positive earnings before extraordinary items in the prior two years; and (d) sufficient data for computing the earnings and returns variables described below. The calendar year constraint was imposed because the market-based forecasts are based upon cross-sectional relationships between earnings and anticipatory returns. Because the parameters of this relationship vary over time (Collins and Kothari (1989)), it is necessary that all firms included in an estimation cross-section have the same fiscal year. Positive earnings in the prior years were required because these earnings are used to scale the earnings changes and to compute price-earnings ratios. The 1990 Compustat data is reasonably complete through calendar 1989. Because the IBES Consensus forecast data begins in 1976, a total of fourteen years, 1976-1989, were available for analysis. A total of 5834 firm-years were available, ranging from a low of 297 firms in 1976, to a high of 516 firms in 1989.

Table 1 reports the cross-sectional means of selected characteristics of the sample firms, both by year (Panel A) and by firm size (Panel B). Panel A shows that the number of eligible firms from the IBES database has doubled over the 14-year analysis period. Panel A also shows the actual percentage changes in earnings each year, as well as the changes predicted by the FAF, MBF and RWDF simple forecasts. The actual percentage changes are highly variable,

---

from seven to fourteen over the entire period studied, 1976-1989.

[6]All techniques for outlier adjustment are by nature arbitrary, and winsorization at ±100% was selected because of its use in a similar context in Brown *et al.* (1980).

ranging from a low of -11.2 percent in 1982, to a high of +22.6 percent in 1976, with an intertemporal average of 5.6 percent. The earnings changes predicted by the three simple forecast sources are considerably less volatile over time. The forecast sources differ noticeably in terms of bias: the financial analyst (FAF) predictions exceed actual earnings in all but two years, and have an intertemporal average of 18.2 percent; the market-based (MBF) predictions exceed actual earnings in ten out of eighteen years, and have an intertemporal average of 12.0 percent; in contrast, the random-walk-with-drift (RWDF) forecasts exceed actual earnings in only six out of eighteen years, and have an intertemporal average of 4.0 percent. This upward bias in analyst forecasts has been noted previously ([7]) and may impair the performance of FAFs relative to the other forecast sources.

Panel B of Table 1 reports the same statistics for a three-part division of the sample firms based upon the market value of common equity measured at the start of the earnings year. The upward bias in the FAF and MBF predictions is present in all size groups, but appears to be higher for firms of smaller size.

Relative performance of simple forecasts: The relative performance of the three simple forecasts is reported in Table 2. Statistical evaluations of the differences in forecast performance for each simple forecast are based upon the fourteen annual measurements of mean errors rather than upon the cross-sectional distributions of the errors. Intertemporal tests are employed because of the considerable amount of cross-sectional dependence that is expected among earnings changes. In addition, because of the time-specific nature of the magnitudes of prediction errors, pairwise (matched-sample) tests are employed.

The comparisons in Table 2 show that forecast error magnitudes are related to firm size: for each of the simple forecasts, the error magnitudes decline with increases in firm size. This decline reflects two factors: lower volatility (hence higher predictability) in the earnings of larger firms; and richer information environments for such firms. To illustrate, the RWDF predictions are based upon the same limited information set (i.e. the historical earnings series) in each size group, and the decline in MSE for this forecast source reflects the lower variability of earnings for larger firms. In contrast, the FAF and MBF predictions are based upon potentially broader information sets, and the richness of the information reflected in forecasts is expected to increase with firm size. This factor is reflected in the fact that the percentage declines in MSE are greater for the FAF and MBF predictions than for the RWDF predictions (for example, for FAFs the prediction MSEs decline by 63.5 percent from the smaller to the larger size firms; for MBFs the decline is 51.9 percent; and for RWDFs the decline is 41.4 percent).

The pairwise comparisons of forecast errors in Table 2 show that MBFs are superior to FAFs for smaller firms, but the two forecast sources are statistically indistinguishable for firms of medium and larger size. FAFs are superior to RWDFs in all but the smaller firm size group, consistent with results in [3] and [11]. The MBFs have significantly lower errors than the RWDFs in all size groups. Overall, the results indicate that if investor analysts were constrained to choose a single forecast source for all firms, then MBFs would be the optimal choice; if the choice was permitted to vary across size groups, then MBFs would be preferred for smaller-size firms, while FAFs would be competitive with MBFs for firms of medium and larger size. The RWDFs would offer no advantage in any size group. The simultaneous availability of all three simple forecasts, however, may allow the construction of composite forecasts with lower errors than any one of the simple forecasts. The remaining empirical tests will address the potential of composite forecasts to improve forecast accuracy.

Two features of the predictive errors from the alternative forecast sources determine the potential benefits of composite forecasts: the portion of MSE that is due to random error, and the degree of correlation among earnings prediction errors (these points were illustrated graphically in Exhibit 1, above). Accordingly, Table 3 provides information on both features for the three simple forecasts. Prediction MSEs are decomposed into the portions due to bias, inefficiency and random error.[7] It was noted in Table 1 that FAFs are strongly upward-biased relative to the other simple forecasts. The decomposition in Table 3 shows that the maximum reduction in MSE due to complete elimination of this bias would be .0174 (or 8.7 percent of total

---

[7]This decomposition was developed by Thiel (1966) and applied to cross-sectional analysis of prediction errors in Klemkosky and Martin (1975).

MSE).[8] The predominant portion of prediction MSE for all forecast sources is random error, and the extent to which the random error can be diversified will substantially determine the benefits of composite forecasts. For example, the RWDFs have the lowest bias and the highest random error. As the weight of RWDFs is increased in a composite forecast, the bias component of MSE will be reduced. The inefficiency and random error portions of the composite MSE may either increase or decrease, however, depending upon the degree of correlation among the forecast errors.

The lower portion of Table 3 reports pairwise correlations among the earnings prediction errors of the alternative simple forecasts.[9] The correlations are sufficiently low to suggest potential benefits from composite forecasting. For example, the highest pairwise correlation is .811, indicating that less than 66 percent of the errors in one simple forecast can be "explained" by linear association with any other simple forecast. Whether these correlations allow error reductions through composite forecasts is the focus of the remaining analysis.

Estimation efficiency based upon *ex post* optimum forecasts: the initial step in evaluating the error-reduction potential of composite forecasts is to determine the estimation efficiency of the alternative weighting schemes.[10] Estimation efficiency is measured as the MSE that results from an *ex post* optimum linear combination of the simple forecast sources. This optimum linear combination is based upon the contemporary variances and covariances among the errors of the simple forecasts. For example, the *ex post* optimum regression weights are obtained by regressing actual earnings changes on the set of three contemporary simple

---

[8]Inefficiency, which reflects the tendency of forecasts above (below) the cross-sectional mean to be too high (low), accounts for 10.7 percent of FAF error and 22.4 percent of RWDF error. This component of forecast error, if stable over time, could be reduced using James-Stein estimation (see for example Landsman and Damodaran (1989)). The ensuing tests of prediction efficiency, however, will show that inefficiency is virtually eliminated in the composite forecasts, so that further attempts to reduce inefficiency are unnecessary in this setting.

[9]The pairwise correlations within each of the three size groups are very similar to those of the combined sample, and so are not reported here.

[10]Guerard and Beidleman (1987) emphasize the distinction between estimation efficiency and prediction efficiency in the construction of composite forecasts. In that study, a regression-based

forecasts, as depicted in expression (7), above. Similarly, the *ex post* RPE weights are based upon the contemporary relative variances of the simple forecast errors, as in expression (6) above. Estimation efficiency, which is based on perfect hindsight, places an upper bound on the reduction in MSE available from constructing composite forecasts. Table 4 reports the MSEs resulting from *ex post* optimum forecasts, which are based upon knowledge of the actual variances and covariances among forecast errors during the forecast period. Both the regression and the RPE weighting schemes permit substantial error reductions for all firms combined, and within each size group. The reductions in forecast errors due to RPE weights are generally below those for regression weights, because the RPE weights rely upon only the relative variances among the errors of the simple forecasts, and ignore the covariances; the regression weights, on the other hand, exploit the full covariance structure among the simple forecasts.

Note also in Table 4 that the potential improvement that composite forecasts offer relative to FAFs declines with firm size, reflecting the increasing quality of FAFs for larger, more closely followed firms. As a consequence, the potential improvements in the other two simple forecasts are positively related to firm size. Although composites offer smaller relative improvements to the MBF predictions, the percentage reductions in MSE are significant statistically in all size groups. It remains to be seen whether these *ex post* reductions in MSE can be obtained in a realistic setting, when composite weights are specified in advance of the forecast period, based upon historical information.

Stability of optimum composite weights over time: the distinction between *ex post* and *ex ante* optimum weighting schemes is necessary because the covariance structure among forecast errors from alternative forecast sources varies over time. Composite forecasts must be constructed at the start of the forecast horizon, based upon information available at that time. A weighting scheme that is optimum *ex post*, such as the regression weighting scheme evaluated in Table 4, may be less useful than a "second-best" weighting scheme, such as RPE weighting, if the weights for the *ex post* optimum composite are more volatile over time. Table

---

composite of analyst forecasts and time-series forecasts enabled significant estimation efficiency

5 addresses this issue: the intertemporal mean weights for the regression and RPE composites are reported, together with their coefficients of variation. The intertemporal means of the estimated regression parameters show a negative average intercept in each size group, reflecting the upward bias in the simple forecasts. The regression weights are highly unstable over time; the intertemporal standard deviations of the intercept and RWDF parameters exceed their intertemporal means in all size groups, and the standard deviations for the weights of the FAF and MBF predictions vary between twenty-three and ninety-eight percent of their means. The RPE weights, on the other hand, are relatively stable over time: the intertemporal standard deviations vary between three and fourteen percent of the mean values. Accordingly, it is expected that prediction MSEs obtained from the use of *ex ante* RPE weights will not differ substantially from the *ex post* optima shown in Table 4. For the regression weights, on the other hand, extreme temporal instability is likely to impair the usefulness of composite forecasts.

Prediction efficiency based upon *ex ante* optimum forecasts: the final set of empirical results assesses the ability of composite forecasts based upon information available at the start of the forecast period, to improve upon *ex ante* optimal simple forecasts. Within each size group, the simple forecast with lowest MSE in the preceding period is chosen as the *ex ante* optimum simple forecast source in the current period. Similarly, within each size group the regression-based and the RPE composites employ the *ex post* optimal weights obtained in the preceding period, in order to form composites of the simple forecasts in the current period. The results from this procedure are displayed in Table 6.

As shown in Table 6, regression-weighted composites do not enable reductions in prediction MSEs below those obtained from the *ex ante* optimum simple forecasts. To the contrary, for all firms combined and in two out of three size groups the prediction errors are increased by the use of the regression-weighted composites. The intertemporal instability in the optimum regression weights is sufficient to nullify the potential benefits from these composites. The RPE-weighted composites, on the other hand, provide significant reductions in prediction errors, for all firms combined and in each of the three size groups. The prediction

---

but did not provide prediction efficiency.

MSEs for the *ex ante* RPE composites reported in Table 6 are just slightly above those reported for the *ex post* RPE composites in Table 4 (the increase is about .002 in each size group). The stability of the RPE weights over time enables substantial reductions in prediction errors through the use of RPE-weighted composites.

Finally, it is instructive to compare the components of MSE that result from the use of the RPE-weighted composite forecasts, which are shown in Table 7, to those reported earlier (in Table 3) for the simple forecasts. The RPE-weighted forecast has virtually eliminated both the bias and the inefficiency components of prediction MSE: together these two elements constitute just 3.7 percent of total MSE. Moreover, the random error component is reduced substantially below that for the simple forecasts shown in Table 3.

IV. Summary and Conclusions

This study has evaluated the potential for composite earnings forecasts to reduce earnings prediction errors. Financial analyst, market-based and time-series forecasts were considered as potential complements in the construction of composite forecasts. Both relative prior error (RPE) and regression-based weighting schemes were examined, and results were provided separately for firms in different size groups. Measures of prediction accuracy were developed annually for an extensive time span (1977-1989) in order to permit formal statistical comparisons of model performance.

Pairwise comparisons of the simple forecasts indicate that both the financial analyst and the market-based forecasts, which potentially are based upon broad information sets, are superior to the time-series forecasts, which are based solely on patterns in the historical earnings series. Market-based forecasts outperform financial analysts for smaller-size firms, while financial analyst forecasts are most accurate for larger-size firms. The RPE-weighted composites, however, enable significant reductions in prediction errors for all size groups, compared to the best *ex ante* forecasts available from the simple forecast sources. Regression-based composites, on the other hand, fail to improve upon the prediction errors of the simple forecasts, which is due to pronounced temporal instability in the covariances among the forecast errors of the simple forecasts. These results are consistent with comparisons of alternative weighting schemes reported in Walz and Walz (1989) and Bunn (1988).

The three forecast sources examined in this study are based upon readily available information. Financial analyst forecasts are widely disseminated; historical earnings numbers amenable to time-series analysis are easily accessible in published financial reports; and market-based forecasts are readily estimated from analyses of historical earnings and market price data. Accordingly, the complementary nature of these simple forecast sources can be exploited at relatively small cost, in order to obtain substantial improvements in earnings prediction accuracy.

The study reflects several limitations that provide directions for further study. IBES consensus forecasts were selected to represent financial analyst forecasts, and the random-walk-with-drift model was selected to represent time-series forecasts. Various other sources of analyst forecasts and various additional time-series models are available, although prior studies offer support for the measures selected in this study. Moreover, there may be merit in combining multiple sources of analyst forecasts and time-series model forecasts, as in Lobo and Nair (1990). The market-based forecasts included in this study, however, potentially are drawn from less-redundant sources of information than would be additional analyst forecasts or time-series model forecasts; for this reason the inclusion of market-based forecasts may offer greater benefits in diversifying unsystematic prediction errors.

The merits of composite forecasts might also be examined over different forecast horizons, or for earnings intervals shorter than a year. For example, the quality of analyst forecasts is known to increase substantially as the earnings year progresses. It is likely that market-based forecasts would reflect similar improvement over time, but it is not clear whether the increasing degree of redundancy between the two forecast sources would obviate the benefits of composite forecasting.

Overall, the study offers strong support for the construction of composite forecasts using a weighting scheme that is based upon information available at the start of each forecast period. In addition, market-based forecasts inferred from the anticipatory behavior of security prices are shown to be important contributors to composite predictions of earnings.

References

Beaver, W. and D. Morse (1978), "What Determines P/E Ratios," Financial Analysts Journal (July/August, 1978), pp. 65-76.

Beaver, W., R. Lambert and D. Morse (1980), "The Information Content of Security Prices," Journal of Accounting and Economics (2), pp. 3-28.

Brown, L., P. Griffin, R. Hagerman and M. Zmijewski (1987), "Security Analyst Superiority Relative to Univariate Time-Series Models in Forecasting Quarterly Earnings," Journal of Accounting and Economics (9), pp. 61-87.

Bunn, D. (1988), "Statistical Efficiency in the Linear Combination of Forecasts," International Journal of Forecasting, 1985, pp. 151-163.

Chatfield, R., S. Hein and R. Moyer (1990), "Long-Term Earnings Forecasts in the Electric Utility Industry: Accuracy and Valuation Implications," The Financial Review (August 1990), pp. 421-439.

Collins, D., S. Kothari and J. Rayburn (1987), "Firm Size and the Information Content of Prices with Respect to Earnings," Journal of Accounting and Economics (9), pp. 111-138.

Collins, D. and S. Kothari (1989), "An Analysis of Intertemporal and Cross-sectional Determinants of Earnings Response Coefficients," Journal of Accounting and Economics (11), pp. 143-182.

Collins, W. and W. Hopwood (1980), "A Multivariate Analysis of Annual Earnings Forecasts Generated from Quarterly Forecasts of Financial Analysts and Univariate Time Series Models," Journal of Accounting Research (Autumn 1980), pp. 390-406.

Conroy, R. and R. Harris (1987), "Consensus Forecasts of Corporate Earnings: Analysts' Forecasts and Time Series Methods," Management Science (June, 1987), pp. 725-738.

Freeman, R. (1987), "The Association Between Accounting Earnings and Security Returns for Large and Small Firms," Journal of Accounting and Economics (90), pp. 195-228.

Fried, D. and D. Givoly (1982), "Financial Analysts' Forecasts of Earnings: A Better Surrogate for Market Expectations," Journal of Accounting and Economics (4), pp. 85-107.

Guerard, J. (1989), "Combining Time-Series Model Forecasts and Analysts' Forecasts for Superior Forecasts of Annual Earnings," Financial Analysts Journal (January/February, 1989), pp. 69-71.

Guerard, J. and C. Beidleman (1987), "Composite Earnings Forecasting Efficiency," Interfaces (September/October 1987), pp. 103-113.

Klemkosky, R. and J. Martin (1975), "The Adjustment of Beta Forecasts," Journal of Finance (September, 1975), pp. 1123-1128.

Landsman, W. and A. Damodaran (1989), "Using Shrinkage Estimators to Improve Upon Time-Series Model Proxies for the Security Market's Expectation of Earnings," Journal of Accounting Research (Spring, 1989), pp. 97-115.

Lobo, G. and R. Nair (1990), "Combining Judgmental and Statistical Forecasts: An Application to Earnings Forecasts," Decision Sciences (Spring, 1990), pp. 446-460.

Shevlin, T. and D. Shores (1990), "Firm Size, Security Returns, and Unexpected Earnings," Working Paper, University of Washington, Seattle.

Thiel, H. (1966), Applied Economic Forecasting New York: North-Holland Publishing Company.

Walz, D. and D. Walz (1989), "Combining Forecasts: Multiple Regression versus a Bayesian Approach," Decision Sciences (Winter, 1989), pp. 77-89.

Watts, R. and R. Leftwich (1977), "The Time Series of Annual Earnings," Journal of Accounting Research (Autumn, 1977), pp. 253-271.

Exhibit 1

Potential Reductions in Prediction Error Variance (MSE) from Composite Forecasts

MSE
$[(1-w_a)F + w_a A]$

Notation:

F,A:	Alternative forecast sources
MSE:	Mean square prediction error
w_a:	Weight of forecast A in a linear composite of forecasts F and A
R(A,F):	Pearson correlation between prediction errors of simple forecasts A and F.
FA:	Locus of MSEs if P(A,F) = +1
FBA:	Locus of MSEs if P(A,F) = -1
FCDA:	Locus of MSEs if P(A,F) = 0
F,C,B:	Minimum MSEs (and optimum weights) based upon P(A,F):

F: $w_a = 0$ (optimum if R(F,A) = +1)

C: $w_a = \dfrac{MSE_F}{MSE_F + MSE_A}$ (optimum if R(F,A) = 0)

B: $w_a = \dfrac{(MSE_F)^{1/2}}{(MSE_F)^{1/2}+(MSE_F)^{1/2}}$ (optimum if R(F,A) = -1)

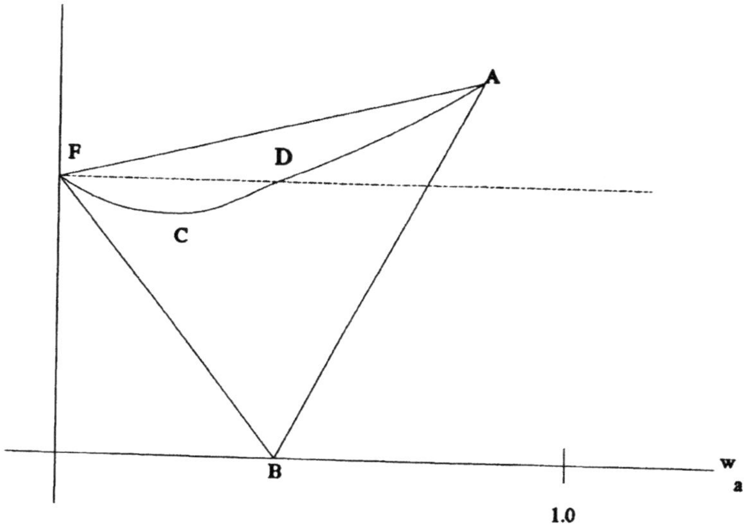

Table 1

Cross-sectional means of selected variables, by year and firm-size groups

	Firms	Firm Size[a] (millions)	Actual % ΔEPS[b]	Predicted % ΔEPS FAFs[c]	MBFs[c]	RWDFs[e]
A. Annual Means						
1976	297	$1,116	22.6%	22.7%	9.9%	5.8%
1977	295	1,507	13.0	17.4	15.7	7.7
1978	348	1,189	16.2	13.8	9.8	6.7
1979	402	1,015	15.7	13.3	16.6	5.7
1980	420	1,114	3.0	10.0	16.3	7.8
1981	420	1,288	4.8	16.8	15.0	7.7
1982	435	1,113	-11.2	14.6	6.8	5.9
1983	428	1,265	12.8	23.3	6.6	2.1
1984	442	1,610	8.2	22.7	13.6	2.1
1985	476	1,592	-8.2	20.4	15.6	-1.7
1986	456	1,951	-.6	20.4	10.7	-0.2
1987	448	2,114	4.2	22.1	11.6	1.7
1988	451	2,209	13.3	21.1	6.3	3.5
1989	516	2,310	-1.5	15.4	13.2	4.9
All Years	5,834	$1,598	5.6%	18.2%	12.0%	4.0%
B. Size-group means[f]						
Smaller	1,942	$ 145	4.2%	22.2%	15.2%	4.3%
Medium	1,942	661	5.5	16.7	10.1	2.9
Larger	1,950	4,376	7.2	15.6	10.5	4.8
All firms	5,834	$1,598	5.6%	18.2%	12.0%	4.0%

Notes:

(a) Market value of common equity, beginning of the earnings year.
(b) Actual percentage change in EPS before extraordinary items.
(c) IBES mean consensus forecast, March of the earnings year.
(d) Market-based forecast.
(e) Random-walk-with-drift forecast
(f) Firms were assigned to market value groups within each year, and each market-value group was pooled over 14 years.

Table 2

Prediction MSEs: Intertemporal Comparisons Across Forecast Sources, by Firm Size Groups

	Intertemporal average MSE, period 1976-1989			Significance tests H_0: $MSE_i - MSE_j = 0$		
	Forecast source			Pairwise comparison t-values[(a)]		
	FAF	MBF	RWDF	(FAF-MBF)	(FAF-RWDF)	(MBF-RWDF)
All firms	.186	.163	.219	2.41**	-2.11*	-4.70***
Size groups:						
Smaller	.296	.235	.292	4.08***	.13	-3.46***
Medium	.154	.141	.194	1.36	-2.09*	-3.73***
Larger	.108	.113	.171	-.53	-3.42**	-3.37***

(a) Intertemporal t-values are based upon the distributions of the 14 annual measurements of the MSEs for the years 1976-1989.

Significance levels:
*: 0.10
**: 0.05
***: 0.01

Table 3

Decomposition of Forecast MSEs and Correlations Among Forecast Sources

A. Decomposition of Forecast MSEs[a]

$$MSE = \frac{1}{N}\sum_{i=1}^{N}(A_i - F_i)^2$$

$$= \underbrace{(\bar{A} - \bar{F})^2}_{\text{Bias}} + \underbrace{(1 - s)^2 \, VAR(F)}_{\text{Inefficiency}} + \underbrace{(1 - R^2)\, VAR(A)}_{\text{Random error}}$$

where A = actual percentage change in earnings
F = forecasted percentage change in earnings
s = slope coefficient from OLS regression of A on F
R^2 = squared correlation between A and F

Portion (and percentage) of MSE due to:

		Bias		Inefficiency		Random error		Total[b]	
Forecast	FAF	.0174	(8.7%)	.0214	(10.7%)	.1620	(80.6%)	.2008	(100%)
	MBF	.0054	(3.1%)	.0054	(3.1%)	.1625	(93.8%)	.1733	(100%)
	RWDF	.0001	(0.0%)	.0518	(22.4%)	.1794	(77.6%)	.2313	(100%)

B: Pairwise correlations among earnings prediction errors:

R(FAF,MBF)	R(FAF,RWDF)	R(MBF,RWDF)
.811	.605	.764

(a) This decomposition is developed in Thiel [1966].
(b) Total MSEs differ from those in Table 2 because the error decompositions were computed from a pooling of all cases over the 13-year period 1977-1989 while the MSEs in Table 2 are intertemporal averages of annual means.

Table 4
Estimation Efficiency Based upon Ex Post Optimal Composites:
Simple Forecasts vs. Regression and Relative Prior Error (RPE) Composites

Simple forecast			Ex post optimum forecast MSEs					
			Regression composite[a]			RPE composite[b]		
	Source	MSE[c]	MSE	Percent reduction	(t-value)[d]	MSE	Percent reduction	(t-value)
All firms	FAF	.194	.139	28.4%	(4.74)***	.154	20.6%	(4.26)***
	MBF	.168	.139	17.3%	(4.83)***	.154	8.3%	(3.14)***
	RWDF	.224	.139	37.9%	(6.82)***	.154	27.6%	(5.46)***
Size groups:								
Smaller	FAF	.307	.197	35.8%	(4.81)***	.226	26.4%	(4.73)***
	MBF	.240	.197	17.9%	(3.85)***	.226	5.8%	(2.34)**
	RWDF	.295	.197	33.2%	(6.77)***	.226	23.4%	(4.60)***
Medium	FAF	.162	.116	28.3%	(4.53)***	.133	17.9%	(3.48)***
	MBF	.148	.116	21.6%	(5.28)***	.133	10.1%	(2.74)**
	RWDF	.202	.116	42.6%	(5.24)***	.133	34.2%	(4.26)***
Larger	FAF	.113	.085	24.8%	(3.19)***	.102	9.7%	(1.61)
	MBF	.116	.085	26.7%	(5.27)***	.102	12.1%	(2.66)**
	RWDF	.175	.085	51.4%	(4.84)***	.102	41.7%	(4.11)***

(a) Regression parameters estimated in period t are used to form composite forecasts for period t.
(b) RPE weights measured in period t are used to form composites forecasts for period t.
(c) All MSEs are computed based upon 13 annual measurements for 1977-1989, to enable comparisons to later tables. For the simple forecasts, these amounts differ from Table 2 which is based upon 14 annual measurements for 1976-1989.
(d) All t-values are based upon the intertemporal distributions of the MSE differences between the simple and composite forecasts.

Significance levels:
**: 0.05
***: 0.01

Table 5

Intertemporal Stability of RPE and Regression Weights Utilized in Forming Composite Forecasts

	Regression weights				RPE weights		
	Intercept	FAF	MBF	RWDF	FAF	MBF	RWDF
All firms							
Intertemporal mean[(a)]	-.056	.373	.509	.086	.339	.354	.307
Coefficient of variation[(b)]	(.221)	(.40)	(.66)	(4.38)	(.07)	(.03)	(.08)
Size groups:							
Smaller:							
Intertemporal mean	-.068	.218	.591	.053	.324	.356	.320
Coefficient of variation	(2.71)	(.86)	(.84)	(9.32)	(.07)	(.03)	(.09)
Medium:							
Intertemporal mean	-.068	.476	.468	.192	.345	.356	.299
Coefficient of variation	(1.65)	(.68)	(.87)	(3.82)	(.09)	(.05)	(.14)
Larger:							
Intertemporal mean	-.053	.563	.604	-.079	.365	.349	.286
Coefficient of variation	(2.13)	(.23)	(.98)	(6.87)	(.09)	(.08)	(.13)

(a) Average weight over the thirteen annual estimation periods, 1976-1988.
(b) Intertemporal standard deviation as a percentage of the intertemporal mean.

Table 6

Prediction Efficiency Based Upon Ex Ante Optimal Forecasts: Simple Forecasts versus Regression and RPE Weighted Composites

	Ex ante best simple forecast[(a)]	Regression Composite[(b)]		RPE Composite[(c)]	
	MSE	MSE	Percent error reduction	MSE	Percent error reduction
All firms	.179	.181	-1.1%	.156	12.8%***
Size groups:					
Smaller	.248	.263	-6.0%	.228	8.1%**
Medium	.158	.153	3.2%	.135	14.6%***
Larger	.113	.126	-11.5%	.104	8.0%*

(a) The simple forecast source with lowest MSE in year t is used to measure MSE in year t+1.
(b) Regression parameters estimated in year t are used to form composites in year t+1.
(c) RPE weights computed in year t are used to form composites in year t+1.

Significance levels based on the intertemporal distributions of the 13 annual measurements of MSE differences (1977-1989):

* 0.10
** 0.05
*** 0.01

Table 7
Decomposition of Prediction MSE for RPE-weighted Composites

	MSE[a]	Percentage
Source of error:		
Bias	.0046	3.3%
Inefficiency	.0006	0.4
Random error	.1351	96.3
Total	.1403	100.0%

(a) Total MSE differs from that shown in Table 6 for the RPE-weighted composite because the calculation shown above is obtained from a pooling of all cases for the period 1977-1989, while the calculations in Table 6 are based upon mean values for each year. Consequently, the above calculation weights each case equally; the Table 6 calculations weight each year equally in order to permit intertemporal tests of significance.

THE VALUATION OF CROSS-CURRENCY INTEREST-SENSITIVE CLAIMS WITH APPLICATION TO "DIFF" SWAPS

Simon H. Babbs
First National Bank of Chicago

D. Ho and T. Schneeweis (eds.), Applications in Finance, Investments, and Banking, 285–333.

1. INTRODUCTION

The literature on cross-currency contingent claims is dominated by the valuation of foreign exchange contracts. See Amin and Jarrow [1991] (AJ) for a review and numerous references. Foremost amount these contracts are forward and option contracts; some attention has also been given to currency futures and options thereon. While the payoffs on such instruments depend only upon the exchange rate, their pricing depends also upon interest rates in the two countries.

Other cross-currency contingent claims, however, have payoffs depending explicitly upon the domestic and/or foreign term structures. Just two examples are: options to buy "foreign" currency bonds at an exercise price fixed in "domestic" currency[1]; and the "diff" or "switch LIBOR swaps" (see Litzenberger [1992]) which we will describe fully in Section 5.

Much research into the pricing of foreign exchange contracts has treated interest rates as deterministic. Comparative static analysis of the resulting pricing formulae confirms that exchange rate movements usually have far greater impact than changes in interest rates. Nevertheless, interest rates are significant inputs, and can have a major influence on, say, the relative value of an american-style option *vis-a-vis* its european-style counterpart. Allowing stochastic variation in interest rates can therefore play a useful secondary role. Some researchers (AJ cite Feiger and Jacquillat [1979]; Grabbe [1983];

---

[1]Section V in AJ, and an Appendix in Babbs [1990b], are devoted to showing that the pricing results obtained in their respective papers are independent of which currency is labelled "domestic" and which "foreign".

*Currently at First National Bank of Chicago, 1 Triton Square, London NW1 3FN, UK. Email:sbabbs@uk.fcnbd.com; tel: 44 (0) 171 903 4286; fax: 44 (0) 171 528 7185.

Adams and Wyatt [1987]) have done this by adapting Merton's [1973] stochastic interest model to apply to interest rate in each currency. AJ point out that Merton's approach requires a pure discount bond for each cashflow date. Whereas currency forwards and european-style options involve only a single known date, american-style options involve uncertainty as to the exercise date, and the marking-to-market of currency futures involves multiple - or even continuous - cashflows. To handle the latter foreign exchange contracts, therefore, involves going beyond Merton [1973], by incorporating fully fledged models of the domestic and/or foreign term structures. *A fortiori*, the valuation of contingent claims whose payoffs depend explicitly on term structure variables requires, as noted by Litzenberger [1992] in relation to "diff" swaps, "a model of the multivariate distribution of the term structures in each country and the exchange rate".

The programme of extending full term structure models to a cross-currency setting has been undertaken independently by AJ and by Babbs [1990b]. The theoretical models constructed in the two papers are in many ways similar. As regards applications, AJ focus exclusively on exchange rate contracts; assuming instantaneous (co-)variances of returns are deterministic, they derive closed-form expressions for the prices of european-style options on the spot exchange rate, for forward contracts, and for currency futures and options thereon. Babbs, however, restricts his treatment of foreign exchange contracts to rederiving, as a special case, Grabbe's [1983] model for european-style options on the spot exchange rate. He then goes on to obtain a tractable model for more general cross-currency contingent claims, in which the joint dynamics of the two term structures and the exchange rate are captured by three Gaussian state variable processes. Babbs' model generalizes to a cross-currency setting the "extended Vasicek" model for a single term structure (see e.g. Babbs [1990a], Hull and White [1990], and Jamshidian [1990a], [1990b]).

The role of this paper is two fold. Firstly - in Sections 2 and 3 - we present Babbs' [1990b] construction of a general cross-currency term structure model, consistent with the observed initial term structures. This construction is, in many respects, similar to that in Sections I and II of AJ. Readers may nevertheless find the different presentation helpful. AJ and Babbs model the dynamics of the "domestic" and the "foreign" term structure by means of an arbitrage-free diffusion model of the kind independently devised by Heath, Jarrow and Morton [1992] and Babbs [1990a]. The exchange rate also follows a diffusion. The two yield curves and the exchange rate are imperfectly correlated. It is shown that there exists a unique "equivalent martingale measure", under which contingent claims are priced by arbitrage at the expected discounted values of their subsequent payoffs. Babbs' construction also includes a demonstration that the cross-country model can be supported by a general equilibrium; AJ merely show the weaker condition of absence of arbitrage opportunities.

Secondly - in Section 4 - we present Babbs' [1990b] "cross-currency extended Vasicek" specialization of the general model, referred to earlier, under which the evolution of the term structures and the exchange rate are captures by three Gaussian state variable processes. We then go on to illustrate the practical advantages of such a specialization by obtaining a new result in Section 5: namely, a closed-form valuation formulation for "diff" swaps.[2] We present a worked example of the formula, and discuss the comparative statics of the key term.

Section 6 concludes the paper briefly. All proofs are relegated to the Appendix.

2. FORMAL STRUCTURE OF THE MODEL

2.1 THE CONSUMPTION SPACE; AGENTS

As in Harrison and Kreps [1979] (HK), we assume a pure exchange economy over a finite timespan $[0,T]$. A probability space $(\Omega,\mathcal{F},P)$ is given over states of the world $\omega\varepsilon\Omega$.

Agents have preferences over payoffs at the initial date and state-contingent payoffs at the horizon. Payoffs may include amounts in more than one currency. Payoffs which, in all states[3], have the same value when translated into (any) single currency, are equally preferred. For convenience, therefore, we may measure all payoffs in one currency, which we will label "domestic"; the other currency we will call "foreign".[4]

Let $S(t)$ be the exchange rate at time t, devined as the "domestic" price of one unit of

---

[2]Since this paper was first written, Jamshidian [1994] and Turnbull [1994] have independently addressed the valuation of diff swaps. Both papers obtain closed-form expressions by imposing deterministic volatility functions analogous to those in Sections 5-6 of this paper.

[3]Strictly in all states outside a P-null set.

[4]The Appendix to Babbs [1990b] shows that no major feature of the model is affected by which currency we choose to label "domestic".

"foreign" currency for spot (interpreted here as immediate[5]) delivery.

Construct a consumption space $\Re x X$ where

$$X = \{p{:}\Omega \rightarrow \Re \ \text{ such that } \ p, \frac{p}{S(T)} \ \varepsilon \ L^2(\Omega,\mathcal{F},P)\} \tag{1}$$

where each p is a payoff measured in "domestic: currency, and $S(T)$ is the exchange rate at the horizon date T.

A set of conceivable agents, with preference over the consumption space, is constructed as in HK.

2.2 *INFORMATION*

The information available to agents at time $t\varepsilon[0,T]$ is represented by $\mathcal{F}_t \subseteq \mathcal{F}$ where $\{\mathcal{F}_t : t\varepsilon[0,T]\}$ is an increasing sequence of sub-sigma-algebras satisfying the "usual conditions"[6] and where, without loss of generality, $\mathcal{F}_0$ is almost trivial, and $\mathcal{F}_T = \mathcal{F}$.[7]

---

[5]In practice, "spot" foreign exchange contracts are for delivery two business days ahead. To allow for this in our results, the most straightforward approach would probably be to construct a notional rate for immediate delivery by discounting both sides of the transaction at the relevant two day interest rate.

[6]See e.g. Karatzas and Shreve [1987] p10.

[7]See also footnote 26.

2.3 TERM STRUCTURE DYNAMICS

Let $B_f(M,t)$ denote the "foreign" currency price at t of a pure discount bond which pays one unit of "foreign" currency at $M \geq t$. Let $B_d(M,t)$ be the "domestic: currency price at t of the corresponding "domestic" bond.

We describe the term structure dynamics, consistent with any[8] initial term structures, by the Ito processes:

$$\frac{dB_f(M,t)}{B_f(M,t)} = (r_f(t)+\theta_f(t)\sigma_f(M,t))dt + \sigma_f(M,t)dZ_f(t) \tag{2a}$$

$$\frac{dB_d(M,t)}{B_d(M,t)} = (r_d(t)+\theta_d(t)\sigma_d(M,t))dt + \sigma_d(M,t)dZ_d(t) \tag{2b}$$

where $r_f(\ )$, $r_d(\ )$ are the respective instantaneous spot interest rates given by:

$$r_f(t) = -\lim_{M \downarrow t} \frac{\ln B_f(M,t)}{M-t} \tag{3a}$$

$$r_d(t) = -\lim_{M \downarrow t} \frac{\ln B_d(M,t)}{M-t}\ ; \tag{3b}$$

$\Theta_f(\ )$, $\Theta_d(\ )$ are non-anticipative processes relating, in some way, [9] to the "price of interest rate risk" on bonds in the two currencies; $\sigma_f(\ )$, $\sigma_d(\ )$ are also non-anticipating functions, representing bond price volatilities; and $Z_f(\ )$, $Z_d(\ )$ are standard Brownian motions whose innovations have the correlation process given by:

$$dZ_f(t).dZ_d(t) = \rho_{fd}(t)dt \tag{4a}$$

---

[8]Strictly, any initial structures $B_f(M,0)$ and $B_d(M,0)$ differentialble with respect to M.

[9]We elucidate this relation fully in Remark 3.3 below.

where ρ_{fd} is a further non-anticipating function. (2a) (equally (2b)) represents the most general single factor Ito process model for term structure dynamics consistent with the absence of arbitrage opportunities between bonds of different maturities. Obviously, (4a) constitutes a completely unrestrictive description of the correlation structure of the two Brownian motions. We could generalize these term structure dynamics to multi-factor models by adding further risk premium and Brownian motion terms of the same general form as those shown; our analysis extends readily to the multi-factor case, and we use one factor per term structure solely in the interests of brevity. The only real restriction, therefore, is the use of Ito processes rather than more general semi-martingales; in particular, we exclude the possibility of jumps.

Babbs [1990a] has shown[10] that such Ito processes can be constructed in a well-defined manner, and that bond prices converge to par at maturity, with probability one.

2.4 *EXCHANGE RATE DYNAMICS*

We describe the exchange rate dynamics, by the Ito process:

$$\frac{dS(t)}{S(t)} = \mu(t)dt + \sigma_s(t)dZ_s(t) \tag{5}$$

where $\sigma_s(\ )$ is a strictly positive non-anticipating process, representing exchange rate volatility; and $Z_s(\ )$ is a standard Brownian motions whose innovations have correlations with those of $Z_f(\ )$, $Z_d(\ )$ given by:

---

[10]Chapter 4 pp104-129.

$$dZ_f(t).dZ_S(t) = \rho_{fS}(t)dt \tag{4b}$$

$$dZ_S(t).dZ_d(t) = \rho_{Sd}(t)dt \tag{4c}$$

Since σ( ) is a strictly positive process, we can define a new process $\Theta_S(\ )$ by expressing μ( ) in the form:

$$\mu(t) = r_d(t) - r_f(t) + \Theta_s(t)\sigma_s(t) \tag{6}$$

(5) represents the most general single factor Ito process model of exchange rate dynamics, and (4b)-(4c) leave the correlations with the term structures totally unrestricted. An increase in the number of Brownian motions in (5) would not significantly enrich the dynamics, since the exchange rate is a scalar quantity.[11]

2.5 *TRADING STRATEGIES*

We define trading strategies as in Babbs [1997], adapted slightly to cope with inter-currency translations, as follows.

Let *I* be an index to the collection of securities traded in the markets. We initially restrict *I* to cover only pure discount bonds in either currency, but we will word our definition to assist generalization later in this paper.

Provisional Definition 2.5.1 *A trading strategy is provisionally defined as: a non-*

[11]The point of this is that a single factor model could be regained by suitably combining the various Brownian motions employed.

negative integer n; a selection of securities, indexed as $i_1,\dots,i_n \in I$ *; together with an n-dimensional real valued stochastic process* $\psi : [0,T]\times\Omega \to \Re^n$. *The kth component,* ψ_k, *of the process represents holdings of security* i_k. *The process must satisfy the following requirements:*

(i) ψ *is predictable;*[12]

(ii) *the stochastic integrals in (8) are well-defined;*[13]

(iii) $\psi_k(t) = 0$ *if security* i_k *matures strictly before t;*

(iv) *terminal value in the terminal consumption space:*

$$\sum_{k=1}^{n} \psi_k(T)V_k(T) \in X \tag{7}$$

where $V_k:[0,T]\times\Omega \to \Re$ *is the price of security* i_k, *as measured in "domestic" currency;*

(v) *"self-financing":* $\forall t,\omega$:

$$\begin{aligned} V(t) &= \sum_{k=1}^{n} \psi_k(t)V_k(t) \\ &= V(0) + \sum_{k=1}^{n} \int_0^t \psi_k(u)dV_k(u) \end{aligned} \tag{8}$$

---

[12] A process is said to be predictable if it is measurable with respect to the sub-sigma-algebras generated by left-continuous adapted processes. Making this requirement prevents arbitrage opportunities arising from exploiting price jumps (see Harrison and Pliska [1981] p237).

[13] Babbs [1990a] achieves this condition by means of the stronger requirement that holdings of securities are locally bounded (see e.g. Dellacherie [1980]. The benefit of the present approach is that, as Harrison and Pliska [1981] pointed out, the replication of even some bounded contingent claims in eg the Black-Scholes economy requires strategies which are not locally bounded.

3. VIABILITY AND PRICING BY ARBITRAGE

We normalize security prices and trading strategy wealth processes by dividing through by the price of a numeraire security, whose payoffs consist precisely of a unit payoff at the terminal data, in all states $\omega\epsilon\Omega$. This security is, of course, precisely[14] the "domestic" pure discount bond maturing at T.

If is convenient at this stage to re-express $Z_f(\ )$, $Z_f(\ )$, and $Z_S(\ )$, in terms of three orthogonal standard Brownian motions $W_1(\ )$, $W_2(\ )$, $W_3(\ )$, where

$$dZ_i(t) - \sum_{j-1}^{3} \alpha_{ij}(t) dW_j(t); \quad i-f,d,S \tag{9}$$

The following technical condition, which will always be satisfied in practice, will simplify the mathematical elaboration of our model:

<u>**Non-degeneracy Assumption**</u> *With probability one, none of the correlations* $\rho_{fd}(\ )$, $\rho_{fS}(\ )$, $\rho_{Sd}(\ )$ *is ever perfect (i.e. ±1). Likewise, none of the volatilities* $\sigma_f(M,t)$, $\sigma_d(M,t)$, $\sigma_S(t)$ *is ever zero, except for* $M=t$.

If we write

(10)

[14]Strictly, the bond matures at par only for all states outside a set of probability zero.

$$\begin{pmatrix} \alpha_{f1} & \alpha_{f2} & \alpha_{f3} \\ \alpha_{d1} & \alpha_{d2} & \alpha_{d3} \\ \alpha_{S1} & \alpha_{S2} & \alpha_{S3} \end{pmatrix} = A$$

then (2a)-(2b), (4a)-(4c) and (5) together imply that:

$$A'A = \begin{pmatrix} 1 & \rho_{fd} & \rho_{fS} \\ \rho_{fd} & 1 & \rho_{Sd} \\ \rho_{fS} & \rho_{Sd} & 1 \end{pmatrix} \tag{11}$$

i.e. A is the square root[15] of the correlation matrix.[16] Note that, barring degenerate cases, A is invertible.

We are now in a position to consider the normalized "domestic" currency price processes of "foreign" pure discount bonds. We know, from HK, that both these, and the corresponding processes for "domestic" bonds, must be martingales, under an "equivalent martingale measure":

---

[15]Priming matrices denotes transposition.

[16]If, in particular, we choose W_1, W_2, W_3 so that $\alpha_{d1} \equiv \alpha_{d2} \equiv \alpha_{f1} \equiv 0$, then

$$A = \begin{pmatrix} 0 & \sqrt{1-\rho_{fd}^2} & \rho_{fd} \\ 0 & 0 & 1 \\ \dfrac{\sqrt{1-\rho_{fd}^2-\rho_{Sd}^2-\rho_{fS}^2+2\rho_{fS}\rho_{Sd}\rho_{fd}}}{1-\rho_{fd}^2} & \dfrac{\rho_{fS}-\rho_{fd}\rho_{Sd}}{\sqrt{1-\rho_{fd}^2}} & \rho_{Sd} \end{pmatrix}$$

Definition 3.1 *A probability measure P^* on $(\Omega,\mathcal{F})$ is said to be an equivalent martingale measure (EMM) if and only if the following thee conditions hold:*

(i) *P^* and P are equivalent, ie have the same null sets. A necessary and sufficient condition for this is that the Radon-Nikodym derivative* $\frac{dP^*}{dP}$ *be strictly positive.*[17]

(ii) *after adjusting for incremental required returns, normalized security price processes (in "domestic" currency terms) are martingales under P^**

(iii) $$\frac{dP^*}{dP} \in L^2(\Omega,\mathcal{F},P) \qquad (12)$$

Lemma 3.2 *The normalized "domestic" price process of the "foreign" pure discount bond maturing at $M \in [0,T]$ satisfied the stochastic differential equation:*

$$\frac{d\{B_f(M,t)S(t)/B_d(T,t)\}}{B_f(M,t)S(t)/B_d(T,t)}$$

[17]Note that, since P, P^* have the same null sets, we may use the term "almost sure" without qualification as to which probability measure is intended.

$$- \sum_{j=1}^{3} \{\sigma_f(M,t)\alpha_{fj}(t) + \sigma_S(t)\alpha_{Sj}(t) - \sigma_d(T,t)\alpha_{dj}(t)\} \times \{ \; [\theta_j^{(d)}(t) - \sigma_d(T,t)\alpha_{dj}(t)]dt + dW_j(t) \; \} \tag{13}$$

where

$$\begin{pmatrix} \theta_1^{(d)} \\ \theta_2^{(d)} \\ \theta_3^{(d)} \end{pmatrix} = A^{-1} \begin{pmatrix} \theta_f + \sigma_S \sum_{j=1}^{3} \alpha_{fj}\alpha_{Sj} \\ \theta_d \\ \theta_S \end{pmatrix} \tag{14}$$

Remark 3.3 We can now clarify the roles of $\Theta_f(\ )$, $\Theta_d(\ )$ and $\Theta_S(\ )$ as prices of risk. From (14), we see that $\Theta_f(\ )$, $\Theta_d(\ )$ and $\Theta_S(\ )$ jointly specify the price of the risks corresponding to innovations in $W_1(\ )$, $W_2(\ )$, and $W_3(\ )$.

Our next, and first major, result states, especially, that our model has a unique set of risk-adjusted probabilities (with respect to our chosen numeraire).

Theorem 3.4 *The model specified in Section 2 has at most one EMM. If this EMM, $P^{(d)}$, exists, then*

$$\xi(t) = \prod_{j=1}^{3} \exp\{-\int_0^t \{\theta_j^{(d)}(u) - \sigma_d(T,u)\alpha_{dj}(u)\} dW_j(u) \qquad - \frac{1}{2}\int_0^t \{\theta_j^{(d)}(u) - \sigma_d(T,u)\alpha_{dj}(u)\}^2 du\}$$

is a P-martingale, with $\xi(T) \; \varepsilon \; L^2(P)$ *(15)*

and $P^{(d)}$ *has Radon-Nikodym derivative*

$$\frac{dP^{(d)}}{dP} = \xi(T) \tag{16}$$

Conversely, if (15) holds, define a probability measure, $P^{(d)}$*, by (16). Then a sufficient condition for* $P^{(d)}$ *to be an EMM is that:*

$$\prod_{j=1}^{3} \exp\{\int_0^t \{\sigma_d(M,u) - \sigma_d(T,u)\}\alpha_{dj}(u) dW_j^{(d)}(u)$$

$$- \frac{1}{2}\int_0^t \{\sigma_d(M,u) - \sigma_d(T,u)\}^2 \alpha_{dj}^2(u) du\}$$

is a $P^{(d)}$*-martingale* $\forall M \varepsilon [0,T]$*, and that* *(17a)*

$$\prod_{j=1}^{3} \exp\{\int_0^t \{\sigma_f(M,u)\alpha_{fj}(u) + \sigma_S(u)\alpha_{Sj}(u) - \sigma_d(T,u)\alpha_{dj}(u)\} dW_j^{(d)}(u)$$

$$-\frac{1}{2}\int_0^t \{\sigma_f(M,u)\alpha_{fj}(u)+\sigma_S(u)\alpha_{Sj}(u)-\sigma_d(T,u)\alpha_{dj}(u)\}^2 du\}$$

(17b)

is a $P^{(d)}$-martingale $\forall M \varepsilon [0,T]$ where $W_1^{(d)}(\ \ )$, $W_2^{(d)}(\ \ )$, $W_3^{(d)}(\ \ )$ are the standard Brownian motions under $P^{(d)}$, given by (A16).

<u>Remark 3.5</u> By the Novikov condition,[18] (17a)-(17b) will always be fulfilled if volatilities and correlations are deterministic. Thus (15) is sufficient for the existence of a unique EMM for that case.

If we now impose the following:

<u>Regularity Condition</u> *The conditions (15) and (17a)-(17b) of Theorem 3.4 are fulfilled.* and impose on trading strategies an additional requirement:

<u>Definition 3.6</u> *Define a trading strategy by the Provisional Definition 2.5.1, supplemented by the following additional requirement:*

(vi) $V(.)\ /\ B_d(T,.)$ is a $P^{(d)}$-martingale

then we can derive a further important result:

---

[18] See e.g. Karatzas and Shreve [1987] Corollary 3.5.13 p199.

Theorem 3.7 *Our model is viable. Arbitrage opportunities and "suicide" strategies are precluded. Moreover, every* $x \varepsilon X$ *is uniquely priced by arbitrage at a value:*

$$V_x = B_d(T,0)\mathrm{E}^{(d)}[\, x \,] \tag{18}$$

where $\mathrm{E}^{(d)}$ *denotes expectations under* $P^{(d)}$.

The theorem states that our model is consistent with general equilibrium, and that there is a unique pricing operator for cross-currency interest-sensitive claims. This operator takes the form of discounting the expected payoff, the expectation being taken under the risk-adjusted probabilities.

As in Babbs [1990a], the above analysis extends readily to contingent claims maturing before T:

Definition 3.8 *A european contingent claim produces a single payoff at some fixed date, which is a function of the prices, at that date, of some fixed finite collections of "foreign" and "domestic" pure discount bonds. Thus, formally, it consists of: some fixed* $M \varepsilon [0,T]$; *a collection* $M_1,\ldots,M_n \subset [M,T]$; *and a payoff function:*

$$x(\, h_f,\, h_d, S(M))$$

satisfying the regularity condition:

$$\frac{x}{B_d(T,M)} \in X \tag{19}$$

where h_f, h_d, *are n-dimensional vectors with respective kth elements* $(k=1,\ldots n)$:

$$h_{fk} = B_f(M_k, M)$$

$$h_{dk} = B_d(M_k, M)$$

So far our analysis has focussed on contingent payoffs receivable at the end date of the economy, T. Having now introduced the idea of european contingent claims paying off at some fixed prior date, M, out next result indicates that, of course, we can value them by reinvesting their payoffs until T and applying Theorem 3.7 - this gives us (20). We also show, however, that this valuation can also be obtained by taking the expected payoff itself under a new risk-adjusted probability measure specific to M and discounting from that date - this is (21).

<u>**Proposition 3.9**</u> *A european contingent claim is priced by arbitrage at:*

$$V_x(0) = B_d(T,0)E^{(d)}\left[\frac{x}{B_d(T,M)}\right] \tag{20}$$

which can conveniently (for many purposes) be re-expressed as

$$V_x(0) = B_d(M,0)E^{(d),(M)}[x] \tag{21}$$

where $E^{(d),(M)}$ *denotes expectations under a probability measure* $P^{(d),(M)}$ *on* $(\Omega, \mathcal{F}_M)$*, equivalent to P, and having Radon-Nikodym derivative*

$$\frac{dP^{(d),(M)}}{dP} = \prod_{j=1}^{3} \exp\{-\int_0^M (\theta_j^{(d)}(u) - \sigma_d(M,u)\alpha_{dj}(u))dW_j$$
$$-\frac{1}{2}\int_0^M (\theta_j^{(d)}(u) - \sigma_d(M,u)\alpha_{dj}(u))^2 du\} \tag{22}$$

So far, our analysis has restricted trading strategies to employing "domestic" and "foreign" pure discount bonds (see Provisional Definition 2.5.1). We now show that our model allows agents to trade in any claim, so long as the prices are consistent with those established by Proposition 3.9:

Theorem 3.10 *Let the Regularity Condition above hold. Define $P^{(d)}$ by (15) and (16). Let all european contingent claims have measurable price processes V_x:[0,M] x $\Omega \rightarrow \Re$. Expand the index I of traded securities to admit such claims. Then the model is viable if and only if the contingent claims are priced by the relation*:

$$V_x(t) = B_d(T,t)E^{(d)}[\frac{x}{B_d(T,M)}] \quad \forall t \in [0,M] \tag{23a}$$

$$= B_d(M,t)E_t^{(d),(M)}[x] \tag{23b}$$

4. "CROSS-CURRENCY EXTENDED VASICEK"

The framework developed in Sections 2-3 admits a wide range of models for term structure and exchange rate dynamics. It might be imagined, therefore, that our valuation formula (23b), established by Theorem 3.10, while of great theoretical power, might not lend itself particularly readily to explicit calculation. However, this is far from the case.

For example, Babbs [1990b] shows that Grabbe's [1983] closed-form expression for the value of a european-style option on the spot exchange rate can be obtained by requiring the various volatility and correlation functions, $\sigma_f(\ )$, $\sigma_d(\ )$, $\rho_{fd}(\ )$, $\rho_{fS}(\ )$ and $\rho_{Sd}(\ )$ to be deterministic.[19]

Our focus in this Section, however, is on cross-currency contingent claims with payoffs depending explicitly on term structure variables. By assuming that volatilities and correlations are deterministic, and that, moreover, bond price volatilities take a particular functional form, we obtain a cross-currency version of the "extended Vasicek" model of a single yield curve. In our cross-currency model, we shall see that the joint evolution of the two term structures and the exchange rate is described by three Gaussian state variable processes. This yields a readily computable valuation formula for arbitrary european-style contingent claims. We illustrate the tractability of this formula by deriving a closed-form valuation expression for "diff" swaps.

We retain[20] Grabbe's [1983] restriction that volatilities and correlations are deterministic. Babbs [1990a] has shown, in a single term structure context, that the adoption of a single factor model with state-independent volatility does not necessarily imply that there is a single state variable for the whole term structure at some future date.[21]

[19] AJ obtain a similar result.

[20] We reiterate the illustrative intent of the restrictions we will make in this section. Comparable results may be possible under altogether different specializations of the general model constructed in Sections 2 to 3, incorporating different dynamics.

[21] See especially Babbs' [1990a] discussion in the Appendix to chapter 7, pp179-81.

Indeed such a variable exists if and only if volatility has a particular functional form.[22] In order, therefore, to minimize the number of state variables statistics required for an arbitrary european contingent claim, we impose this functional form in both currencies:

$$\sigma_k(M,t) = \{G_k(M)-G_k(t)\}\ \lambda_k(t); \qquad k=f,d \tag{24}$$

where G_k and λ_k are essentially arbitrary functions, but (without loss of generality) we can take $G_k(0)=0$.

The two factor model discussed in Heath, Jarrow and Morton [1992] pp91-2 involves two volatility functions which are special cases of the above specification. A full discussion of the properties of our specification of volatility is found in Babbs [1990a]. Briefly, however, (24) is necessary and sufficient for each term structure to be described in terms of a single state variable process (given by 26b) below). If we demand also that volatility be multiplicatively separable as the product of terms depending respectively upon residual term to maturity, $M - t$, and calendar time, t, then σ_k is forced to adopt the form which we discuss and employ in the worked example in Section 5.1 below.

Of especial note are the implications for the processes for the instantaneous spot rate of interest (we drop the f and d suffixes, since the two processes are otherwise identical):

$$dr(t) = \mu'(t)dt + \frac{G''(t)}{G'(t)}\{\mu(t)-r(t)\}dt + G'(t)dY(t) \tag{25}$$

where

[22]See Babbs [1990a] Chapters 6 and 7 pp153-81.

$$\mu(t) = f(t) + G'(t)\int_0^t [G(t)-G(u)]\lambda^2(u)du \tag{26a}$$

$$dY(t) = \Theta(t)\lambda(t)dt + \lambda(t)dZ(t) \tag{26b}$$

and $f(\ )$ is the initial instantaneous forward rate curve:

$$f(t) = -\frac{\partial}{\partial t}\ln B(t,0) \tag{26c}$$

Equations (25)-(26c) look complicated, but on closer inspection can be seen to represent a generalized mean-reverting random walk, where the mean is a volatility-adjusted version of the initial forward rate curve. They may therefore be regarded as making the mean-reversion model of Vasicek [1977] consistent with whatever initial term structure is actually observed, when simultaneously liberalizing the mean-reversion, volatility, and risk parameters. As regards empirical evidence, Dybvig [1997] derived encouragement for a single-factor Vasicek-type model from US data.

Having set up the dynamics of the model, we can now establish a valuation formula for arbitrary european contingent claims. The formula depends merely on computing the expectation of a function of a tri-variate Normal distribution. It is thus readily calculable; moreover, as we shall see in relation to "diff" swaps, it can yield closed-form results for quite complex products.

Theorem 4.1 *Let x be an arbitrary european contingent claim. Then under the* *dynamics discussed in this subsection, the price process of x is given by:*

$$V_x(t) = B_d(M,t)E_t^{(d),(M)}[\ x(h_f,h_d,S(M))\ ] \tag{27}$$

where the kth elements of h_f, h_d $(k=1,...,n)$ are given by:

$$h_{fk} = B_f(M_k,M) - \frac{B_f(M_k,t)}{B_f(M,t)}\exp\{\beta(M_k,M)+\{G_f(M_k)-G_f(M)\}Y_f\} \tag{28a}$$

$$h_{dk} \equiv B_d(M_k,M)$$

$$- \frac{B_d(M_k,t)}{B_d(M,t)} \times\exp\{-\frac{1}{2}\int_t^M\{\sigma_d(M_k,u)-\sigma_d(M,u)\}^2du+\{G_d(M_k)-G_d(M)\}Y_d\} \tag{28b}$$

and

$$S(M) = \frac{B_f(M,t)S(t)}{B_d(M,t)}\exp\{-\frac{1}{2}C(t,M) + Y_S\} \tag{28c}$$

where

$$\beta(M_k,M) = -\int_t^M\{\sigma_f(M_k,u)-\sigma_f(M,u)\}\{\rho_{fS}(u)\sigma_S(u)-\rho_{fd}(u)\sigma_d(M,u)\}$$
$$+ \frac{1}{2}\sigma_f^2(M_k,u) - \frac{1}{2}\sigma_f^2(M,u)\ du \tag{29}$$

and Y_f, Y_d, Y_S are trivariate Normally distributed under[23] *$P^{(d),(M)}$ with zero means and the following variances and covariances:*

---

[23] $P^{(d),(M)}$ was defined by (22) above.

$$E_t^{(d),(M)}[Y_f^2] = \int_t^M \lambda_f^2(u)du \tag{30a}$$

$$E_t^{(d),(M)}[Y_d^2] = \int_t^M \lambda_d^2(u)du \tag{30b}$$

$$E_t^{(d),(M)}[Y_S^2] = C(t,M) \tag{30c}$$

$$E_t^{(d),(M)}[Y_f Y_d] = \int_t^M \lambda_f(u)\rho_{fd}(u)\lambda_d(u)du \tag{30d}$$

$$E_t^{(d),(M)}[Y_f Y_S] = \int_t^M \lambda_f(u)\{\sigma_f(M,u) + \rho_{fS}(u)\sigma_S(u) - \rho_{fd}(u)\sigma_d(M,u)\}du \tag{30e}$$

$$E_t^{(d),(M)}[Y_f Y_d] = \int_t^M \lambda_d(u)\{\rho_{fd}(u)\sigma_f(M,u) + \rho_{Sd}(u)\sigma_S(u) - \sigma_d(M,u)\}du \tag{30f}$$

where C( ) is given by:

$$C(t,M) = \int_t^M \{\sigma_f^2(M,u) + \sigma_S^2(u) + \sigma_d^2(M,u) - 2\sigma_f(M,u)\rho_{fd}(u)\sigma_d(M,u) + 2\sigma_f(M,u)\rho_{fS}(u)\sigma_S(u) - 2\sigma_S(u)\rho_{Sd}(u)\sigma_d(M,u)\}du \tag{31}$$

5. APPLICATION TO "DIFF" SWAPS

"Diff" swaps consist of the exchange of streams of regular floating rate interest payments on some notional principal. The floating interest rate used for one stream is "foreign" currency LIBOR; the other is some constant margin above "domestic" currency LIBOR. In contrast to the arrangements under a conventional cross-currency swap, however, both interest rates are applied to the same "domestic" currency notional principal amount, without regard to the evolution of the exchange rate between the two currencies. Such an arrangement enables the counterparties to expose themselves to movements in international interest rate differentials, without taking on any explicit exchange rate exposure.

The value of such a swap equals the sum of the values attributable to each successive interest period. Thus it will suffice to focus henceforth on an individual period. The net payment to the party receiving the "foreign" interest rate is:

$$p = (r_f - m - r_d)\,\delta \tag{32}$$

where: r_f is the "foreign" LIBOR; r_d is the "domestic" LIBOR; m is the margin; and δ is the accrual factor for the interest period. Note that the payment is made in "domestic" currency, and at the end of the interest period.

Both LIBOR rates will refer to interbank deposits to be placed on the start date of the interest period. However, the maturity dates of those deposits may differ as a result of bank holidays in the two countries. Moreover, the dates at which the LIBOR rates are determined may differ, according to national conventions as to how long before the placing of funds the interest rate is agreed.[24] Thus the relation between the LIBOR rates and the term structure processes in each currency may differ.

Let us denote the start and end of the "diff" swap interest period by M^S, M^E; the ends of the corresponding deposit periods by M_f^E , M_d^E ; and the LIBOR determination dates by M_f, M_d. Then r_f, r_d are related to the term structure processes by:

$$r_k = \left\{\frac{B_k(M^S, M_k)}{B_k(M_k^E, M_k)} - 1\right\} \div \delta_k; \qquad k = f,d \tag{33}$$

where δ_k is the accrual factor for the relevant deposit contract.

It follows that p can be regarded as the difference between two contingent payments, determined at M_f,M_d , with respective amounts:

$$p_f = r_f\delta \tag{34a}$$

$$p_d = (r_d+m)\delta \tag{34b}$$

Allowing for the fact that payments of these amounts does not occur until M^E, we can regard these two payments as european-style contingent claims maturing at M_f,M_d respectively, with (discounted) values at those respective dates of:

$$r_f\delta B_d(M^E, M_f) \tag{35a}$$

$$(r_d+m)\delta B_d(M^E, M_d) \tag{35b}$$

---

[24] In US dollars, and most other currencies, the rate is agreed two business days before the placing of the funds. In the UK, by contrast, funds are deposited on the date the rate is agreed.

We now proceed to apply Theorem 4.1 to each of these contingent claims individually. The result can be stated as:

Proposition 5.1 *The value of the "diff" swap net payment for the period* $[M^S, M^E]$, *at some date* $t<M_f, M_d$ *is given by the discounted present value of the payment, calculated using adjusted forward interest rates, namely:*

$$V_{diff}(t) = B_d(M^E,t)[\hat{r}_f - m - \hat{r}_d]\delta \tag{36}$$

where the adjusted forward interest rates[25] *are given by:*

$$\hat{r}_k = \{\exp\{\int_t^{M_k} A_k(u)du\}\frac{B_k(M^S,t)}{B_k(M_k^E,t)} - 1\} \div \delta_k; \quad k=f,d \tag{37}$$

where

$$A_f(u) = \{\sigma_f(M_f^E,u) - \sigma_f(M^S,u)\} \text{ x }$$

$$\{\sigma_f(M_f^E,u) + \rho_{fS}(u)\sigma_S(u) - \rho_{fd}(u)\sigma_d(M^E,u)\} \tag{38a}$$

$$A_d(u) = \{\sigma_d(M_d^E,u) - \sigma_d(M^E,u)\}\{\sigma_d(M_d^E,u) - \sigma_d(M^S,u)\} \tag{38b}$$

Remark 5.2 Note that exchange rate effects play a role--a purely indirect role--in the valua-tion formula, through the appearance of the exchange rate volatility, σ_S, and the correlation between innovations in the exchange rate and in "foreign" bond prices, ρ_{fS}, in (38*a*).

---

[25]The forward rates implicit in the term structure at time t are obtained by replacing M_k by t in (33). Comparison of the resulting formula with (37) and (38a)-(38b) clearly justified the term "adjusted forward rates".

Remark 5.3 Note also, from (38*b*), that $A_d(\ )$ will be identically zero if - as is commonly the case - the end of the period corresponding to the "domestic" interest rate reference index, M_d^E, coincides with the end of the swap interest period, M^E. The "adjusted domestic forward rate" as given by (37) then reduces to the market forward rate. Indeed the adjustment to the "domestic" rate will, in practice, always be negligible, unless M_d^E and M^E differ markedly. This last can only occur through the tenor of the reference index differing from the length of the swap period (eg by using a 6-month index for a quarterly swap); the resulting effect is attributable solely to such mismatches rather than to the use of such a mismatch within a diff swap.

5.1 WORKED EXAMPLE

In this sub-section, we provide a worked example of the closed-form diff swap valuation formula given by Proposition 5.1. While purely illustrative, this example demonstrates both the computational tractability of the model, and also the size of the differences between the adjusted forward rates, $\hat{r}_f$ and $\hat{r}_d$, and their market counterparts, F_k:$k=f,d$, which are given by (37) with $A_k(\ )$ set identically equal to zero.

A crude model for diff swap valuation would apply (36), but using market forward rates instead of the adjusted rates in that formula. Practitioner interest in Proposition 5.1 will therefore focus not on the valuation formula directly, but upon the magnitude of the adjustments made to market forward rates. We noted in Remark 5.3 that the adjusted "domestic" rate will be at most insignificantly different from its actual counterpart, so long as the tenor of the "domestic" interest rate index equals the length of the swap interest period. In our example we will assume quarterly interest periods and 3-month reference rates. It will therefore be appropriate for us to focus solely on the adjustment to "foreign" forward rates:

$$\varepsilon_f \equiv \hat{r}_f - F_f$$

$$- \left(\exp\left\{\int_t^{M_f} A_f(u)du\right\} - 1\right) \frac{1+F_f\delta_f}{\delta_f} \tag{39}$$

The interest rate adjustment, ε_f, given by (39) depends on the integral of the function $A_f()$ from the current time, t, to the determination date, M_f, of the reference interest rate. Clearly therefore, the adjustment will be negligible for imminent interest periods, but may grow substantially for remote periods. It is therefore of interest to investigate the size of the adjustment as a function of the time to the start of the diff swap interest period.

Apart from various dates and corresponding accrual factors, and the margin on the swap, the inputs we require are: "foreign" discount factors for various dates; and bond price and exchange rate volatility and correlation functions.

Academics and practitioners are familiar with a range of techniques to infer discount factor curves from market data. Having obtained discount factors, our computation will be as easy or as difficult as the evaluation of the integral

$$\int_t^{M_t} A_t(u)du$$

At worst, this will be an exercise in numerical integration, based on whatever volatility and correlation functions we specify.

The most general functional of bond price volatility in the extended Vasicek model was given by (24). For practical purposes, however, it would seem intuitively desirable to be able to express that volatility as a product of two terms: one a function of calendar time and expressing how the volatility of the yield curve as a whole varies over time ("when is the volatility occurring?"); and the other a function of residual term to maturity, *M-t*, expressing how the volatility of the yield curve as a whole impacts individual maturities ("what is the volatility happening to?"). Babbs [1990a] and others have shown that imposing this requirement on (24) can only be achieved if $G_k(\ )$ takes the form:

$$G_k(u) = \frac{1-e^{-\xi_k u}}{\xi_k} \tag{40a}$$

for some constant ξ_k, with the degenerate ($\xi_k=0$) case:

$$G_k(u) = u \tag{40b}$$

whence we can re-write (24) as:

$$\frac{1-e^{-\xi_k(M-t)}}{\xi_k}\kappa_k(t)$$

where

$$\kappa_k(t) = e^{-\xi_k t}\lambda_k(t)$$

Note that with $G_k(\ )$ agiven by (40a) or (40b), the short rate process (25) becomes:

$$dr(t) = \mu'(t)dt + \xi\{\mu(t)-r(t)\}dt - \Theta(t)\kappa(t)dt - \kappa(t)dZ(t) \tag{41}$$

Thus, we can interpret ξ as the rate of mean reversion of the short rate, and $\kappa(\ )$ as its variability (ie instantaneous standard deviation of <u>arithmetic</u> movements) over time. Numerous authors[26] have shown that the Ho and Lee [1986] "two-parameter" model corresponds to the degenerate ξ=0 case of (41).

Purely for ease of exposition, we will treat the "foreign" and "domestic" variability functions, the exchange rate volatility function, and the correlations between "foreign" and "domestic" bonds, and between the exchange rate and "domestic" bonds, as constant. Substitution into (38a) then gives us:

$$A_f(u) = \frac{e^{-\xi_f(M^S-t)}-e^{-\xi_f(M_f^B-t)}}{\xi_f}\kappa_f\{a_1e^{\xi_f(u-t)}-a_2e^{2\xi_f(u-t)}+a_3e^{(\xi_f+\xi_d)(u-t)}\} \tag{42}$$

where

$$a_1 = \frac{\kappa_f}{\xi_f} + \rho_{fS}\sigma_S - \frac{\rho_{fd}\kappa_d}{\xi_d} \tag{43a}$$

(43*b*)

[26]A particularly full treatment is given in Babbs [1990a] chapter 20.

$$a_2 = \frac{\kappa_f}{\xi_f} e^{-\xi_f (M_f^E - t)} \qquad a_3 = \frac{\rho_{fd} \kappa_d}{\xi_d} e^{-\xi_d (M^E - t)} \tag{43c}$$

Integrating analytically gives us:

$$\int_t^{M_f} A_f(u)\,du = \frac{e^{-\xi_f (M^S - t)} - e^{-\xi_f (M_f^E - t)}}{\xi_f} \kappa_f \{ a_1 \frac{e^{\xi_f (M_f - t)}}{\xi_f} - a_2 \frac{e^{2\xi_f (M_f - t)} - 1}{2\xi_f} + a_3 \frac{e^{(\xi_f + \xi_d)(M_f - t)} - 1}{\xi_f + \xi_d} \} \tag{44}$$

If we now ignore the (numerically insignificant) gap that may exist between the reference determination date, M_f and the start of the diff swap interest period, M^S, and make the simplifying assumption that reference and swap interest periods are exactly 91 days long, with interest accruing on an actual days over 360 day basis (ie the standard money market practice in most countries), the "foreign" interest rate adjustment becomes a function solely of the time, M^S-t, to the start of the interest period, and of the forward interest rate, F_f, and of the model parameters. Note that, for individual diff swap periods, we could take account of the exact date details without increasing the computational burden significantly.

We take the following illustrative, but plausible, inputs:

Foreign forward rate, F_f=7% (use at each maturity)

Foreign reversion, ξ_f=0.1

Foreign short rate variability, κ_f=1.4%

Domestic reversion, ξ_d=0.15

Domestic short rate variability, κ_d=1.2%

Correlation between "foreign" and "domestic" bonds: ρ_{fd}=0.4

Exchange rate volatility, σ_S=12%

We combine these parameter values with either positive or negative between "foreign" bonds and exchange rate, ρ_{fS}=±0.15

The positive sign for the latter correlation signifies that a rise in "foreign" bonds (ie a fall in "foreign" interest rates) tends to be associated with a depreciation of the foreign currency.

For these inputs, the corresponding "foreign" interest rate adjustments are plotted in Figure 1.

Figure 1 indicates that the size of the adjustment required to "foreign" forward rates can be appreciable, especially at longer maturities. The size of the adjustment - and even its sign - depends on the values of the model parameters (see further below).

Comparative static analysis of the adjustment with respect to changes in model parameters can be derived by appropriate partial differentiation of (39) and (44):

$$\frac{\partial \varepsilon_f}{\partial \rho_{fS}} > 0 \tag{45a}$$

$$\frac{\partial \varepsilon_f}{\partial \sigma_s} \begin{cases} > 0, \text{ if } \rho_{fs} > 0 \\ \leq 0, \text{ if } \rho_{fs} \leq 0 \end{cases} \tag{45b}$$

$$\frac{\partial \varepsilon_f}{\partial \rho_{fd}} < 0 \tag{45c}$$

If $\rho_{fd}>0$, then

$$\frac{\partial \varepsilon_f}{\partial \xi_d} > 0; \quad \frac{\partial \varepsilon_f}{\partial \kappa_d} < 0 \tag{45d}$$

while, if $\rho_{fd} \leq 0$, then

$$\frac{\partial \varepsilon_f}{\partial \xi_d} \leq 0; \quad \frac{\partial \varepsilon_f}{\partial \kappa_d} \geq 0 \tag{45e}$$

The sensitivities to ξ_f, κ_f take either sign in more complex fashion. Since $A_f(\ )$ can take either sign, so can the sensitivities of ε_f to maturity, and to the forward rate, F_f.

The unambiguous sensitivities can be interpreted intuitively. A positive correlation between "foreign" bond prices and the value of the "foreign" currency, enhances the attractiveness of "foreign" bonds.[27] This reduces the expected "foreign" bond prices - and thus increases the expected interest rates - that would be required under risk

[27]This operates through a "heads I win more/tails I lose less" effect, as rises (falls) in "foreign" bond prices in local currency terms tend to be translated into "domestic" currency at higher (lower) exchange rates.

neutrality. In turn this increases the value of receiving the "foreign" rate in the diff swap, giving us (45a). The scale of this effect depends in part, of course, upon the scale of exchange rate movements, whence (45b).[28] In a similar vein, a positive correlation between "foreign" and "domestic" bond prices - and thus as a positive correlation between interest rates also - means that the benefits (costs) through the diff swap of higher (lower) "foreign" rates will be tend to be partially offset by the need to discount the resulting cashflows at higher (lower) "domestic" rates, whence (45c). The scale of this effect (whose direction is, of course, reversed for a negative correlation), depends in part on the variability of prospective "domestic" rates; whence (45d) or (45e) as appropriate.

Table 1 illustrates the magnitudes of the various sensitivities, for the adjustment applicable for a swap interest period starting five year ahead.

Note that of the sensitivities unambiguously signed in the comparative static analysis above, that to the correlation, ρ_{fS}, between "foreign" bonds and the exchange rate is by far the largest.

6. CONCLUSIONS

We have achieved an integration of the analysis of foreign exchange and term structure contingent claims by constructing a general framework capable of admitting a wide

---

[28]A negative correlation turns the "heads I win more/tails I lose less" effect (see previous footnote) into a "heads I win less/ tails I lose more" effect.

range of term structure and exchange rate dynamics. Extending the work of Harrison and Kreps [1979], we have shown that our framework is viable, and that all contingent claims are priced by arbitrage.

By specialising the various volatility and correlation functions, we have obtained a cross-currency version of the "extended Vasicek" yield curve model. The resulting model has been expressed in terms of three Gaussian state variable processes, giving rise to a readily calculable valuation formula for arbitrary european contingent claims. We have illustrated the practical potential of this model by deriving a new result: a closed-form valuation expression for the "switch LIBOR" or "diff" swaps discussed by Litzenberger [1992], and presented a worked example, including a discussion of comparative statics.

APPENDIX

<u>**Proof of Lemma 3.2**</u> Trivial by Ito's lemma.

<u>**Proof of Theorem 3.4**</u> Suppose that there exists an EMM, $P^{(d)}$. By definition of an EMM,

$$\frac{dP^{(d)}}{dP} \in L^2(P) \tag{A1}$$

Hence

$$\eta(t) = E\left[\frac{dP^{(d)}}{dP} \middle| F_t\right] \tag{A2}$$

is a square-integrable P-martingale with

$$\eta(0) = E\left[\frac{dP^{(d)}}{dP}\right] = 1 \tag{A3}$$

We can therefore apply martingale representation theory[29] to obtain that[30]

$$\eta(t) = 1 + \sum_{j=1}^{3}\int_0^t \beta_j(u)dW_j(u) \tag{A4}$$

for some P-square-integrable processes $\beta_j(\ );j=1,2,3$

By (2b),

$$\frac{d\{B_d(M,t)/B_d(T,t)\}}{B_d(M,t)/B_d(T,t)} = \{\sigma_d(M,t)-\sigma_d(T,t)\}\times[\{\theta_d-\sigma_d(T,t)\}dt+dZ_d] \tag{A5}$$

which, by (9) and (14),

$$= \{\sigma_d(M,t)-\sigma_d(T,t)\}$$

---

[29]See e.g. Liptser and Shiryayev [1977] Theorem 5.5 p162, essentially the Kunita-Watanabe Representation Theorem.

[30]We have generally not felt the need to make explicit the various measurability conditions involved in the stochastic calculus we have been undertaking. The validity of (A4) however depends on the assumption that the increasing family $\{\mathcal{F}_t;t\in[0,T]\}$ with which our probability space is equipped is that generated by $Z_f(\ )$, $Z_d(\ )$, and $Z_g(\ )$.

This restriction states that agents' information consists precisely of the history of the term structures and the exchange rate. Such restrictions are not uncommon in the literature, having been introduced by HK (foot of p394, plus discussion at foot of p395. Babbs and Selby [1998] explore the robustness of arbitrage-based pricing results when this restriction is dropped.

$$\times \sum_{j=1}^{3} \alpha_{dj}[\{\theta_j^{(d)} - \sigma_d(T,t)\alpha_{dj}\}dt + dW_j] \tag{A6}$$

Since $P^{(d)}$ is an EMM, $B_d(M,t)/B_d(T,t)$ is a $P^{(d)}$-martingale; implying[31] that $B_d(M,t)\eta(t)/B_d(T,t)$ is a P-martingale. Applying Ito's lemma,

$$\frac{d\{B_d(M,t)\eta(t)/B_d(T,t)\}}{B_d(M,t)/B_d(T,t)} = \{\sigma_d(M,t)-\sigma_d(T,t)\}\sum_{j=1}^{3} \alpha_{dj} y_j dt + \sum_{j=1}^{3} [\{\sigma_d(M,t)-\sigma_d(T,t)\}\eta + \beta_j] dW_j \tag{A7}$$

where:

$$y_j(t) = \eta(t)\{\Theta_j^{(d)}(t) - \sigma_d(t,t)\alpha_{dj}(t)\} + \beta_j(t) \tag{A8}$$

Now an Ito process is a martingale only if[32] if has zero drift. Thus we require

$$\sum_{j=1}^{3} \alpha_{dj}(t) y_j(t) = 0 \tag{A9}$$

Applying similar arguments to "domestic" currency returns from holding "foreign bonds, as given in the Lemma above, we require also:

$$\sum_{j=1}^{3} \{\sigma_f(M,t)\alpha_{fj}(t) + \sigma_s(t)\alpha_{sj}(t) - \sigma_d(T,t)\alpha_{dj}(t)\} y_j(t) = 0 \tag{A10}$$

---

[31]See e.g. Liptser and Shiryayev [1977] Lemma 6.6 p226.

[32]It is well known that this condition is necessary but not sufficient. Its necessity flows from the result that, on a finite interval, a continuous local martingale of finite variation is constant (see eg Elliott [1982] Lemma 11.39 p121).

Multiplying (A9) by $\sigma_d(T,t)$ and adding to (A10), followed by setting $M=t$,[33] and dividing through by $\sigma_S(t)$ gives us:

$$\sum_{j=1}^{3} \alpha_{Sj}(t)y_j(t) = 0 \tag{A11}$$

Similarly, adding $\sigma_d(T,t)$ times (A9) and $\sigma_S(t)$ times (A11) to (A10), followed by dividing through by $\sigma_f(M,t)$ gives us:

$$\sum_{j=1}^{3} \alpha_{fj}(t)y_j(t) = 0 \tag{A12}$$

In geometric terms, (A9) and (A11)-(A12) tells us that the vector $y(t)$ is perpendicular to each of the rows of $A(t)$, which, by the non-degeneracy assumption, are not all coplanar. Hence,

$$y(t) = 0 \tag{A13}$$

Applying (A13) to (A8) gives us a stochastic differential equation for $\eta(\ )$, whose solution is

$$\eta(\ ) = \xi(\ ) \tag{A14}$$

whence (15) holds.

Thus, if $P^{(d)}$ is an EMM, then $\xi(\ )$ is P-martingale with

$$\xi(T) = \eta(T) = \frac{dP^{(d)}}{dP} \in L^2(P) \tag{A15}$$

Conversely, if the condition (15) in the theorem is fulfilled, then, by the Girsanov Theorem[34], (16) defines a

---

[33]We use here that $\sigma_d(t,t) = 0$. See chapter 4 of Babbs [1990a] for details.

[34]See e.g. Karatzas and Shreve [1987] Theorem 3.5.1 p191.

probability measure $P^{(d)}$ equivalent to P, under which we construct three orthogonal standard Brownian motions

$$W_j^{(d)}(t) = W_j(t)+\int_0^t \{\theta_j^{(d)}(u)-\sigma_d(T,u)\alpha_{dj}(u)\}du;\; j=1,2,3 \tag{A16}$$

as we may re-express the discounted process (13) as

$$\frac{dB_d(M,t)/B_d(T,t)}{B_d(M,t)/B_d(T,t)} = \{\sigma_d(M,t)-\sigma_d(T,t)\}\sum_{j=1}^{3}\alpha_{dj}(t)dW_j^{(d)} \tag{A17a}$$

Similarly,

$$\frac{d\{B_f(M,t)S(t)/B_d(T,t)\}}{B_f(M,t)S(t)/B_d(T,t)} = \sum_{j=1}^{3}\{\sigma_f(M,t)\alpha_{fj}(t)+\sigma_S(t)\alpha_{Sj}(t)-\sigma_d(T,t)\alpha_{dj}(t)\}dW_j^{(d)} \tag{A17b}$$

The unique solutions of (A17a) and (A17b) are the respective $P^{(d)}$-supermartingales:

$$\frac{B_d(M,t)}{B_d(T,t)} = \frac{B_d(M,0)}{B_d(T,0)}\prod_{j=1}^{3}\exp\{\int_0^t\{\sigma_d(M,u)-\sigma_d(T,u)\}\alpha_{dj}(u)dW_j^{(d)}$$

$$-\frac{1}{2}\int_0^t\{\sigma_d(M,u)-\sigma_d(T,u)\}^2\alpha_{dj}^2(u)du\} \tag{A18a}$$

and

$$\frac{B_f(M,t)S(t)}{B_d(T,t)} = \frac{B_f(M,0)S(0)}{B_d(T,0)} \quad \times\prod_{j=1}^{3}\exp\{\int_0^t\{\sigma_f(M,u)\alpha_{fj}(u)+\sigma_S(u)\alpha_{Sj}(u)-\sigma_d(T,u)\alpha_{dj}(u)\}dW_j^{(d)}$$

$$-\frac{1}{2}\int_0^t \{\sigma_f(M,u)\alpha_{fj}(u)+\sigma_S(u)\alpha_{Sj}(u)-\sigma_d(T,u)\alpha_{dj}(u)\}^2du\}$$

(A*18b*)

If (17a) and (17b) hold, the RHS of (A18a) and (A18b) are, in fact, $P^{(d)}$-martingales: thus, $P^{(d)}$ is an EMM as required. •

<u>**Proof of Theorem 3.7**</u> The first assertion follows immediately from the above Assumption and Theorem 3.4. Arbitrage and suicide strategies are readily shown to be precluded by requirement (vi) on trading strategies. The final assertion follows from a result[35] of Babbs [1990a].

<u>**Proof of Proposition 3.9**</u> Essentially trivial. Details similar to those in chapter 6 of Babbs [1990a]. •

<u>**Proof of Theorem 3.10**</u> By Theorem 3.4, $P^{(d)}$ is the sole candidate EMM. Equation (23a) is precisely what is required to ensure that the discounted price processes of contingent claims are $P^{(d)}$-martingales. The result (using (23a)) now follows by the unique existence of the EMM, just as in Theorem 3.7 above. Equation (23b) follows from (23a) by the same manipulations as required to prove Proposition 3.9. •

<u>**Proof of Theorem 4.1**</u> Under $P^{(d),(M)}$, we can construct[36] orthogonal standard Brownian motions:

---

[35]Chapter 5 Section 2.4 Corollary p140. Essentially, that result extends the analogous result in HK (Section 3 Corollary p392) to a term structure context.

[36]Cf. (A16).

$$W_j^{(d),(M)}(t) = W_j(t) + \int_0^t \{\theta_j^{(d)}(u) - \sigma_d(M,u)\alpha_{dj}(u)\} du; \quad j=1,2,3 \tag{A19}$$

Substituting (A19) into (A6) and undertaking simple manipulations yields:

$$\frac{d\{B_d(M_k,t)/B_d(M,t)\}}{B_d(M_k,t)/B_d(M,t)} = \{\sigma_d(M_k,t) - \sigma_d(M,t)\} \sum_{j=1}^{3} \alpha_{dj}(t) dW_j^{(d),(M)}(t) \tag{A20}$$

Applying a similar procedure to (13) yields

$$\frac{d\{B_f(M_k,t)S(t)/B_d(M,t)\}}{B_f(M_k,t)S(t)/B_d(M,t)} = \sum_{j=1}^{3} \{\sigma_f(M_k,t)\alpha_{fj}(t) + \sigma_S(t)\alpha_{Sj}(t) - \sigma_d(M,t)\alpha_{dj}(t)\} dW_j^{(d),(M)}(t) \tag{A21}$$

Using Ito's lemma to take logarithms in each of the above equations and integrating over [t,M] gives:

$$lnB_d(M_k,M) = \ln\frac{B_d(M_k,t)}{B_d(M,t)} - \int_t^M \{\sigma_d(M_k,u) - \sigma_d(M,u)\}^2 du \quad + \sum_{j=1}^{3} \alpha_{dj}(u)\{\sigma_d(M_k,u) - \sigma_d(M,u)\} dW_j^{(d),(} \tag{A22}$$

and

$$\begin{aligned} \ln\{B_f(M_k,M)S(M)\} &= \ln\frac{B_f(M_k,t)S(t)}{B_d(M,t)} - \\ &-\frac{1}{2}\sum_{j=1}^{3}\int_t^M \{\sigma_f(M_k,u) - \alpha_{fj}(u) + \sigma_S(u)\alpha_{Sj}(u) - \sigma_d(M,u)\alpha_{dj}(u)\}^2 du \\ &+\sum_{j=1}^{3}\int_t^M \{\sigma_f(M_k,u)\alpha_{fj}(u) + \sigma_S(u)\alpha_{Sj}(u) - \sigma_d(M,u)\alpha_{dj}(u)\} dW_j^{(d),(M)} \end{aligned} \tag{A23}$$

Setting $M_k=M$ in (A23) gives

$$\ln(S(m) - \ln\frac{B_f(M,t)\,S(t)}{B_d(M,t)}) -$$

$$-\frac{1}{2}\sum_{j-1}^{3}\int_t^M \{\sigma_f(M,u)\alpha_{fj}(u) + \sigma_S(u)\alpha_{Sj}(u) - \sigma_d(M,u)\alpha_{dj}(u)\}^2 du \tag{A24}$$

$$+\sum_{j-1}^{3}\int_t^M \{\sigma_f(M,u)\alpha_{fj}(u) + \sigma_S(u)\alpha_{Sj}(u) - \sigma_d(M,u)\alpha_{dj}(u)\}\; dW_j^{(d),(M)}$$

whence, subtracting from (A23),

$$lnB_f(M_k,M) - \ln\frac{B_f(M_k,t)}{B_f(M,t)} - -\sum_{j-1}^{3}\int_t^M \alpha_{fj}(u)\{\sigma_f(M_k,u) - \sigma_f(M,u)\}$$

$$\times\left\{\frac{\sigma_f(M_k,u) + \sigma_f(M,u)}{2}\alpha_{fj}(u) + \sigma_S(u)\alpha_{Sj}(u) - \sigma_d(M,u)\alpha_{dj}(u)\right\}du \tag{A25}$$

$$+\sum_{j-1}^{3}\int_t^M \{\sigma_f(M_k,u) - \sigma_f(M,u)\}\alpha_{fj}(u)\; dW_j^{(d),(M)}$$

If we now make use of (24) and (31), define

$$Y_f - \sum_{j-1}^{3}\int_t^M \alpha_{fj}(u)\lambda_f(u)dW_j^{(d),(M)} \tag{A26a}$$

$$Y_d - \sum_{j-1}^{3}\int_t^M \alpha_{dj}(u)\lambda_d(u)dW_j^{(d),(M)} \tag{A26b}$$

$$Y_S = \sum_{j=1}^{3} \int_t^M \{\alpha_{fj}(u)\sigma_f(M,u) + \alpha_{Sj}(u)\sigma_S(u) - \alpha_{dj}(u)\sigma_d(M,u)\} dW_j^{(d),(M)} \tag{A26c}$$

and undertake straightforward manipulations, (28a)-(29) emerge as required.

It follows directly from (A26a)-(A26c) that, under $P^{(d),(M)}$, Y_f, Y_d, Y_S, are trivariate. Normally distributed with zero means and the variance and covariances given by (30a)-(30f).

The result now follows by (23b). •

<u>**Proof of Proposition 5.1**</u> In (35a) and (35b) substitute for the LIBOR rates using (33). Substitute for the pure discount bond prices at the relevant LIBOR determination dates, using (28a) or (28b) as appropriate. The result follows from taking expectations under $P^{(d),(M_f)}$ for the payoff in (35a), under $P^{(d),(M_d)}$ for the payoff in (35b), and carrying out tedious but entirely elementary manipulations. •

BIBLIOGRAPHY

P D Adams and S B Wyatt (1987) "Biases in Option Prices: Evidence from the Foreign Currency Option Market" *Journal of Banking and Finance*, 549-62.

K I Amin and R A Jarrow (1991) "Pricing Foreign Currency Options under Stochastic Interest Rates" *Journal of International Money and Finance* 10, 310-29.

S H Babbs (1990a) "The Term Structure of Interest Rates: Stochastic Processes and Contingent Claims" Unpublished PhD Thesis, London University (November 1990).

S H Babbs (1990b) "The Valuation of Cross-Currency Interest-Sensitive Claims" unpublished working paper.

S H Babbs (1997) "A Family of Ito Process Models for the Term Structure of Interest Rates" in *Vasicek and Beyond*, L Hughston, ed., London: Risk Publications, 253-271.

S H Babbs and M J P Selby (1998) "Pricing by Arbitrage in Incomplete Markets" *Mathematical Finance* 8:2, 163-168.

C Dellacherie (1980) "Un Survol de la Theorie de l'Integrale Stochastique" *Stochastic Processes and their Applications* 10, 115-44.

P H Dybvig (1997) "Bond and Bond Option Pricing Based on the Current Term Structure" in *Mathematics of Derivatives Securities*, M A H Dempster and S R Pliska, eds., New York: Cambridge University Press, 271-293.

R J Elliott (1982) *Stochastic Calculus and Applications* Applications of Mathematics 18, Springer Verlag.

G Feiger and B Jacquillat (1979) "Currency Option Bonds, Puts and Calls on Spot Exchange and the Hedging of Contingent Foreign Earnings" *Journal of Finance*, 1129-39.

J O Grabbe (1983) "The Pricing of Call and Put Options on Foreign Exchange" *Journal of International Money and Finance* 2, 239-53.

J M Harrison and D M Kreps (1979) "Martingales and Arbitrage in Multiperiod Securities Markets" *Journal of Economic Theory* 20, 381-408.

J M Harrison and S R Pliska (1981) "Martingales and Stochastic Integrals in the Theory of Continuous Trading" *Stochastic Processes and their Applications* 11, 215-60.

D C Heath, R A Jarrow and A Morton (1992) "Bond Pricing and the Term Structure of Interest Rates: a New Methodology for Contingent Claims Valuation" *Econometrica* 60, 77-105.

T S Y Ho and S-B Lee (1986) "Term Structure Movements and Pricing Interest Rate Contingent Claims" *Journal of Finance* 41, 1011-29.

J Hull and A White (1990) "Pricing Interest-Rate Derivative Securities" *Review of Financial Studies 3*, 573-92.

F Jamshidian (1990a) "Bond and Option Evaluation in the Gaussian Interest Rate Model" to appear in *Research in Finance 9*.

F Jamshidian (1990b) "The Preference-Free Determination of Bond and Option Prices from the Spot Interest Rate" to appear in *Advances in Futures and Options Research* 4, 51-67.

F Jamshidian (1994) "Hedging Quantos, Differential Swaps and Ratios" *Applied Mathematical Finance* 1, 1-20.

I Karatzas and S E Shreve (1987) *Brownian Motion and Stochastic Calculus* Graduate Texts in Mathematics 113, New York: Springer-Verlag.

R S Liptser and A N Shiryayev (1977) *Statistics of Random Processes I: General Theory* Springer-Verlag.

R H Litzenberger (1992) "Swaps: Plain and Fanciful" *Journal of Finance* 47, Presidential Address, 831-50.

R C Merton (1973) "Theory of Rational Option Pricing" *Bell Journal of Economics and Management Science* 4, 141-83.

S Turnbull (1994) "Pricing and Hedging Diff Swaps" *Journal of Financial Engineering* 2, 297-333.

O A Vasicek (1977) "An Equilibrium Characterization of the Term Structure" *Journal of Financial Economics* 5, 177-88.

Figure 1: Adjustment to "foreign" forward interest rate

Table 1: Sensitivities * of adjustment for "foreign" 3-month interest rate, 5 years forward, to specified increases in parameters

F_f,	+1%	+0.04bp
ξ_f,	+0.05	-3.00bp
κ_f,	+0.1%	+2.31bp
ξ_d,	+0.05	+0.37bp
κ_d,	+0.1%	-0.44bp
ρ_{fd},	+0.1	-1.32bp
σ_S,	+1%	0.27bp
ρ_{fS},	+0.1	+6.56bp

* initial parameter values: F_f=7%; ξ_f=0.1; κ_f=1.4%; ξ_d=0.15; κ_d=1.2%; ρ_{fd}=0.4; σ_S=12%; ρ_{fS}=0.05. Corresponding adjustment 14.75bp.

Advances in Computational Economics

1. A. Nagurney: *Network Economics.* A Variational Inequality Approach. 1993 ISBN 0-7923-9293-0
2. A.K. Duraiappah: *Global Warming and Economic Development.* A Holistic Approach to International Policy Co-operation and Co-ordination. 1993 ISBN 0-7923-2149-9
3. D.A. Belsley (ed.): *Computational Techniques for Econometrics and Economic Analysis.* 1993 ISBN 0-7923-2356-4
4. W.W. Cooper and A.B. Whinston (eds.): *New Directions in Computational Economics.* 1994 ISBN 0-7923-2539-7
5. M. Gilli (ed.): *Computational Economic Systems.* Models, Methods & Econometrics. 1996 ISBN 0-7923-3869-3
6. H. Amman, B. Rustem, A. Whinston (eds.): *Computational Approaches to Economic Problems.* 1997 ISBN 0-7923-4397-2
7. G. Pauletto: *Computational Solutions of Large-Scale Macroeconometric Models.* 1997 ISBN 0-7923-4656-4
8. R.D. Herbert: *Observers and Macroeconomic Systems.* Computation of Policy Trajectories with Separate Model Based Control. 1998 ISBN 0-7923-8239-0
9. D. Ho and T. Schneeweis (eds.): *Applications in Finance, Investments, and Banking.* 1999 ISBN 0-7923-8294-3

KLUWER ACADEMIC PUBLISHERS – DORDRECHT / BOSTON / LONDON

GPSR Compliance

The European Union's (EU) General Product Safety Regulation (GPSR) is a set of rules that requires consumer products to be safe and our obligations to ensure this.

If you have any concerns about our products, you can contact us on ProductSafety@springernature.com

In case Publisher is established outside the EU, the EU authorized representative is:

Springer Nature Customer Service Center GmbH
Europaplatz 3
69115 Heidelberg, Germany

Batch number: 10755284

Printed by Printforce, the Netherlands